Bloom's Modern Critical Interpretations

The Adventures of
   Huckleberry Finn
The Age of Innocence
Alice's Adventures in
   Wonderland
All Quiet on the
   Western Front
Animal Farm
The Ballad of the Sad
   Café
Beloved
Beowulf
Black Boy
The Bluest Eye
The Canterbury Tales
Cat on a Hot Tin Roof
Catch-22
The Catcher in the Rye
The Chronicles of
   Narnia
The Color Purple
Crime and
   Punishment
The Crucible
Cry, the Beloved
   Country
Darkness at Noon
Death of a Salesman
The Death of Artemio
   Cruz
The Diary of Anne
   Frank
Don Quixote
Emerson's Essays
Emma
Fahrenheit 451
A Farewell to Arms
Frankenstein
The Glass Menagerie
The Grapes of Wrath
Great Expectations

The Great Gatsby
Gulliver's Travels
Hamlet
Heart of Darkness
The House on Mango
   Street
I Know Why the
   Caged Bird Sings
The Iliad
Invisible Man
Jane Eyre
The Joy Luck Club
Julius Caesar
The Jungle
King Lear
Long Day's Journey
   into Night
Lord of the Flies
The Lord of the Rings
Love in the Time of
   Cholera
Macbeth
The Man Without
   Qualities
The Merchant of
   Venice
The Metamorphosis
A Midsummer Night's
   Dream
Miss Lonelyhearts
Moby-Dick
My Ántonia
Native Son
Night
1984
The Odyssey
Oedipus Rex
The Old Man and the
   Sea
On the Road

One Flew over the
   Cuckoo's Nest
One Hundred Years of
   Solitude
Othello
Persuasion
Portnoy's Complaint
Pride and Prejudice
Ragtime
The Red Badge of
   Courage
Romeo and Juliet
The Rubáiyát of Omar
   Khayyám
The Scarlet Letter
A Separate Peace
Silas Marner
Slaughterhouse-Five
Song of Solomon
The Sound and the
   Fury
The Stranger
A Streetcar Named
   Desire
Sula
The Sun Also Rises
The Tale of Genji
A Tale of Two Cities
"The Tell-Tale Heart"
   and Other Stories
Their Eyes Were
   Watching God
Things Fall Apart
The Things They
   Carried
To Kill a Mockingbird
Ulysses
Waiting for Godot
The Waste Land
Wuthering Heights
Young Goodman Brown

Bloom's Modern Critical Interpretations

William Shakespeare's
Othello
New Edition

Edited and with an introduction by
Harold Bloom
Sterling Professor of the Humanities
Yale University

BLOOM'S
LITERARY CRITICISM
An imprint of Infobase Publishing

Bloom's Modern Critical Interpretations: Othello—New Edition

Copyright © 2010 by Infobase Publishing

Introduction © 2010 by Harold Bloom

Bloom's Literary Criticism

An imprint of Infobase Publishing

132 West 31st Street

New York NY 10001

Library of Congress Cataloging-in-Publication Data

William Shakespeare's Othello / edited and with an introduction by Harold Bloom. — New ed.

    p. cm.—(Bloom's modern critical interpretations)

    Includes bibliographical references and index.

    ISBN 978-1-60413-818-4 (hardcover : alk. paper)

    1. Shakespeare, William, 1564–1616. Othello. 2. Othello (Fictitious character) 3. Tragedy. [1. Shakespeare, William, 1564–1616. Othello. 2. English literature—History and criticism.] I. Bloom, Harold. II. Title: Othello.

    PR2829.W47 2010

    822.3'3—dc22

                          2009046904

Bloom's Literary Criticism books are available at special discounts when purchased in bulk quantities for businesses, associations, institutions, or sales promotions. Please call our Special Sales Department in New York at (212)967-8800 or (800)322-8755.

You can find Bloom's Literary Criticism on the World Wide Web at http://www.chelseahouse.com

Contributing editor: Pamela Loos

Cover design by Alicia Post

Composition by IBT Global, Troy NY

Cover printed by IBT Global, Troy NY

Book printed and bound by IBT Global, Troy NY

Date printed: April, 2010

Printed in the United States of America

10 9 8 7 6 5 4 3 2 1

Contents

Editor's Note

My introduction meditates partially on Iago as an incarnate spirit of war, following a suggestion of Harold Goddard.

R. A. Foakes also turns to Iago and the malignant artistry of a man who elicits the tragic potential in others rather than authoring it himself. In James L. Calderwood's assessment, Iago is the mediator, ever eclipsing the characters' access to the truth.

Edward Berry returns to the issue of racial identity in the play, arguing that Shakespeare particularizes his portrayal of Othello in an attempt to resist both stereotype and the creation of a universalized type. Thomas Moisan then contends that the play's reliance on modes of repetition and interrogation reveals a prevailing ambivalence about language and the distortions of rhetoric.

For Maynard Mack, the audience is led to the same mistaken judgments that will later ensnare the main players in the tragedy. He sees the central preoccupation with irretrievable loss as outweighing a powerful sense of mystery the work would otherwise possess. T. H. Howard-Hill turns his attention to discourse in the play and the linguistic differences that set Cassio and Iago apart.

Edward Pechter casts the play in terms of a search for answers and the emergence of Iago and the qualified information he imparts as the false beacon in that quest. Then, Robert N. Watson links *Othello* to its possible origins in Reformation tragedy and its manifestation of Shakespeare's Protestant valuations and fears.

In the volume's final essay, Joan Ozark Holmer suggests that, in the martial and militaristic world of Venice, Desdemona is the one true warrior represented onstage.

HAROLD BLOOM

Introduction

Iago is the genius or bad angel of *Othello* and of Othello. It marks us that we know more readily how to assimilate Iago than to value Othello. Even my best students are wary of sympathizing with Othello. He baffles them: how can the great captain-general so rapidly collapse into incoherence, murderousness, and apparent self-pity?

If each of us had an Iago as personal spirit, would we do better?

The tragedy *Othello* suffers because it is preceded by *Hamlet*, and followed by *King Lear*, *Macbeth*, and *Antony and Cleopatra*. Othello does not match the protagonists of those dramas, and yet Iago does. The imbalance between Othello and his devilish Ancient or ensign unsettles us these days. But that is part of Shakespeare's design in a play whose peculiar painfulness rivals *King Lear*'s.

Iago has been a fecund ancestor in high literature. His progeny include Satan in Milton's *Paradise Lost*, Claggart in Melville's *Billy Budd*, and Judge Holden in Cormac McCarthy's *Blood Meridian*. Coleridge spoke of Iago's "motiveless malignancy," but when Satan speaks of his Sense of Injured Merit we encounter Iago's fierce motive. He has been passed over for promotion and Cassio, a staff officer and not a warrior, has been given the post by Othello.

The wound to Iago, as we discern, is onto-theological. He had worshipped Othello as war-god. Betrayed, Iago activates his pyromaniac drive to

1

carry war into the camp of peace. A true believer bereft of his fiery faith, Iago uncovers in himself a genius for destroying his captain-general.

Edmund in *King Lear* is the grand strategist of catastrophe, composing the play with the lives of the other characters. Iago, an extraordinary improviser, is rather the tactician of absolute evil. He does not set out with the object of Desdemona's murder by Othello, but embraces the horror when the Moor warns him that he must prove Desdemona a whore or else himself be slain by the overlord of mercenary soldiers.

Magnificent as his triumphalism becomes, Iago remains secondary to the tragic hero, Othello. In the twentieth century, critics like the abominable T. S. Eliot and the equally dogmatic F. R. Leavis deprecated Othello, denying him tragic stature. We can learn from them how not to go about reading so painful a drama as Shakespeare writes.

Othello, like Lear, has never known himself well. A fighter since childhood, he has fully earned his professional eminence. His gift is for commanding others, and for maintaining the separation of war from peace. Serene in his own sublimity, he believes in the honor of arms, and cannot believe that his trust is ever wrongly bestowed. Affinities abound with Antony and with Coriolanus, two other sad captains who fall apart as the contradictions in their own natures encounter overwhelming stress.

How can tragic dignity be maintained if one is reduced to incoherence by Iago's subtle art? Shakespeare is uncanny in preserving a residue of Othello's self-identity that can be reaffirmed in his suicidal final speech. Eliot and Leavis thought that Othello was only cheering himself up at the end, but that is caricature and not accurate analysis.

Hegel, who valued Shakespeare above all other writers, famously thought that tragedy came about as a conflict "between right and right." A.C. Bradley endorsed the Hegelian theory of tragedy, but I find it remote from Shakespearean actuality. There is no right on either side of the contraries that rend Othello apart. The Moor is victimized by a devil, and has no chance whatsoever.

What was Shakespeare trying to do for himself as poet-dramatist by writing *The Tragedy of Othello*? After the impasse of *Hamlet*, *Othello* clears the way for the incredible breakthrough in which *Antony and Cleopatra* followed the composition first of *King Lear* and then of *Macbeth*, thus concluding just fourteen consecutive months in which three masterworks were brought forth. I surmise that the agony of Othello was a kind of ritual sacrifice to the dark gods of creativity so as to enable Lear, Macbeth, and Antony to rise up out of the maelstrom of Shakespeare's capacious spirit.

Times go by turns, and *The Tragedy of Othello* has come back from Eliotic disapproval. Since Eliot was every kind of a racist, including a virulent anti-Semite, we can suppose that Othello's African background also provoked the poet-critic of *The Waste Land*. To this day, there is no critical agreement upon what does or does not happen in the play. I do not believe that the marriage between Desdemona and the Moor ever is consummated. Elliptical at his subtlest, Shakespeare is content to leave it uncertain. The profound sadness of *Othello* is appropriately increased by this dubiety. As readers we must construe for ourselves, and bear the play's shadows as they throng among us.

R. A. FOAKES

The Descent of Iago:
Satire, Ben Jonson, and Shakespeare's Othello

It is the habit of criticism to attend to the chronology of Shakespeare's plays in a general way, usually in terms of convenient groupings, such as the dark comedies, the central tragedies, the late plays, and so on. In this way we can conveniently preserve a sense of the rough placing of any play within the canon, and not worry too much about its specific dating, which in the case of most plays remains to some extent speculative. However, to the extent that we take the dating of the plays for granted, and think of them in conventional groupings, we are liable to ignore details that are both surprising and significant. The dating of *Othello* is a case in point. It is discussed usually in the context of Shakespeare's other tragedies, or, as by Reuben Brower in *Hero and Saint* (1971) or Richard Ide in *Possessed with Greatness* (1980), in the context of heroic tragedy.[1] Observing its position in the chronology of Shakespeare's plays suggests a quite different context. It is generally assumed that the sequence of plays after *Hamlet* is as follows:

> *Troilus and Cressida* about 1602
> *All's Well that Ends Well* about 1602–3
> *Othello* 1602–4
> *Measure for Measure* 1604

From *Shakespeare and His Contemporaries: Essays in Comparison*, edited by E. A. J. Honigmann, pp. 16–30. © 1986 by Manchester University Press.

5

In other words, *Othello* belongs chronologically with the dark comedies. If at first sight this seems absurd, it is at least worth inquiring what significance this might have for an understanding of the play.

The plays of this period, beginning with *Hamlet*, have in general, as is well known, a strong connection with new departures in satire and satirical comedy. Shakespeare's own company staged Ben Jonson's *Every Man in his Humour* (1598), *Every Man out of his Humour* at the end of 1599, and *Sejanus* in 1603, a play in which Shakespeare himself took a leading part, according to the 1616 Folio. He also played in the revised *Every Man in his Humour*, performed at court on 2 February 1605, and perhaps staged earlier in 1604. Shakespeare knew Jonson's plays very well, and could hardly have escaped the impact of Marston too, whose *The Malcontent* was stolen, expanded and performed at the Globe before its publication in 1604. Although Shakespeare is not mentioned among the leading actors who played *Every Man out of his Humour*, this play is particularly interesting because it was the first of Jonson's works to be published, in 1600, and because it constituted a kind of manifesto for comical satire, including 'more than hath been publikely Spoken or Acted'.

The formal verse satires of Hall, Marston, Guilpin and others, published about 1598–9, characteristically invented a satirical spokesman, and various personae for him to attack as examples of vice or folly. In the boldest, most powerful and most sensational satires of this period, those grouped in Marston's *The Scourge of Villainy* (1598), some sketches are developed at considerable length, like that of the braggart soldier in Satire VII, 100–38, or the lover 'Publius' in Satire VIII, who is dramatised in passionate and lascivious adoration of the hairpin he has obtained from his mistress. What she used to allay the itch, he worships in his own extravagant words:

Touch it not (by the Lord sir) tis divine,
It once beheld her radiant eyes bright shine:
Her haire imbrac'd it, o thrice happie prick
That there was thron'd, and in her hair didst sticke. (VIII. 104–7)

The dramatisation of a lover's absurd posturings anticipates the gentler and more humorous treatment of the romantic lover in Jonson's Puntarvolo. Shakespeare also made use of such sketches, as in his creation of the affected courtier Osric, who is exhibited, as it were, by Hamlet (and Shakespeare) the satirist to our mockery in V.ii.

In *Every Man out of his Humour* Jonson went much further both in theory and in practice. Marston's satires range across a spectrum from Juvenalian anger (Satire II) through cynic snarling (Satire VII) and malcontent spleen

(Satire X) to laughter at the affectations of 'humours' (Satire XI). If there is no obvious overall design in Marston's *Scourge of Villainy*, he evidently tried out a variety of masks through which to satirise in different ways the follies and abuses dramatised in the numerous figures sketched within the satires. He also saw himself as a fool to write rhymes to be read by fools, and in Satire VII, he includes himself in condemnation of human degeneracy, showing the satirist to be himself vulnerable to attack, and tarred with the vices found in others. Jonson perhaps was stimulated by Marston's Satire XI, with its display of humours or affectations, to develop a theory of humours as anchored in the whole bent of the personality (*Every Man out of his Humour*, Induction 102–14), and so relate it to the greater depth necessary for developing a character through the five acts of a play. But Shakespeare had already shown, in his creation of figures like Nym, Bardolph, Silence and Shallow, that he did not need theories to teach him how to make characters.

Of much more interest is Jonson's concern with the role of the satirist in drama. His chorus of Cordatus and Mitis serves to explain the 'humours' of the play, to link them with classical antecedents, as in the reference to Plautus preceding III.ix, and to justify the claim that the absurdities of the characters are true to life, while at the same time arguing that they reflect on no one in particular. So in II.iii Cordatus claims it is 'very easily possible' that there should be such a 'humorist' as Puntarvolo, who makes advances to his wife 'in geometrical proportions', and at the end of II.vi, he counters the fears of Mitis by insisting that no 'noble or true spirit in court' will be upset at the display of Fastidious Brisk, any more than a 'grave, wise citizen' will see himself in Deliro. Jonson was evidently giving much thought to what he was about, in seeking to take care of the more obvious objections to satire, and he was also concerned with a profounder issue, which begins to emerge in the very design of his play. The induction presents to us Asper, the righteous man so indignant with the 'impious world' that he must, with a Juvenalian fervour (echoing too Marston's second satire in *The Scourge of Villainy*, which begins 'I cannot hold, I cannot I indure ... my rage must freely runne'), 'strip the ragged follies of the time', expose vice, and be applauded, he thinks, by 'Good men and virtuous spirits' for doing so. Mitis raises an important question by asking, in effect, what gives Asper the right to take this stand:

> *Mitis* I should like it much better, if he were less confident.
> *Cordatus* Why, do you suspect his merit?
> *Mitis* No, but I fear this will procure him much envy.

For the purposes of the action of the play Asper is transformed into 'an actor and a humorist', becoming Macilente, who retains the function of satirical spokesman, as when he comments on the miserly Sordido, 'Is't possible that such a spacious villain / Should live, and not be plagued' (I.iii. 62–3), but whose judgement is undermined by his envy of others. Sordido he can hate and despise, as he can Carlo Buffone, who takes no moral position, 'bites at all, but eats on those that feed him' (I.ii. 203), and turns everything to jest. Carlo Buffone takes pleasure in misleading others, and describes himself in his advice to Sogliardo on his purchase of a coat of arms: 'Love no man. Trust no man. Speak ill of no man to his face: nor well of any man behind his back . . . Spread yourself upon his bosom publicly whose heart you would eat in private' (III.iv. 92–5). Jonson's own distaste emerges in Macilente's comments on him, and in Puntarvolo's linking of Carlo Buffone with Marston as the 'grand scourge; or second untruss of the time' (II.iii. 84–5), the 'black-mouthed cur' (II.ii. 202) whose voice Jonson apparently heard in the violent satire of *The Scourge of Villainy*. If Carlo Buffone deserves in the end to be punished, when Puntarvolo beats him and seals his beard with wax to prevent him from speaking in Act V, should Macilente escape untouched? His envy grows in the course of the play, from his understandable railing on fortune for making the foolish Deliro rich rather than himself, into a readiness to abuse others behind their backs, as Carlo Buffone prompts him to be spiteful about Fastidious Brisk in IV.iv; and finally, in V.i, it turns into mere malice in his poisoning of Puntarvolo's dog.

The treatment of Macilente at the end, when he acts as a supervisor in the discomfiture of Deliro and Fastidious Brisk, leaves him untouched, and able to become Asper again without even changing his appearance. This device enables Jonson to create an interesting and vulnerable character, and at the same time turn him into the upright judge Asper, 'eager and constant in reproof', who could hardly be developed without appearing conceited, self-important and didactic. The problem Jonson was trying to solve might be formulated thus: how is the satirical spokesman in a play to obtain leverage over the other characters? The writer of satires may give more offence by claiming, or appearing to suggest, that he is above the rest of humanity, than by glancing at particular people. Marston probably did so, even though he included himself among the sinners in Satire VII. An Asper stalking through the entire play would be intolerable and dull. So it was a good dramatic instinct which led Jonson to develop Macilente as the 'true picture of spite' (V.viii. 70), more malicious than Carlo Buffone, and distinguished from him by his self-awareness, his asides and soliloquies, which enable him to function to some extent as a moral commentator on the action, and give him a degree of superiority.

The unprincipled jester or railer like Carlo Buffone (a type Shakespeare developed into Thersites, Parolles and Lucio) may expose folly and vice in others, but remains contemptible himself. Even so, he draws our sympathy to the extent that he releases our frustrations by his exposure of others (as in Thersites' mocking of Ajax and Achilles, revealing their conceit and stupidity), or by being simply the thing he is, a scapegoat whose humiliation (as in the case of Carlo Buffone, Parolles and Lucio) soaks up blame for the offences of others, of Macilente in *Every Man out of his Humour*, of Bertram in *All's Well*, of society in *Measure for Measure*. Macilente is more complex, the malcontent scholar who feels his merits go unrecognised, and who knows he should, but cannot, control his 'blood and his affection', and is burnt up with envy. To the extent that we respond to his intellectual superiority (he has the best verse speeches in the play), and to the sense of self-laceration and defeat in one who might be better, our attitude towards him will be ambivalent. We have to balance his acts of petty malice (as when, after accepting a new suit from Deliro, and an introduction at court from Fastidious Brisk, he abuses Brisk as a 'poor fantastic' to Deliro and Fallace) against the justice of his perceptions, for instance, about the court itself:

> Here, in the court! Be a man ne'er so vile
> In wit, in judgement, manners, or what else;
> If he can purchase but a silken cover,
> He shall not only pass, but pass regarded . . . (III.ix. 9–12)

It was Macilente's envy of fools wearing suits of satin (II.v) that led him to accept Deliro's gift: he would be as rich and splendidly dressed as the courtier, but cannot help then turning on those who have been kind to him; so Fallace comments, 'Here's an unthankful spiteful wretch! The good gentleman vouchsafed to make him his companion, because my husband put him in a few rags, and now see how the unrude rascal backbites him!' (IV.ii. 42–5). Carlo Buffone, who 'will sooner lose his soul than a jest' (Prologue), backbites for pleasure, Macilente backbites because he is torn between desire for the possessions of others and scorn of their stupidity or self-deception; and though their motives are different, the effect is similar, so that at this point these two kinds of satirist begin to merge.

The satirist's world is dominated by vice and folly, and the darker it becomes, the harder it is to maintain a comic tone. The genial solutions of a Justice Clement will not do, and Jonson's rescue of Macilente is contrived too palpably. In *The Malcontent*, Marston refined on this concept of the discontented railer who despises others as inferior, but envies them for possessing what he lacks, by creating Malevole/Altofronto. In this play Marston brings his Asper, so to speak, into the play as the good Duke Altofronto, but at the cost of making his *alter ego* Malevole innocuous. Malevole, it is true, strikes malcontent attitudes:

Only the malcontent, that 'gainst his fate
Repines and quarrels—alas, he's goodman tell-clock!
His sallow jaw-bones sink with wasting moan;
Whilst others' beds are down, his pillow's stone. (III.ii. 11–14)

In fact, he appears to be far from wasting with moan, and enjoys himself
hugely in the action by intriguing and stage-managing the 'Cross-capers,
tricks' (IV.iv.13) by which fools and knaves are exposed or discomfited.
The play turns into a comedy in which the wounding of Ferneze in II.iv
is the only harsh moment (since the audience for a short time supposes
he is dead), the nearest thing to Macilente's act of malice in poisoning
Puntarvolo's dog.

The satirist (Macilente-Carlo Buffone) figure finds a more familiar and
comfortable home in tragedy, most successfully in those Italianate plays where
he joins or serves vicious princes like Lussurioso, Brachiano or Ferdinand; in
considering the plays of Tourneur and Webster as tragedies of intrigue and
revenge, it is easy to overlook the connections of Vindice, Flamineo and Bosola
with earlier satirical comedy. It is ironic that the satirist figure of works like
The Scourge of Villainy should, through his envy of others, his own contamina-
tion by the vices he attacks, in fact pass most readily into the service of the
dramatist as the tool-villain of revenge tragedy. In a dramatic action in an evil
world, the satirist, forced to take part in events and no longer merely a commentator, can join that world to serve it, however grudgingly, and he is thus
given dramatic complexity through the conflict in himself as he condemns
evil in others while participating in it himself; alternatively, he can stand aloof
like Asper, in which case he is neutralised and unable to act at all. This is a
difficulty in Jonson's finely wrought *Sejanus* (acted 1603, and another play in
which Shakespeare took a part); in it Silius, Arruntius, Sabinus and Lepidus
all function to greater or lesser degree as satiric commentators on the action,
but can do nothing against Sejanus, Macro or Tiberius; they are reduced to
following the counsel of Agrippina: 'stand upright, / And though you do not
act, yet suffer nobly' (IV.i. 73–4). The strongest action possible, indeed the
only one, is suicide, as staged in the presence of the Senate by Silius in III.i. In
this world only Fortune, the goddess Sejanus prays to and denounces in V.iii,
may one day bring a change, and the virtuous remain ineffectual.

The interest in the uses of satirical figures in drama at this time was
shared by Shakespeare, as is evident in his dark comedies, and I would now
like to consider what bearing this has on *Othello*, the tragedy that in time of
composition most closely relates to *Troilus and Cressida* and *All's Well*. Here
another factor has to be taken into account, namely Shakespeare's concern in
this period with love, war and the heroic. This is implicit in *Hamlet*, in the

hero's idealisation of his father as Mars or Hercules, his envy of Fortinbras, whose name embodies the heroic attribute of *fortezza*, and perhaps his rejection of Ophelia. It becomes explicit in *Troilus and Cressida*, which turns on the clash between love or lust and war, and in *All's Well*,[2] which shows Bertram as anxious to be off to the wars and dedicate himself to Mars, even as Helena abandons Diana for Venus (II.iii. 74–5) and chooses him for a husband. The play's action develops the tension between love and war, and allows neither to emerge unscathed. Perhaps Shakespeare had in mind the Renaissance vision of the hero as the godlike man, figured in Aeneas or Hector, and of love as an appropriate theme for an heroic poem, as proposed by Tasso, and exemplified in *The Faerie Queene*; perhaps too he conceived Othello, as Reuben Brower argues,[3] in relation to the conventional image of the tragic epic hero, but if so, he also had the experience of satire in mind, as an actor in *Every Man in his Humour, Sejanus* and perhaps other plays staged by his company. A familiar figure in the satires of the period is Marston's 'heroic' warrior, the 'dread Mavortian' of Satire VII, Tubrio, who swaggers with his experience of fighting in the low countries, but is wasted 'In sensuall lust and midnight bezeling' (VII.124). He reappears in Satire VIII as analogous to Hercules enslaved to Omphale, the warrior given over to the couch of Venus. Satire opened up new perspectives on the heroic by questioning the possibility of true nobility or moral authority and including all in the degenerate condition of man. Macilente envies the lover and the soldier, though one, Puntarvolo, is foolish, the other, Shift, a contemptible swaggerer. The most devastating critique of the heroic is perhaps Jonson's in *Sejanus*, in which no possibility of heroic action is left, merely stoic resignation in the face of corruption so pervasive and powerful that no individual can challenge it.

In its emphasis on love and war, *Othello* belongs thematically as well as chronologically with the early dark comedies. In them the image of the heroic warrior is challenged not only through the satirical commentary of Thersites and the empty flourishes of Parolles, but also in the presentation of Achilles as a 'dread Mavortian' corrupted by his lust for Polyxena and his 'masculine whore' Patroclus, and even of Hector as seduced by a desire for personal gain in pursuing to the death a Greek warrior solely for the sake of his rich armour. Here war itself is depicted less in terms of heroism and the 'chivalry' Hector speaks of, than as a matter of savage butchery and revenge. *Othello* at first sight offers a complete contrast in the figure of the noble, dignified Moor as he appears in Act I, stopping a brawl in the streets, or addressing the Senate in Venice; yet I think it has to be seen not as a kind of answer to *Troilus and Cressida*, an altogether different view, but rather as a play arising out of the same questioning that prompted both *Troilus and Cressida* and *All's Well that Ends Well*.

Othello's 'occupation' as a warrior has to be taken on trust, since he is not involved in any fight in the action of the play; what fighting there is involves Cassio, set on by Roderigo on the watch in Cyprus in II.3, and again attacked by Roderigo at Iago's behest in V.i. Othello's image as a warrior is created entirely in language, and the play has to do not with heroism, but again with the hero ensnared by love, and laid open to corruption. Implicitly, too, the critique of war itself is continued. Othello as warrior exists as a public figure: through much of the play he is seen with followers in the streets, at a meeting of the Senate, arriving with a crowd at Cyprus, or dealing with public business. By engineering the cashiering of Cassio, Iago is enabled to convert a business occasion into a personal conversation with Othello in III.iii, and so prompt his jealousy. Othello has no *private* scene alone with Desdemona until the murder in Act V, other than the scene in which he treats her as a whore in a brothel, converting this meeting in imagination into a less than private occasion, with Emilia transformed into a bawd listening at the door. The 'Pride, pomp and circumstance of glorious war' belong in the world of public affairs, and in so far as this is Othello's world, it leaves him without a private role.

Indeed, it might be claimed that Othello's habituation to 'glorious war' has incapacitated him for domesticity. Othello is not merely an alien black man of mysterious origin in the white world of Venice, and thus alone, but solitary too as a fighter who from his 'boyish days' (I.iii. 132) has known nothing but war and adventure in the perpetual motion of the professional soldier. He has no intimates,[4] until he is seduced into a kind of intimacy with Iago, as he has no small-talk, lacking 'those soft parts of conversation / That chamberers have' (III.iii. 268–9). His natural mode of utterance, as has often been noted, is magniloquent, a grand Othello music, 'spirit-stirring', like the drums of war, and splendid for calming a riot, ordering the watch and maintaining command. It also serves to tell the story of his life, which bowls over Desdemona, wooed not in a growing intimacy, but incidentally by a narrative of adventures in war. Summoned to Cyprus immediately after their marriage, and sailing in different ships, Othello and Desdemona are reunited there in the one moment they have of sheer delight in their union: here they embrace and kiss, the one occasion when the text requires them to do so before the murder scene in Act V. Even their greeting in Cyprus, however, is not a moment of simple intimacy. Othello may lose himself momentarily in the absolute content of finding her safe on land after the storm at sea (he uses the word 'content' three times in the space of a dozen or so lines), but he seems to be aware, too, as an audience must be, that he is speaking in public. His ship arrives after the others, and he makes his entry late in II.i, when there are assembled on stage a group of Cypriots (Montano, three Gentlemen and a Messenger), Cassio, Desdemona, Iago, Roderigo, Emilia and attendants. Othello enters with more 'attendants' on to a crowded stage, containing nine or ten actors with speaking parts, and an unspecified number of extras. This scene of his reunion with Desdemona is thus at the same time the biggest crowd scene, the largest public gathering, in the play, after the scene of the Senate meeting in II.iii. Othello greets her

> O my fair warrior!
> *Des.* My dear Othello!
> *Oth.* It gives me wonder great as my content
> To see you here before me. O my soul's joy!
> If after every tempest come such calms,
> May the winds blow till they have waken'd death,
> And let the labouring bark climb hills of seas
> Olympus-high, and duck again as low
> As hell's from heaven. If it were now to die
> 'Twere now to be most happy; for I fear
> My soul hath her content so absolute
> That not another comfort like to this
> Succeeds in unknown fate. (II.i. 130–91)

The last few lines, combining a sense of foreboding that their union cannot last, with the hint of sexual consummation in 'to die', might be thought of as privately addressed to Desdemona, but the whole speech is at the same time a grand public declaration heard by all, as indeed the first part of the speech could be addressed to the assembled company.

Othello is very much a public figure inhabiting the public arenas of war and leadership. He is cut off from the play's private relationships, and the scenes in which characters engage in small talk, convey a sense of being relaxed, are those between Iago and Roderigo, the drinking scene (II.iii) in Cyprus, the scenes between Cassio and Desdemona, Cassio and Bianca, Desdemona and Emilia. Othello is marked off by his distance from these others, by the extent to which he exists, is defined by, his role or 'occupation', his public standing as a great warrior. The play establishes a gap between public and private worlds, between war and peace. Brabantio's private anguish, his 'particular grief' (I.iii. 55), seems a small matter in relation to the threatened war with the Turks, but the arrival of Othello in Cyprus, where he greets Desdemona ironically as 'my fair warrior', coincides with the end of hostilities, as he announces 'our wars are done' (II.i. 200). Othello's 'occupation' is already gone, and Iago exploits his inability to adapt to peace, to domestic life, by filling his unoccupied mind with hideous suspicions.

Thus although it is important to start from the 'recognition of greatness' which Brower sees as essential in a reading of *Othello*, the 'heroic simplicity' of the 'noble moor',[5] the play is far from being an exposition of the noble perplexed by the diabolic. It seems to me rather that it stands in contrast to *Sejanus*: Jonson's play postulates a world almost wholly vicious, in which the few upright characters become innocuous Aspers, just satirical commentators reduced to impotence; *Othello* postulates a world almost wholly good, in which the one malicious character fulfils what is implicit in Macilente's 'true envy', which, followed out in its implications, leads not back to Asper as in *Every Man out of his Humour*, but on to Iago. In *Othello* the pursuit of Desdemona by Roderigo is made to seem absurd, as his folly is exploited by Iago, rather than wicked, and his ambitions would evaporate but for Iago's cunning exploitation. Also the peccadilloes of Cassio in getting drunk and later tangling with Bianca are not generally seen as blemishes on 'the daily beauty in his life' (V.i. 19) shown in his loyalty to Othello. In the world of the play, Roderigo and Cassio are not identified as corrupt, except in so far as Iago exploits their weaknesses.

In formal satires the poet or persona speaking takes on a role as presenter of characters displayed usually in savage caricature, such as Marston's Luxurio:

> looke who yon doth goe,
> The meager lecher, lewd Luxurio,
> Tis he that hath the sole monopolie
> By patent, of the suburb lecherie ...
> (*The Scourge of Villainy*, Satire XI, 136ff.)

Macilente begins in similar vein in the early scenes in *Every Man out of his Humour*, as in his commentary on Carlo Buffone at the end of I.ii, or his railing, something in the fashion of Marston's cynic satirist in *The Scourge of Villainy*, Satire VII or Sordido:

> Is't possible that such a spacious villain
> Should live, and not be plagued? Or lies he hid
> Within the wrinkled bosom of the world,
> Where heaven cannot see him? ... (I.iii. 62ff.)

Here Sordido is on stage reading a 'paper' brought to him by a 'Hind', so that Macilente becomes a kind of presenter, and not merely a commentator (in I.ii he comments on Carlo Buffone directly to the audience when alone on the stage). As the play goes on, he inevitably becomes more involved, until in the final act Macilente functions as a kind of stage-manager within the action in putting characters out of their humours; he 'begins to be more sociable on a sudden', as Mitis points out at the end of Act IV, but only so as to 'unleash the torrent of his envy' in directly manipulating affairs. He thrives on the misery of others, 'O, how I do feed upon this now and fat myself! Here were a couple unexpectedly dishumoured: well, by this time, I hope, Sir Puntarvolo and his dog are both out of humour to travel . . .' (V.iii. 67–70); and in the final scene he gloatingly exposes and comments on the folly of Deliro, Fallace and Fastidious Brisk. The satirist as presenter of character-sketches and commentator on them naturally develops further dimensions in drama as a manipulator and intriguer exploiting the weaknesses of others in order to expose them for what they are.

Apart from his act of 'pure envy' in poisoning Puntarvolo's dog, this is where Macilente stops, and the resolution of the play is comic, allowing his conversion into Asper. In *Othello*, Iago may be seen as a Macilente developed into a tragic villain. A. C. Bradley thought of him as an artist, a figure into whom Shakespeare had put a good deal of himself, and Iago has sometimes been seen as expressing the malign as opposed to the benign artist (Prospero).[6] The connection with Macilente helps to show why this view is overpitched; Iago is not a creator, but a manipulator of what comes his way, an opportunist staging events he in the end cannot control, as they gather a momentum he does not foresee, when, for example, Othello demands that he kill Cassio (III.iii. 476–7), and when Roderigo and Iago together fail in the attempt. Like the satirist, Iago sees the worst in the other characters, and reveals their vices and follies; but he goes beyond the satirist in using this exposure to destroy others.

The play begins with the disturbance he stages in the streets of Venice, using Roderigo to work on the racial prejudice of Brabantio. Roderigo is the least plausible character in the play,[7] a 'silly gentleman' (I.iii. 307), doting so much on Desdemona that he does what Iago incites him to, however outrageous or dangerous, a prosaic fool who can nevertheless rise to the dignity of a powerful blank verse, as at I.i.120ff., that seems out of keeping with his general nature. Roderigo serves, of course, as a necessary tool for Iago in bringing about the dismissal of Cassio from his office as lieutenant, and in the attempted murder of Cassio later; but we never hear the 'further reason' (IV.ii. 242) that might have persuaded Roderigo to such an implausible deed. Shakespeare is casual about this, and safely so, since our attention is so gripped by the main action involving Othello and Desdemona at this stage of the play that we do not stop to question why Roderigo turns murderer. The main function of Roderigo is not here, but in his role as interlocutor, setting off Iago's commentary, as a cynical and envious satirist, on the world.

The long dialogues between the two, each dominated by Iago, at I.i. 1–80, I.iii. 301–79 and II.i. 211–79 establish Iago's perspective on everyone. Like Marston's cynic, all Iago sees is changed for the worse, as in his version of Othello's promotion of the 'counter-caster' Cassio, or is explicable in terms of appetite and sensuality; love becomes a 'sect or scion' of lust, and Desdemona's courtesy to Cassio in II.i is an 'index and obscure prologue to the history of lust and foul thoughts'.

The second and third of these prose exchanges end with the exit of Roderigo, while Iago remains on stage to deliver a verse soliloquy. In these two scenes, and also at II.iii. 325–51 and III.iii. 325–33, Iago, as it were, takes the audience into his confidence in speeches that are not, as Hamlet's soliloquies may be understood, largely expressions of an inner debate, over-heard by an audience thinking of him as meditating on his own, but rather a means of subtly involving the audience in Iago's schemes and rationalisings. To describe them as direct self-explanation is not sufficient; through the first part of the play, Othello and Desdemona are seen only as public figures in crowd scenes, but we see Iago not merely in private talk with Roderigo, but with the audience too. His motives for 'practising' on Othello and Cassio may be unconvincing, but cannot be simply discounted as motive-hunting.[8] There is just enough plausibility in them to make them faintly disturbing; he has been passed over in promotion; Moors were assumed to be 'lusty', and the rumour that Othello had seduced Emilia might seem not incredible; Cassio is a 'proper man', and his courtesies to Desdemona and Emilia could easily be misinterpreted (indeed his kissing of Emilia and taking Desdemona 'by the palm', II.i. 166, parallel exactly the behaviour of Polixenes and Hermione which provokes such violent jealousy in Leontes). The point is that even if we reject Iago's particular imputations as unreliable or false, nevertheless, because of his privileged placing in the play's development, which allows him to con-fide in the audience directly, he involves us, draws us into a kind of complicity in his designs.[9]

His particular imputations may seem merely gross, but we have to assent in some measure to the general assumptions implicit in what he says, the assumptions of the envious satirist who sees folly and vice everywhere:

> And what's he then that says I play the villain?
> When this advice is free I give and honest,
> Probal to thinking, and indeed the course
> To win the Moor again? (II.iii. 325–8)

Iago's advice is indeed good, but it forces us to see Cassio and Othello in the satirist's perspective. Cassio's easy manner towards Desdemona and Emilia in II.i shows that he is 'handsome, young and hath all those requisites in him that folly and green minds look after' (II.i. 245–7); his loose behaviour with Bianca further warrants this perspective, suggesting how easily his constant suit to Desdemona to recover his office may be misconstrued, but in his self-concern Cassio is blind, and his contemptuous, self-satisfied dismissal of Bianca as a 'customer', a 'fitchew', in Othello's hearing, provides for him the final 'proof' of Desdemona's infidelity. Othello, of course, mistakenly supposes Cassio is speaking of his wife, but Cassio is to blame too, as Iago makes us see 'how he laugh'd at his vice' (IV.i. 167). Iago also exposes Othello, making us realise the gap in age, sympathy and manners between him and Desdemona (II.i. 218ff.), that incongruity which lends credence to the insinuation that the marriage cannot last, and is reinforced by general beliefs about the nature of moors, as lustful barbarians, 'changeable in their wills' (I.iii. 348). Iago generalises the prejudices that distort Brabantio's attitude to his daughter's marriage.

He also makes us see Desdemona in the context of general assumptions about women, jokingly brought out in the satirical verses with which he responds to Desdemona's invitation to praise her in II.i; his 'praise' of women is summed up in the lines

> There's none so foul, and foolish thereunto,
> But does foul pranks which fair and wise ones do. (II.i. 141–2)

It is appropriate for the envious satirist to praise 'the worst best', as Desdemona says, to turn virtue itself into pitch, because he is 'nothing if not critical' (II.i. 119). Iago reiterates to Roderigo later in this scene, what he had argued in I.iii, that Desdemona is no different from other women, and as likely to do 'foul pranks' when she comes to her senses about the unnatural marriage she had made, and begins to 'heave the gorge' at it. If he misjudges Desdemona's virtue, he nevertheless forces us to be sharply aware of the incongruity in her marriage, the gap in colour, age, sympathy and temperament between her and her husband; he also makes us realise the potential fragility of a love that was excited by Othello 'bragging and telling her fantastical lies' (II.i. 221), an exaggeration too near the truth for comfort.

In these ways Iago's general satirical perspective in the first half of the play, his emphasis on the worst tendencies in human behaviour, shapes our view of the action. It is sometimes said that Iago poisons or infects Othello's mind, as evidenced by Othello's adoption of the animal imagery characteristic of Iago's perception of the beast in man; but Iago only draws out what is already there. He is at least partly right about Cassio, who laughs too easily about his 'vice', and about Othello, whose ability to transform in imagination Desdemona into a prostitute in V.ii confirms the possibility that the 'noble Moor' is at the same time an old black ram, whose world of experience includes a familiarity with the ways of brothels. The terrifying nature of the tragedy in this play is that it is brought about not by Iago, who can only trigger events, or take advantage of accidents, but by the potential for vice and folly that lies in everyone, and is held in check by a delicate balance that is easily disturbed. Iago knows this: 'If the balance of our lives had not one scale of reason to poise another of sensuality, the blood and baseness of our natures would conduct us to most preposterous conclusions' (I.iii. 329–34). All he has to do is create a disturbance, and let the 'baseness of our natures' work.

If Desdemona escapes the general imputation of baseness, she is shown as headstrong and foolish, and again a partial truth emerges in Iago's perspective. The gap between her and Othello is also one of knowledge, and her innocence in part is mere ignorance, which leaves her amazed when he shows anger to her:

> My lord is not my lord; nor should I know him
> Were he in favour as in humour alter'd. (III.iv. 125–6)

It is her failing that she does not 'know' him, and knows the world so little that she does not conceive how her advocacy of Cassio might be misinterpreted. So Iago's perception that 'her delicate tenderness will find itself abus'd' (II.i. 232) proves correct. Iago as the envious satirist serves as a presenter of the early stages of the action in *Othello*. He is the figure closest to the audience, who uses Roderigo as a foil in elaborating a general satirical vision of human beings as given to folly and vice, and makes us see Othello, Desdemona and Cassio in this context. In his soliloquies he talks us into a kind of complicity with him, to the extent that we are forced to allow his perceptiveness, to concede there may be some truth in what he says, and to enjoy his wit. As he 'knows' Othello, Desdemona and Cassio better than they know themselves, so we 'know' him better than we do the other characters, and because of this, his perspective provides a controlling view up to the third act. The key to the play is not the extent to which Othello is infected by Iago, but the extent to which we in the audience are seduced by him. For it is impossible to reject altogether the satirist's vision, even while we recognise and are horrified by the malice of a Macilente or Iago, since his truths come too near home. The power of Iago is rooted in the context of satirical poetry and drama which fed Shakespeare's imagination during the years that brought *Othello* to completion. A recognition of the connections between *Othello*, the dark comedies which belong chronologically with it, and the satire of the period, especially as represented in Jonson's *Every*

Man out of his Humour, provides a context which helps us both to understand Shakespeare's method in constructing his play, and to explain why Iago is such a disturbing figure.[10]

NOTES

1. The main traditions in the criticism of the play are outlined by Robert Hapgood in the section on *Othello* in *Shakespeare: Select Bibliographical Guides*, ed. Stanley Wells (Oxford, 1973), pp. 159–70. If there has been a change in the years since then, it is best seen in a decline of interest in such questions as whether the Moor is noble or ignoble, and in a greater willingness to recognise what Hapgood called a 'full spectrum of interpretative possibilities' (p. 162), as marked, for instance, in the five different interpretations of Iago sketched in Stanley Hyman's *Iago* (1970). The most recent full-length study of the play, however, Janet Adamson's *Othello as tragedy: some problems of judgment and feeling* (Cambridge, 1981), returns to old issues, dismissing Hyman's book (p. 65), and treating the characters as autonomous, 'real', and capable of being objectively analysed. She takes us back to the self-dramatising Othello of F. R. Leavis, and for her 'Iago . . . is an essentially simple mind, for whom life is correspondingly simple' (p. 76). A subtler interpretation of Iago's 'secret motives' is offered in E. A. J. Honigmann's *Shakespeare: Seven Tragedies* (London, 1976), pp. 78–88. I have tried to show how varying, even contradictory interpretations of Othello and Iago are suggested by the text in 'Iago, Othello and the critics', printed in *De Shakespeare à T. S. Eliot: Mélanges offerts à Henri Fluchère* (Paris, 1976), pp. 61–72.

2. In *The Comic Matrix of Shakespeare's Tragedies* (Princeton, 1979), Susan Snyder relates *Othello* to Shakespeare's romantic comedies, and sees in the action up to the reunion of Othello and Desdemona in Cyprus 'a perfect comic structure in miniature' (p. 74). This seems a strained argument to me. Much more germane to the general issue here, though not concerned with *Othello* itself, is Lee Bliss's *The World's Perspective: John Webster and the Jacobean Drama* (New Brunswick, New Jersey, 1983), especially Chapter 1, 'The art of distance 1: Tragicomedy', pp. 13–53.

3. In R. A. Brower, *Hero and Saint*, (Oxford, 1971) p. 28ff.

4. It is true that Desdemona says Othello has known Cassio a long time (III. iii. 11), and speaks of him as many a time coming 'awooing' with Othello (III.iii. 71), but we are never *shown* this closeness between the two men, and what Desdemona says is contradicted by Cassio's complete ignorance about Othello's marriage in I.ii, and about the identity of his bride at I.ii. 52.

5. Brower, *Hero and Saint*, pp. 2, 28.

6. A. C. Bradley, *Shakespearean Tragedy* (London, 1904), pp. 225–32; see also Honigmann, *Shakespeare: Seven Tragedies*, pp. 78–82, and Hyman, *Iago*, pp. 61–100.

7. Roderigo is reminiscent of the comic butts satirised in plays like *Every Man out of his Humour* (see p. 18 above), but is presented without an assurance (as in the case of Jonson's Puntarvolo), that such extreme behaviour is 'very easily possible'. In his quirky, brilliant essay on *Othello*, published in *The Dyer's Hand* (London, 1963), and reprinted in *Shakespeare Othello: A Casebook*, edited John Wain (London, 1971), pp. 199–223, W. H. Auden remarked on the implausibility of Roderigo, and noted that 'when we first see Iago and Roderigo together, the situation is like that in a Ben Jonson comedy' (p. 204).

8. I am thinking, of course, of Coleridge's famous formulation, 'the motive-hunting of motiveless malignity' (*Coleridge's Shakespearean Criticism*, ed. T. M. Raysor, 2 vols., London, 1930, I. 49).

9. Moralistic critics tend to see Iago as a character designed 'precisely to arouse our intolerant loathing' (Adamson, *Othello as Tragedy*, p. 86); Nevill Coghill went so far as to claim that the function of Iago's soliloquies is to distance him from the audience and 'create hatred for him' (*Shakespeare's Professional Skills*, Cambridge, 1964, p. 147). Such approaches are insensitive to the way Shakespeare makes Iago fascinating through what Giorgio Melchiori calls 'The rhetoric of character construction in *Othello*', *Shakespeare Survey*, 34 (1981), 61–72. (He notes that Iago speaks 32.58 per cent of the words in the play, and Othello 24.09 per cent; however, Iago's proportion of the dialogue is even higher in Acts I and II, in which he has 43 per cent of the lines, about 606 out of 1398, and provides the dominant voice and perspective on the action.) See also Marvin Rosenberg's study of the acting tradition relating to Iago, which led him to observe, in *The Masks of Othello* (Berkeley and Los Angeles, 1961), p. 183, that 'The drives we have learned to recognise as a badge of humanity are twisted and magnified in Iago, but we cannot disown them'.

10. *Every Man out of his Humour* is quoted from *The Complete Plays of Ben Jonson*, ed. G. A. Wilkes, Vol. I (Oxford, 1981).

JAMES L. CALDERWOOD

The Properties of the Play

1. Iago and Inbetweenness

Since at least 1817, when Hazlitt called Iago "an amateur of tragedy in real life," critics have remarked on the theatrical artistry of Othello's ancient.[1] Stanley Edgar Hyman makes the most concentrated case, picking up on Bradley's claim that "Shakespeare put a good deal of himself into Iago" and arguing that "for Shakespeare, Iago is a merciless self-portrait as artist-criminal . . . and a therapeutic symbolic action of purging away the guilt of Shakespeare's Faustian craft."[2] What this means in Hyman's subsequent discussion is that Iago mimics the playwright's craft in staging scenes and manipulating people, in creating illusions, in improvising to meet occasions, and in exhibiting a full repertory of lies ranging from the "flat untruth" to the "artistic suggestion-in-non-suggestion."

Cataloging Iago's stage practices is less meaningful, however, than registering their staginess. In the tradition of the theatrical villain he takes a showy pleasure in sharing with the audience his knavery, his many motives, his manipulative cleverness, even the labor pains of his creative plotting—"How, how?—Let's see" (1.3.395). By staginess, then, I mean mediation. Situated between two idealists, Othello and Desdemona, who believe they communicate not *in* but through words and bodies—that is, who think signs and referents (and signifiers and signifieds) are so fast married that communication

From *The Properties of Othello*, pp. 113–34, 152–54. © 1989 by the University of Massachusetts Press.

is virtually intuitive—Iago stands for mediation, for inbetweenness and the shaped made-up-ness of things.

The logocentric assumption of Othello and Desdemona that signifiers and signifieds are covertly married is emblematized by their own covert marriage, by the fact that they themselves appear on stage as husband and wife sans signifier—without any declarative ceremony. On the other hand, when Iago "marries" Othello at the end of Act 3, Scene 3, he insists on ceremony:

> Do not rise yet.
> [*Kneels*] Witness, you ever-burning lights above,
> You elements that clip us round about,
> Witness that here Iago doth give up
> The execution of his wit, hands, heart,
> To wronged Othello's service! Let him command,
> And to obey shall be in me remorse,
> What bloody business ever. [*They rise.*]

Although much of his insidious wooing is accomplished without words, relying on the suspiciousness of silence, when it comes to murder, Iago, like a bride marrying above her rank, is especially anxious to seal his good fortune in ritual. Or, rather, in a parody of ritual, for his business is to subvert mediation in all its forms, to set down the pegs that make not merely music but traditional ceremonies, honest words, gestures, facial expressions—signs, in short.

Indeed *en*-signs.

. . . [I]t is no accident that Iago is Othello's ancient or ensign, his flag-carrier. He himself makes a point of it as he prepares to leave the streets and join the Moor:

> Though I do hate him as I do hell-pains,
> Yet for necessity of present life,
> I must show out a flag and sign of love,
> Which is indeed but sign. That you shall surely find him,
> Lead to the Sagittary the raised search,
> And there I will be with him. (1.1.156)

Iago's stress on signs here draws attention to mediation, to signs as signs, to false signs that are indeed "but signs"—those in which the shadow of evil intent falls *between* sign and referent to fashion a lie, as Iago's shadow will fall between Othello and the truth of Desdemona to fashion a murder. It draws attention also to the centaurian sign of the Sagittary which shows out a flag of barbarism, which is indeed but sign, before the inn where the Moor and his bride are presumably attempting to consummate a marriage.

But Iago's inbetweenness is manifested not only within the play, in Venice. His puns on his emblematic military rank also get in between the audience and the Bradley-like illusion of Iago the Venetian. He is literally, he reminds us, a flag or sign of a man—in short, a character, not a person.

Or, rather, he is a metacharacter. As such, he undoes what is usually regarded as the business of the actor: to create a convincing illusion of reality by converting dialogue into speech, script into natural behavior. Instead, Iago turns his own seemingly impromptu speech back into dialogue and script, into the stuff of the stage. For him to say "I am not what I am" (1.1.66) and swear "by Janus" (1.2.33) is appropriate not merely because his Janus-like profile reveals knavery to us in the Globe while exhibiting "honesty" to his fellows in Venice but also because it reveals artifice to us and "reality" to them. As a walking lie he emblematizes the pervasive doubleness of Shakespeare's task, simultaneously to make and match: to make a play that matches life.

Iago's soliloquies illustrate this perfectly. In them he at once muses silently in Venice and speaks publicly in the Globe. Insofar as soliloquy is a means of suggesting depth and inwardness of character, his soliloquies lend him a certain substance as a real "person" in Venice, the only person with an articulate inner life; but insofar as soliloquy is a device to keep an audience informed, they sabotage his reality and declare him an artificial stage figure, a nephew of the old Vice, the only character who knows and unabashedly admits he is a character in a play—hence, a metacharacter. When Iago comes forward to address the audience in soliloquy, he denies his equality with the other characters. He strides into the mirror of art, only to pause half-in half-out and assert both his metadramatic discreteness from the realities of Venice and his illusionistic discreteness from the realities of London. This violation of the realistic "rules" of the play observed by the other characters on stage is a theatrical equivalent to his violation of the communal mores observed by other "people" in Venice.[3] To him, rules, norms, and principles, wherever they exist, are items of blind faith to which he issues a devilish *non serviam*. Only fools like Othello have such faith, and they pay dearly for it.[4]

Iago's doubleness is in the Freudian sense uncanny—the familiar given an eerie turn. For doubleness on stage is familiar enough. As Bert O. States points out, the actor never quite fully invests his role:

> He is always slightly quoting his character. . . . No matter how he acts, there is always the ghost of a self in his performance (not to be confused with egotism). Even the most unsophisticated theatergoer can detect something else in the characterization, a

superconsciousness that could be nothing other than the actor's awareness of his own self-sufficiency as he moves between the contradictory zones of the illusory and the real, *vraisemblance* and *vrai*, seeming and being. . . .[5]

I wonder, however, if Iago may not invert this slight divestiture. In his case, is it not the character rather than the actor who is the ghost, so that instead of an actor quoting Iago's lines we have Iago speaking his own lines through the voice of the actor? In other words, does Iago the demonic character take parasitic possession of the actor who plays him? Well, of course that's fanciful. But surely not unactable. To gain such an impression, the actor would have to play not just Iago but himself as well—himself in the role of an actor possessed by a character, compelled at times almost against his will, somewhat puppetlike, to say what he says and do what he does. At the end of Act 3, Scene 3, when Iago says to Othello "I am your own forever," the diabolic spirit would pass like ectoplasm from the actor playing Iago to him who plays Othello. Thus exorcised, the actor would now be free to play his role as Iago like everyone else, and Iago would return to being merely a character. Now it is Othello who becomes possessed and driven by an alien spirit, who turns Janus-faced and double, who in his worst moments—say, in the dialogue leading up to his epilepsy—finds his voice uncannily taking on the accents of Iago.

In any event, just as Iago gets in between and destroys the marriage of Othello and Desdemona, so he gets in between and deconstructs the audience's theatrical marriage to the illusion of reality in Venice. As a johannes factotum of the theater himself—actor, director, playwright, prompter—Iago is the antithesis of realism. Of course as a tempter to evil he relies on the realistic appearance of honesty, and philosophically his view of the world is crudely realistic. Metadramatically, however, he makes it clear that the emperor of Realism is clothed in highly visible quotation marks when he is around. Without him, we would religiously indulge our Coleridgean poetic faith, our natural talent for seeing through signs and suspending disbelief. Taking a cue from the idealistic Othello and Desdemona, we might well assume that our epistemological marriage to the events in Venice were made in heaven, not fashioned by vulgar theatrical ceremonies on the boards of the Globe. But Iago intervenes—the impediment to the marriage of true minds in the theater as well as in Venice. Instead of saying "the perfect ceremony of love's rite," which is the poet's proper function (Sonnet 23), Iago the poet *manqué* substitutes an imperfect ceremony, a black mass parody of a wedding in which he takes Desdemona's place and speaks fair words with devilish meanings. Had Desdemona played the interior playwright, surely we should have had a true troth plighted betwixt us and the depicted world. But in between us and the light of her truth appears Iago, to cast the shadow of a lie across Shakespeare's stage.

Not that Shakespeare is defining his craft as a lie. Rather, I should think, he is defining it in this case as a tragedy. To say "the perfect ceremony of love's rite" is the proper function of the comic rather than the tragic poet, and in that role Shakespeare does more than his share of haling young lovers before the altar of his hymeneal art. The perfect ceremony of tragedy, however, is not a wedding but a killing, and as a participant in that ceremony Iago is functional in the extreme: Shakespeare wields him like a ritual knife in an action that drives straight to the heart. Thus in creating Iago, Shakespeare had no need to purge himself of the "guilt of his Faustian craft," as Hyman suggests. His craft is the tragic craft; it calls for Iago to do as he murderously does and for Shakespeare to write as he murderously writes. It is no sin for a man to labor in his vocation.

2. Iago's Motives

Because Iago is functional in the extreme, so is Shakespeare's plot. Anyone talking about *Othello* is almost obliged to say "The plot is superbly constructed, with virtually every element skillfully exploited by Iago so as to hasten the final catastrophe."[6] But although everyone agrees the plot is well motivated, few agree about how well motivated Iago is. Hence an entire book by Hyman titled *Iago: Some Approaches to the Illusion of His Motivation*.

Hyman explains his lengthy subtitle by putting as much distance as he can between himself and Bradley. "Let me say this as firmly as possible: as a character in a play, not a person, Iago has no motivation. His entire existence consists of words on a page: he has no psychology, no character or personality, no history (he had no past before the play began, and has no future after it ends)" (pp. 4–5). Rudely exposed like this, stripped bare of mimetic reality, Iago can only clutch at fig leaves of motivation offered him by a playwright who would a little o'erstep the immodesty of nature. Shakespeare, that is, "must create the illusion (again by means of words on the page) that such a figure as Iago is motivated in everything that he does" (pp. 5–6).

One problem with this otherwise admirable proclamation is that it endows motivation with an illusionary status no more peculiar to it than to anything else in the theater. When speech comes from a script and clothing from a costume box, when faces are painted, actions rehearsed, and scenes set, what makes motivation so particular? By this exacting criterion, to write about any theatrical matter would require our saying "Some Approaches to the Illusion of [Speech, Action, Scene, Clothing, etc.]." In fact Hyman should have titled his own book not *Iago* but *The Illusion of Iago*, because like everything else in the play Iago is, as he admits, not what he is.

In short, we are talking about a play. Which is entirely acceptable to Iago. That is, to label anything about him an illusion is rather redundant when that is precisely what he himself, honest in duplicity, repeatedly does. Othello and Desdemona are riveted to their realistic identities; they would be appalled to discover not only that they are in a theater as well as in Venice but also that they are not in fact Othello and Desdemona but Richard Burbage and a boy actor (and married to boot!). Iago, however, freely acknowledges what he both is and is not, and revels in his revelry. Thus he is sign-like both in the Saussurian sense that attributes meaning to what a sign is not and in the Derridean sense of what a sign is not yet. He is the very non-essence of semantic deferral; no matter how much he tells us about himself and his motives we never feel we have come to an end-stopped truth. Meaning is never identical with itself, and neither is Iago. His being consists in not-being, his meaning in what is not meant.

In this light, then, the question Coleridge posed in his famous phrase "the motive-hunting of motiveless malignity" is actually "Is the illusion of Iago's motivation illusory?" Does Iago protest too much? Is he really fuming with indignation because he was passed over for the lieutenancy? Is he consumed with a desire for vengeance because he suspects Othello and Cassio of bedding his wife? Perhaps, perhaps not.[7] The actor must decide, as he must also decide whether to play Iago—or to be played by Iago—as a latent homosexual, a xenophobic racist, a sadist, a misogynist, a satanic demi-devil, a Machiavellian misanthrope, and so forth.[8] Obviously no one can bring all of these Iagos on stage in one performance. But whichever one(s) the actor chooses to play, he will be false to his role if he fails to incorporate into his performance something of Iago the artist.

One tangential virtue of Coleridge's famous phrase is its suggestion that in the character of Iago Shakespeare has demystified the concept of motivation. Insofar as motivation is held to be originary and inward, at the source of things, it is normally taken to be more real than the behavior it produces— especially when *real* is defined as "originary and inward, close to the source of things." However, if Iago is indeed motive hunting, then motivation is not the source of his behavior but merely another form of it, as fictional as his lies. In that case we are obliged to search for the motives for his motive hunting, a search that takes us backward like a crab into an infinite regress. Since we can always find something prior to a point of origin—the chaos before Creation or another universe in which our Big Bang was a black hole—we must at some point cry out like Aristotle "Enough!" and posit an Unmoved Mover. In *Othello* or any other Shakespearean play the likeliest candidate for Unmoved Mover is the elusive playwright from Stratford, if only because our ignorance of *his* motives is more infinite than any regress. Thus there is no better place to cry "Enough!" than the point at which a search for Iago's motives becomes a search for Shakespeare's motives.

At the same time, however, an attempted transition from Iago to Shakespeare is instructive, because at that point a merger of motives does take place in what might be called, if not motiveless malignity, something rather similar and nearly as sinister—aesthetic disinterestedness. For the one motive we can safely attribute to Shakespeare is the desire to write a good play—a good murderous tragedy that will strew the stage with bodies and bring the audience's collective heart into its constricted throat. Thus his own malignity toward his characters, his blithe willingness to subject them to anguish and agony, is, monstrous as it sounds, aesthetically motivated. Which is to say that it is not malignantly motivated at all, because far from bearing ill will toward Othello and Desdemona, Shakespeare must surely be delighted with the Moor and his bride, even as the one smothers the other. Contemplating them with one auspicious and one dropping eye, he must murmur

> How sad, how sorry, how brutal—but how marvelously right! That villain Iago wrought well. Now, let me revive Desdemona just for an instant—it will pump a little hope into the audience—then smother her again. A final gasping moment of struggle and terror, then death. There, that's it, perfect! Anne, Anne, where are you? Listen to this....

And, to be sure, Iago must be sitting somewhere too, smitten with awe and wonder, thinking "Ah, that villain Shakespeare, what a clever dog! To be sure, I was not bad myself—aesthetically, that is. We do make a fine team. Now, if he will just get me out of this play alive, like Falstaff, perhaps we can do something else—King Lear, for instance—I could play Edmund...."

So I suggest that Iago's "motives" can be attributed less to Iago the man (the illusion of a man with motives) than to Iago the artist, the shadow of Shakespeare the artist, with whom he shares a total absence of malignant intent, whatever he says, and a maximum interest in doing whatever it takes to maneuver this play to its gratifying tragic conclusion.

Of course I exaggerate the role of artifice in Shakespeare's art. Desdemona's terror and Othello's anguish in the deathbed scene issue not from a self-conscious preoccupation with dramaturgical technique but from a sympathetic imagination in which human feeling flows into artful feeling with, by this time in Shakespeare's career, scarcely a ripple of resistance. Still, even if they are resolved as if by second nature, artful considerations are inevitably present. Subtract all human feeling and they alone remain, in the shape of a character called Iago.

Let me take this a bit further by returning to the efficiency of Shakespeare's tragic plot and to Iago as master plotter. That Iago is a plotter goes without saying. He revels in plots, sees them everywhere—suspects Othello of wearing his nightcap, suspects, now that he thinks of it, Cassio of lusting for it too, and may even be casting mock-suspicious glances at handsome nobles in the boxes as he says all this. When he is not suspecting plots in others, he is inventing them himself. The opening words of the play catch him in midplot, or in midplots, for to accomplish one plot (making his fool his purse) he has been pretending to be busy with another one (bribing Desdemona into Roderigo's bed). In this respect too he resembles Shakespeare, who, not content with the one plot he inherited from Cinthio, has conjured Roderigo out of thin air and thrust him on stage so Iago will have someone to practice on before he turns his attentions to Othello.

Roderigo is an addition to Cinthio's plot; his presence multiplies plots and emphasizes the superfluous in Shakespeare's art, the superfluous that largely constitutes his art. Superfluous because the Iago-Roderigo plot functions as an analog to the Iago-Othello plot, and analogs are superfluous where plot is concerned. In the evolving action, analogs do not add or subtract, multiply or divide; they are an "equals" sign that goes nowhere, a form of doubling that defers the causal thrust, much as the artful ornamentation of a sword is superfluous and if carried too far may prove a hindrance to its cutting action. Iago and Shakespeare both take an interest in plotting that exceeds the needs of their own master plot—Iago because he enjoys plotting for plotting's sake, Shakespeare because his dramatic craft does not live by plot alone but presupposes doublings, recursions, correspondences, symmetries—a making of patterns as well as a shaping of clean efficient actions.

Still, let us focus on efficient actions, on plots that are, as Aristotle said they should be, causative and well motivated. Unfortunately, however, *cause* and *motive* are Janus-faced concepts. On the one hand they refer to points of origin the pursuit of which leads into infinite regresses. Iago himself is no introspective hunter of origins. He trots out his motives and causes quickly, mounts himself and his plot on them, and gallops off with never a backward glance. Even at the end of the play when he is given a grand opportunity to justify and/or to brag about his villainies, he locks himself in silence: "What you know, you know." Is he being secretive to vex his audience? Is he overcome by the enormity of his deeds? Or is he unable to answer because he knows no more than they why he has done as he has done? In any case, the motives have disappeared, as though for him and Shakespeare they served their purpose, made a beginning, and there's an end on it.

On the other hand, they may have made their beginning because of their end, for causes and motives are ends as well as beginnings. A motive is within the agent before he acts, generating his action, but it is also the projected result of that action. To the question "Why?" that hangs in the air at the end of the play, Iago might have replied "Because I had grievances, suspicions, hatreds" or, equally logically, "To destroy his marriage." Similarly, the cause in Othello's "It is the cause" is both the driving force that initiates his murder of Desdemona—his indignation at her supposed betrayal—and the terminal effect aimed at—his desire to prevent her from betraying more men. Moreover, as one would expect from Othello, the cause is hierarchical as well as temporal—there is the low degrading sexual cause that must not be revealed to the chaste stars and the transcendent "altruistic" cause of preserving the honor of other men.

Looked at this way, a cause may itself be the result of a cause—not a prior cause but a subsequent one. The end—Aristotle's final or telic cause—may as it were precede and precipitate the beginning, or efficient cause, to bring about an aesthetic form.[9] This is especially true in tragedies, because although the gestating playwright may not yet know where his play will take place, who his hero will be, or how his plot will develop, he does know precisely how everything will end—in death. The hero will die. Moreover, he will die because of something he himself does, because of an act triggered by *hamartia*. Why does he perform this act? "Because he must die" is as proper an answer as "Because of a tragic flaw within him." Whatever the latter may be, whatever the playwright chooses it to be—hubris, impulsiveness, jealousy, ambition, nobleness grown to a pleurisy—it will be an aesthetic product of his future death: the beginning of a plot must be pregnant with its own end. Here again, Iago's motives are aesthetically rather than realistically motivated. Their excessive number—his nonpromotion, his love for Desdemona, his various fears of cuckoldry—calls such extravagant attention to motivation as to demystify it. Iago seems to be saying "I am about to do terrible things. I must have reasons. What could they be?"—very much as Shakespeare seems to be saying "I am going to have Iago do terrible things. He must have reasons. What could they be?" (The nearest analog to this seems to me the demystification of the classical unity of time, and the exposition it entails, by Prospero and Miranda in Act 2, Scene 1 of *The Tempest*.) In any event, a play with an ending fraught with so much pity and fear requires a well-motivated plot and plotter, a plot whose causal design depends on villainous designs.

Design, with its semantic three-way stretch, is a word tailor-made for Iago; it fits him as "motive or aim," as "pattern," and, in hyphenated form (*de-sign*), as "de-meaning." In true Iago style, these various senses of the word efface one another. For example, aesthetic design (design as "pattern") suppresses signs as symbols of meaning by foregrounding formal elements such as congruence, symmetry, and recurrence. Meaning yields to geometry. Thus Iago "de-signs" or demeans signs not only when he divests words of meaning

by lying but also when he transforms meaningful humans into causal elements or phases of his plot. For causation converts integral ends into opportunistic means. Cassio must be gotten drunk so he will provoke a riot so he
will be cashiered so he will solicit Desdemona for reinstatement so Othello
will grow suspicious and, after a few more *so*'s, kill his wife. At each point a
person is reduced to a function, and his or her action is stripped of its nuances
of human feeling and meaning in order to become a link in a causal chain. If
B advances the plot from *A* to *C*, it has done its job and can retire unlamented.
Plotting and causation dehumanize in the interests of a design that can be
achieved only by using up and discarding each of its functional components.
And one of the things plotting dehumanizes is the plotter himself. Become a
tragic plotter and you are sure to be maligned. People will say you came into
the world upside-down and gnashing like Richard Crookback, or they will
long to bury you neck-deep in the earth like Aaron the Moor. If you become
really good at plotting they will call you demi-devil, stare suspiciously at your
feet, and stab you in a spirit of scientific inquiry.

   Surely there is a paradox here. The aesthetic impulse is supposed to treat
things not as means but as ends. It is supposed to paint fruit whose artfulness
paralyzes the observer's salivary glands, to shape plays that convert the audience from Desdemona-rescuing Partridges into deeply moved but wisely passive Wordsworths. Very often, however, the aesthetic impulse does not work
so gently in playwrights, who to achieve their aesthetic ends are notoriously
ruthless in employing both people and characters. Playwriting tends to leave
in its wake a lot of damp ex-friends muttering things like "If I had any idea
he was going to put Andrew and me into his play as those dolts Aguecheek
and Belch he'd have had damned fewer cakes and ale at our expense!" Nor
is it any less ruthless with characters. Shakespeare's reworkings of Cinthio's
tale—"Let me age and blacken the Moor, invent the gull Roderigo, erase
Iago's genuine love for Desdemona, tone down the brutality of the murder,
and get rid of the long horror story in which Desdemona's relatives take their
revenge"—are as blandly manipulative as Iago's evil schemings: "Let me move
Roderigo there, station Othello here, bring in Cassio with a handkerchief"
and so on. Here again is motiveless malignity in the role of aesthetic disinterestedness—the kind of disinterestedness that exploits friend and foe alike,
that humiliates and murders a Desdemona as readily as a Roderigo, and that
steals from Cinthio, Plutarch, Holinshed, and Belleforest without a blush.
When your aim is fine designs, everything is grist for the mill.

3. Satisfaction and Form

But fine designs do have drawbacks. The very reason perfect forms are
aesthetically satisfying—because they are perfect—may also render them

dissatisfying. They have achieved the state Othello claims for himself when he boasts of his "perfect soul" and the Senate calls him "all in all sufficient" (4.1.266). What is truly all in all sufficient—whether a person, a play, or a polyhedron—is closed off to the imagination and essentially dead. The closure of a curved line on itself gives birth to a circle but kills possibility; it leaves no openings, has no future, and while its closure may be deeply satisfying to the scientist, it cannot but make the critic grieve. Perhaps that is why Shakespeare associates Othello's moments of emotional repletion, his feeling of all in all sufficiency in war and love, with death.

If we adopt Kenneth Burke's psychological definition of form—"the creation of an appetite in the mind of the auditor, and the adequate satisfying of that appetite"[10]—then we can see in Shakespeare's craft a metadramatic parallel to Iago's craftiness. For Iago is busily engaged in creating an appetite in Othello. "Would I were satisfied!" Othello cries, and Iago, anxious to please, replies—

> I see, sir, you are eaten up with passion.
> I do repent me that I put it to you.
> You would be satisfied?
>   OTH. Would? Nay, and I will.
>   IAGO And may; but how? How satisfied, my lord?
> Would you, the supervisor, grossly gape on?
> Behold her topped? (3.3.396)

As an interior playwright, Iago's business is to promise the satisfactions of a completed action but also to postpone their arrival. A small example occurs when Othello responds to the story about Cassio's sensual dream as though all his doubts were satisfied and only revenge remains: "I'll tear her all to pieces." But this is too easily accomplished; it offends Iago's artistic sensibilities. "Nay," he interrupts, "but be wise. Yet we see nothing done; / She may be honest yet." What an evil genius lies in those two *yets*, holding out as they do the tantalizing possibility that nothing has been done but factoring in a cynical assumption that even if it be not now, yet it will come; the readiness—a jealous anguish sustained at the level of almost-certainty, of almost-form—is all.

More widely, the action of the play begins on two fronts, love and war, with Othello apparently in command of both. However, the action of love seems less to begin than already to have concluded; we begin where comedies end, with man and maid already married. But *has* this action really been completed? At the risk of immodesty, we must ask how long were the newlyweds in the Sagittary, and what were they doing when Iago called Othello forth. In short, has the Moor actually bedded his wife?

Iago seems to answer these questions with his pruriencies about white ewes being tupped "even now, now, very now," but Iago knows no more than we do of the matter—he later queries Othello with the wink and nudge of one married man to another, "But, I pray you, sir, / Are you fast married?" (1.2.10). Iago doesn't know, the audience doesn't know, and as for Shakespeare, he keeps his counsel.

Thus it seems *theatrically* plausible that Desdemona remains unbedded or incompletely bedded throughout the play.[11] I say "theatrically" here in reference to the infamous "double time scheme," for as everyone knows the stage portrayal of events leaves no time for Cassio to bed Desdemona (if he is supposed to do so after the marriage), and as though to obviate this problem Shakespeare inserts various suggestions that a longer period of time has elapsed during which adultery could have been committed (and the marriage consummated).

Even without a double time scheme, however, the absence of an opportunity to commit adultery passes unnoticed in the theater simply because it is never mentioned ("Nonsense, how is this possible?") and because the audience knows it is a lie anyhow. On the other hand, the possibilities of an unconsummated marriage are clearly advertised: we hear of Othello's being called forth from the Sagittary on his wedding night; we hear his vehement denials of erotic desire before the Senate; we hear him assign Desdemona to a separate ship; we see their separation dramatized in the arrival of the ships at Cyprus; we hear him invite Desdemona to bed with the words "The purchase made, the fruits are to ensue; / The profit's yet to come 'tween me and you" (2.3.10); and we hear him accept with remarkable equanimity a second arousal from bed—"'Tis the soldiers' life / To have their balmy slumbers waked with strife" (2.3.251).

In Burke's terms then, Shakespeare creates an appetite in the audience, a curiosity about the consummation of the marriage, that instead of being satisfied is sustained throughout the play. Not of course that we expect ocular proof—a theatrical reenactment of the moment when the gods gathered about to watch the net of Hephaestus drop on Ares and Aphrodite—but we might have expected something to negate the interruptions and separations that give us doubtful pause. As it is, we remain uncertain until the Murder Scene, when we obtain ocular proof indeed.[12] Grossly gaping on as Desdemona is at last bedded, we are perversely satisfied, for we find that satisfaction and death coincide—our satisfaction, Othello's satisfaction, Desdemona's death.

But is *satisfaction* really the right word? Do we actually take some kind of pleasure in the smothering of the innocent Desdemona? Alas, so it would seem. A pleasure analogous to that which I attributed to Shakespeare earlier: "How sad but how marvelously right!" As possibility evolves into probability and then into inevitability, a sense of formal completion yields aesthetic pleasure—the kind we experience when Oedipus is blinded, Faustus carried off, or Samson Agonistes crushed. Thus we too participate in that disinterestedness that borders on motiveless malignity. Not that heartless pleasure is all we feel. Rather, like Othello, we are torn between a soft-hearted pity for Desdemona and a stony-hearted devotion to a "cause" that requires her death to fulfill its destined logic.

Of course this stony-hearted aesthetic pleasure ought to be evoked at the end of any tragedy. But in *Othello* Shakespeare takes special pains to call it forth. It is a matter of satisfaction. In the previous chapter I mentioned that whether or not there is a *coitus interruptus* in the play there is certainly a *miles interruptus* when the anticipated battle with the Turks fails to materialize. Thus the energies that drive Othello toward his violent ends are generated, I argued, less by sexual than by martial frustrations.

Othello, however, is not the only person deprived of satisfaction by the disappearance of the Turks. We too have been led to expect a battle, to look forward to experiencing some measure of the pomp and glory and the downright violence that Othello speaks of later. But then, inexplicably, the Turks vanish in an offstage tempest, the battle comes to nought, and we must content ourselves with this weak piping time of peace.

Here is a perfect example of Burke's psychology of form subverted. An appetite is created in the audience, only to be frustrated. Precisely what we would expect of Iago, but the villain here is Shakespeare. What Iago keeps doing to Roderigo (and will later do to Othello), Shakespeare does to us. Curiously enough, precisely at this point Iago seeks to rekindle Roderigo's desire to put money in his purse by assuring him that Desdemona's marital content cannot last, that she already fancies Cassio:

> Mark me with what violence she first loved the Moor, but for bragging and telling her fantastical lies. And will she love him still for prating? Let not thy discreet heart think it. Her eye must be fed; and what delight shall she have to look on the devil? When the blood is made dull with the act of sport, there should be, again to inflame it and to give satiety a fresh appetite, loveliness in favor, sympathy in years, manners, and beauties—all which the Moor is defective in. (2.1.222–30)

Trust Iago to have made a study of desire and to know it arises from human defect. Humans are not complete, nor were meant to be; they lust because they want, and they want because they are wanting. That includes not merely the Desdemonas and Roderigos but us in the audience as well, who are here because we too lack and want, because we lack and therefore want form, eloquence, beauty, and, to be sure, the satisfactions and consummations of violence. But satisfaction is hard come by and harder kept. Satiety cannot succeed satiety without something to rekindle desire, and nothing kindles desire like frustration.

In some degree then, by playing on our desire for aesthetic form, for the completion of an action and the satisfaction of an appetite, Shakespeare seduces us into wanting Iago's violent plot to succeed. If we cannot have warfare between Turks and Venetians, let us have it elsewhere, in love and revenge. So the impulse to battle is displaced onto sex, issues of state divert into domestic channels, and violence to others turns reflexive. "Are we turned Turks," Othello demands of the rioters on Cyprus, "and to ourselves do that / Which heaven hath forbid the Ottomites?" (2.3.164). But this random drunken swordplay between Cassio and a few Cypriots is no substitute for the Turkish wars; only something with shape and tragic size to it can satisfy us now—and Othello too for that matter. "You would be satisfied?" Iago asks.

"Would? Nay, and I will."

And so he is. Increasingly it is he who is turned Turk on the painful wheel of Iago's lies, and this Turk will not disappear until he gets the violence he wants. Thus, killing a whore he has his revenge, and at the same time a perverted sexual climax. Iago too has his satisfaction as his plot rounds to a successful close. And as it succeeds, our formal desires are satisfied as well. The fatal bedding of Desdemona consummates the marriage and our aesthetic expectations at once. With Othello standing in for the Turk, and Desdemona for Cyprus, everyone rests content in the perfection of form. Except that . . .

4. Dissatisfaction and Unity

. . . as I said before, perfect form satisfies dissatisfyingly. Surely it does in *Othello*, where the perfection of Iago's and Shakespeare's plots entails the disintegration of perfection in the hero—the collapse of Othello's absolute content and all in all sufficiency. Yet even the perfection of those plots is called in doubt. The moment of success, when Othello is content that he has dealt harsh justice to a whore, and Iago is content that his design is complete, is shattered by Emilia's screechings of "Villainy!" Suddenly all is thrown into doubt and confusion, and as the satisfactions of completed action dissolve, it becomes apparent that no action is complete until it is understood, until the question "What has happened here?" is satisfactorily answered.

What *has* happened here?

Emilia discloses what she knows up to a point, the point of Iago's sword, which is still stained with the blood of Roderigo, who might have told far more. With both of them dead, only Iago knows the truth. "Will you, I pray, demand that demi-devil / Why he hath thus ensnared my soul and body?"

To which Iago famously replies, "From this time forth I never will speak word." And, true to his word for once, later on when Othello has increased the "tragic loading of this bed" with the weight of his own body and Lodovico declares "This is thy work" and pauses, or should pause, to invite an explanation, Iago says nothing.

What then are Lodovico and Gratiano to report to the Senate? The situation casts them jointly in the role of Horatio, commandeered by the dying Hamlet to tell his story to the yet unknowing world. Horatio's is no easy task, even though Hamlet had earlier filled in the gaps of the story for his friend by passing on the Ghost's tale, for instance, and by recounting the ocean voyage episode. But Lodovico and Gratiano have a more difficult task, for the biggest gaps in their knowledge of Othello's story—the events that occurred back in Venice and the temptation of Othello by Iago—although they could be, will not be filled in by the schemer who was there. When Iago lapses into silence Othello's story disappears too—or would have if it weren't for some incriminating messages conveniently discovered in the pockets of Roderigo and Iago: a couple of letters passed between the two villains plus "a discontented paper" of Iago's. These provide just enough information to call forth from Othello a breast-beating "O fool, fool, fool!"

But letters must be interpreted, because as recent philosophy has made abundantly clear, writing keeps its intentions to itself. Refusing to answer questions, to explain itself, it says only "What you know, you know," or "What is written is written," and withdraws into an Iago-like silence. Shakespeare's play is similarly unresponsive, and for a similar reason. For despite its dialogue and speeches, it is as much a written document as that original focus of hermeneutics, the Bible. The actor who plays Iago can no more answer our questions than the villain he plays. His speech is not authentic speech, an invitation to dialogue, but spoken writing; and we know Hamlet's opinion of those who "speak more than is set down for them"—"That's villainous!"

If Hamlet the dramaturge is right, then Iago is no villain. He says precisely what is set down for him, no more, no less. And what is set down for him is nothing—which accords perfectly with the fact that no one knows better than he that there is nothing, no definitive truth, to repeat at this point, even if he wanted to repeat it. As the very spirit of mediation he knows that the act of reaching out for knowledge fends it off, that ocular proof is blind and certainty uncertain. Iago stands for nothing—or, rather, for Nothing, for the negative that shadows all positives. Thus his first gesture of deception takes the form of "Ha! I like not that" as Cassio departs (3.3.35). Then to Othello's "What dost thou say?" he replies "Nothing, my lord; or, if—I know not what." In these first two lines of his as tempter, he issues three nega-tives—two *nots* and one *nothing*—and one curious positive negative, *know*. These supply us with our first hint of the *no* lurking within *know*, of the fact that Iago's insinuations, in a diabolic version of creation ex nihilo, mold the empty substance of "nothing" into the illusion of its homonym "noting."

Othello picks up this negative style immediately by saying, not as we would expect "Was that Cassio?" but "Was *not* that Cassio parted from my wife?" The repetition of *not* is insidious for two reasons—because it casts the shadow of *naught* across both Othello's discourse and Desdemona's conduct, precisely the shadow Iago wants to have cast, and because its presence here precludes a true answer to Othello's question. Had Othello said "Was that Cassio?" a straightforward "Yes" would have delivered the truth. Phrased as it is, however, a reply of "Yes" would merge bafflingly with "No," since it could mean either "Yes, it was not" or "Yes, it was." But Iago always avoids the word *yes*, even when it would prove cunningly ambiguous. In this case he replies typically with another question—"Cassio, my lord?"—and then drifts into troubled conjecture: "No, sure, I cannot think it."

Inasmuch as Othello's "Was not that Cassio parted from my wife?" invites an equivocal response it forecasts his later ambivalence. He wants ocular proof and an end to doubt, yet he covets ignorance and blindness. He would have been happy, he says, if the "entire camp" had "tasted her sweet body, / So I had nothing known" (3.3.351). No in-betweens for him—he would know either everything or nothing; and his desire here to know nothing leads inevitably to his obliteration of all offensive knowledge in an epileptic loss of conscious-ness. The irony of course lies in the fact that, as with all of Iago's lies, there is nothing to be known. "By heaven, I'll know thy thoughts!" Othello demands, but Iago's dark thoughts cannot be brought to light, because, quite simply, he has no dark thoughts about Desdemona.

At the same time Iago specializes in the knowledge of the unacknowl-edged. He knows and suggests with sidelong smiles and dark hints what, he implies, all Venetians know but never express, that all men are knaves and lechers at heart, all women whores, and under the lapel of every virtue is a sales tag. Such knowing is negative by necessity—unacknowledged knowl-edge, the truths culture says "no" to in order to survive as culture.

But Iago knows, and plays the knowing game to perfection. "Good sir, be a man," he implores Othello:

Think every bearded fellow that's but yoked
May draw with you. There's millions now alive
That nightly lie in those unproper beds
Which they dare swear peculiar; your case is better.

> O, 'tis the spite of hell, the fiend's arch-mock,
> To lip a wanton in a secure couch,
> And to suppose her chaste. *No*, let me *know*;
> And *knowing* what I am, I *know* what she shall be. (4.1.65)

Every *know* that comes into Iago's gravitational field here is warped into a *no*, so that "knowing what I am" becomes a kind of *no-ing* or nullifying of self in the sacred act of achieving self-knowledge. What can be known, contra Othello, is not what one is but only what one is not, as Iago declared earlier when he said "I am not what I am." Then, with this non-knowledge of self intact, he will "know what she shall be." Here the *no* within *know* not merely nullifies self-knowledge but destroys the self—"what she shall be" is no-thing, a whore, a dead whore.

The nullity at the center of knowing is brought forth climactically when Iago's knowledge of Othello's story is demanded, and he delivers his tautological reply,

> Demand me nothing. What you know, you know.
> From this time forth I never will speak word.

Absorbing some of the negative radiation from *nothing* in the first sentence and *never* in the third, the otherwise invisible *no* within the twice repeated *know* of the second sentence begins to glow with an oxymoronic, cross-canceling energy. To *know* is to *no*, to deny; knowledge in this bad world is self-negating—what you know cannot be acknowledged. Since society is grounded on that which is unspoken, I shall not speak. Or, inversely, what you *no* you *know*—what you negate by a failure to acknowledge, you nevertheless *do* know, we all do; hence explanations are superfluous. Make of it what you will.

So the truth we are so anxious to know (whatever words like that might mean after Iago's final speech) dissolves into silence. Not, however, Emilia. Under the force of her clamoring accusations, Iago's seemingly perfect plot shatters. Of course this destruction of Iago's plot contributes to the construction of Shakespeare's. Not even Shakespeare's plot is perfect, however. In fact, if Iago's last speech undermines the concept of a causal beginning, Othello's last speech undermines the concept of an actional end; and both combine to make an assault on formal perfection.

As I said before, no action is complete until it is understood. Unfortunately no action is ever completely understood, for the signs of its understanding, the terms of its definition, are unending; there is always more that could be said. Every action, however unequivocal in appearance, attenuates into a series of fragmentary and conflicting interpretations or, less contentiously, flows into a sea of discourse.

That Shakespeare is conscious of this seems evident from Othello's closing address, which constitutes the first interpretation of his unlucky deeds. The first, for his is by no means the final story—in fact not even a story at all, but hints and instructions to those who will tell his story: "Then must you speak of. . . ." But hints and instructions must be interpreted, just as the letters Lodovico and Gratiano are shortly to write must be interpreted by the senators who read them. Othello's "unlucky deeds" forge a link in a chain of interpretation that stretches as far as this book and, however astonishing and painful to contemplate, even beyond.

5. Theatrical Property

We could put these matters in terms of property—theatrical property. In Chapter 2 I mentioned that theft could be regarded as a kind of communicative process in reverse, in which the sequence "sender-message-receiver" becomes "owner-property-thief." Translating *message* into *property* merely brings out a metaphor already latent in the sender-message-receiver formulation. For that sequence suggests that verbal expressions are, as messages, somewhat objectlike or propertylike; they bottle up meanings and pass them inviolate from person to person irrespective of speaker, hearer, or context.[13] Like an Aristotelian plot, there is a distinct beginning, middle, and end to such a process, and an element of shared ownership: my private ideas, packaged and shipped to you, become yours as well.

This notion of meaning as either private or public property seems written into *Othello*. That is, questions about ownership of property in the play, such as "Who owns Roderigo's purse or Othello's handkerchief?" or most critically "Who owns Desdemona herself?" give rise to the larger question, "Who owns *Othello*?"

The answer depends on who does the answering. Othello, advocate of unitary truths and private property, would reply "Shakespeare, of course." But a jurist of the day would have been less certain. He might have pointed out that a script in itself, however valuable, was not really property, although the writer had personal rights to it. But of course Shakespeare did not keep his script to himself; he sold it to his acting company for from six to ten pounds. Only then, "in the hands of an acting company," Joseph Loewenstein notes, "did the work begin to acquire abstract property values that needed protection: the right to exclusive performance and the right to control the reproduction of the manuscript, either by release to a scrivener or by sale of a copy to a printer or publisher."[14] Normally once the script had been sold to an acting company the playwright no longer had any rights in it. But the ownership of

Othello would have been complicated by the fact that Shakespeare was, like Iago, something of a johannes factotum of the theater—not only playwright and actor but also shareholder in his company and householder of the Globe. Thus he was selling his script in part to himself and buying it in part from himself. To the (let us say) ten pounds he got for *Othello* (a ten-pound play if ever there was one!) he could pocket his share of the take as actor (if he played a role) and as shareholder-householder as well, not to mention his share of the modest fee (two or three pounds) paid by a stationer to print it, had any printer done so during his lifetime. Thus, although he would still have a manifold financial interest in *Othello*, his authorial property rights, as we understand them today, were not so much forfeited as simply nonexistent to begin with.

And quite properly so, Iago would have said, thinking along other lines. For if Othello would answer "Shakespeare, of course" to the question "Who owns *Othello*?," Iago would surely demur—

> Shakespeare, my lord? No, sure, I cannot think it. Let me remind you that this fellow Shakespeare is himself little better than a thief. How do you think this script came into his keeping? I'll tell you. This piratical Stratfordian boarded a land-carrack named the *Hecatommithi*, captained by one Giovanni Battista Giraldi Cinthio, an honest countryman of mine, and, without so much as a "By your leave," he plucked a precious story from its hold, pocketed it up, and went his way. Oh, I grant you, he may have improved on it somewhat, but that does not make it his, any more than your marrying Desdemona made her yours. After all, she passed from her father to you and, so it seemed, from you to Cassio and (who knows?) perhaps to the entire camp, pioners and all. These stories, my lord, are like these women; we can call the creatures ours, but not their appetites. Look to't.

Translated from the Italian, Iago apparently means that Shakespeare can add to, subtract from, divide, and multiply Cinthio's story in an effort to make it his own—he can funnel into it his own meanings to suit his own designs and declare "This play is *my play*, as true a reflection of my truth as Desdemona is of Othello's, as unchanging as she, and . . ."—and, alas, as doomed to death as she. To claim the play as his private property, the repository of his fixed and constant truths, is to deprive it of its theatrical life and transform a live script into a dead text. The mode of existence of a play, insofar as it is based on sharing, discourages even the thought of authorial property rights. Even to bring it to theatrical being, the playwright must yield it up, first to the players and then to the audience, all of whom will swarm aboard and make off with chests of meanings they will claim for their own. The players are to the playwright who hands them his script as the listening Lodovico and Gratiano are to the Othello who tells them his version of his story. And lined up behind the players is a series of audiences who, like the senators back in Venice, will hear of these matters and interpret them each in its own way. This being the case, Shakespeare can no more claim exclusive title to his play than Othello can to his identity.

This does not mean that Shakespeare renounces his ownership entirely, although his apparent indifference to the publication of his plays might suggest as much. His modesty, I imagine, is on the sly side, as if he were to admit that his play is no more than a strumpet, as Pandarus implies at the end of *Troilus and Cressida* when he bequeaths the audience his diseases. But in *Othello* the strumpet Bianca longs for marriage to Cassio, and the so-called strumpet Desdemona is in reality true to her troth. Like the Desdemona of Othello's imagination, the play may "turn, and turn, and yet go on / And turn again," proving almost wantonly obedient to all who pay the fee and enjoy its favors. But of course these turnings are not as degrading as they might sound. The inconstancy of the play is a measure of its vitality. From age to age it is revivified in the interpretive imaginations of audiences. If it loses the integrity of a fixed monument in this process, it gains the integrity of an ever-changing but constant fountain.

Moreover, like a fountain its randomness is in some degree constrained by its source. Or, to return to the marriage metaphor, the play is also faithfully plighted to Shakespeare. It keeps its troth in the sense that it, like Sonnet 76, remains "so far from variation or quick change . . . That every word doth almost tell [his] name." No one but he could have made it so, and no matter how hospitable it is to our interpretive incursions, we cannot have it entirely as we like it. Like language itself, the play may be something of a strumpet, but in the keeping of a husband like Shakespeare it is also something of a beloved and honest wife. If it is no one's exclusive property, neither is it everyone's common goods.

Notes

1. Stanley Edgar Hyman sums up the critical line from Hazlitt through Hudson, Bradley, and Granville-Barker to Kenneth Burke in his chapter "Iago and Prospero," in *Iago: Some Approaches to the Illusion of His Motivation* (London: Elek Books Ltd, 1971). On Iago's artistry, see William Hazlitt, *Characters of Shakespeare's Plays* (Boston: Wells and Lilly, 1818), pp. 60–76; A. C. Bradley, *Shakespearean Tragedy*, 2d ed. (1904: reprint ed., London: Macmillan, 1908), pp. 175–242; Harley Granville-Barker, *Prefaces to Shakespeare*, 2 vols. (Princeton: Princeton University Press, 1947), vol. 2, esp. pp. 98–112; Harold Goddard, *The Meaning of Shakespeare*, 2 vols. (Chicago: Chicago University Press, 1951), 2: 69–106; Heilman, *Magic in the*

Web, esp. "The Iago World: Styles in Deception," pp. 45–98; and Sidney Homan, *When the Theater Turns to Itself* (East Brunswick, N.J.: Associated University Presses, 1981), pp. 104–20, and his "Coda on *A Midsummer Night's Dream* and *Othello*," in Shakespeare *Theater of Presence* (Lewisburg, Pa.: Bucknell University Press, 1986), pp. 196–202.

2. Hyman, *Iago*, p. 61.

3. Janette Dillon makes the insightful observation about Richard III that his breaking free from the illusion of reality during his soliloquies parallels his breaking free from the social and moral order in England; see her chapter on *Richard III* in *Shakespeare and the Solitary Man* (Totowa, N.J.: Rowman and Littlefield, 1981), pp. 49–60, esp. p. 59.

4. Speaking of Iago's *non serviam* stresses of course his diabolic rebellion, not against God but against standards of morality and decency usually held to take their source in divinity. Similarly, Othello the Christian convert does not lose his faith in God but in an earthly substitute, the "divine Desdemona." See in this connection Norman Rabkin, *Shakespeare and the Common Understanding*, pp. 57–73.

5. Bert O. States, *Great Reckonings in Little Rooms: On the Phenomenology of Theater* (Berkeley and Los Angeles: University of California Press, 1985), p. 125. See also the chapter "The World on Stage" for a brilliant discussion of signs and images in the theater.

6. David M. Zesmer, *Guide to Shakespeare* (New York: Barnes and Noble, 1976), p. 309. On the other hand, H. A. Mason regards the play as badly constructed (Shakespeare *Tragedies of Love* [London: Chatto and Windus, 1970], pp. 59–162); and Ned B. Allen argues that Shakespeare wrote the play rather backwards, the last three acts first, the first two last (which accounts, he feels, for the so-called double time scheme)—"The Two Parts of *Othello*," *Aspects of Othello*, ed. Kenneth Muir and Philip Edwards (Cambridge: Cambridge University Press, 1977), originally published in *Shakespeare Survey* 21 (1968).

7. Robert B. Heilman and Bernard Spivack have addressed the question of Iago's motivation most thoroughly, in *Magic in the Web* (pp. 25–44), and in *Shakespeare and the Allegory of Evil* (New York and London: Columbia University Press, 1958), pp. 3–25.

8. Psychoanalytic critics in particular have not been content with Coleridge's "motiveless malignity." On the whole they locate the source of Iago's evil in sadism and homosexuality. See for instance Martin Wangh, "*Othello*: The Tragedy of Iago," *Psychoanalytic Quarterly* 19 (1950): 202–12; Shelley Orgel, "Iago," *American Imago* 25 (1968): 258–74; Robert Rogers, "Endopsychic Drama in *Othello*," *Shakespeare Quarterly* 20 (1969): 205–16; M. D. Faber, "*Othello*: The Justice of It Pleases," *American Imago* 28 (1971): 228–46; and Leslie Y. Rabkin and Jeffrey Brown, "Some Monster in His Thought: Sadism and Tragedy in *Othello*," *Literature and Psychology* 23 (1973): 59–67. See also Randolph Splitter, "Language, Sexual Conflict, and 'Symbiosis Anxiety' in *Othello*," *Mosaic* 15, no. 3 (1982): 17–26.

9. Aristotle's remarks on causation take their most concentrated form in *Physics*, Book 2 and passim; *Metaphysics*, Book 5; and *Posterior Analytics*, Book 2.

10. Burke, "Psychology and Form," in *Counter-Statement* (1931; Berkeley and Los Angeles: University of California Press, 1968), pp. 29–44.

11. Arguments against the consummation of the marriage are presented by William Whallon, *Inconsistencies*, pp. 68–81, and by T. G. A. Nelson and Charles Haines, "Othello's Unconsummated Marriage," pp. 1–18.

12. In his study of *Othello*, "The Stake of the Other," Stanley Cavell says "My guiding hypothesis about the structure of the play is that the thing *denied our sight* throughout the opening scene—the thing, the scene, that Iago takes Othello back to again and again, retouching it for Othello's enchafed imagination—is what we are shown in the final scene, the scene of the murder" (p. 132).

13. For a discussion of the prevalence and incorrectness of this communicative metaphor, see Michael Reddy, "The Conduit Metaphor," in *Metaphor and Thought*, ed. A. Ortony (Cambridge: Cambridge University Press, 1979), and George Lakoff and Mark Johnson, *Metaphors We Live By* (Chicago: University of Chicago Press, 1980), pp. 10–13.

14. Joseph Loewenstein, "The Script in the Marketplace," in *Representing the English Renaissance*, ed. Stephen J. Greenblatt (Berkeley and Los Angeles: University of California Press, 1988), p. 266. In the following discussion of ownership I'm indebted to Loewenstein's informative article. See also Gerald Eades Bentley, *The Profession of Dramatist in Shakespeare's Time, 1590–1642* (Princeton: Princeton University Press, 1971), pp. 88–110.

EDWARD BERRY

Othello's Alienation

Critics have tended to ignore or underplay the issue of Othello's race. The topic of race has always been explosive, particularly when it involves miscegenation, and invites evasiveness. A more significant impulse, however, has been the widespread critical assumption that Shakespeare's plays depict not the particularities but the essentials of the human condition. A.C. Bradley, for example, asserts that "in regard to the essentials of his character" Othello's race is unimportant, and that Shakespeare would have laughed if anyone had congratulated him on "the accuracy of his racial psychology."[1] Robert Heilman calls *Othello* a "drama about Everyman, with the modifications necessary to individualize him."[2] Harold Clarke Goddard argues that Othello is "neither a Negro nor a Moor" but "any man who is more beautiful within than he is without."[3] Jane Adamson claims that Othello's Moorishness "matters only in so far as it is part of a much larger and deeper" issue—the distinction in life between "the 'fated' and the 'free' aspects of the self."[4] This tendency to transcend the particulars of race or culture is not restricted to those critics most sympathetic to Othello, for, in their famous critiques of Othello's egotism and self-delusion, neither F.R. Leavis nor T.S. Eliot even alludes to such matters; both treat Othello's moral flaws as universals.[5] The weight of critical tradition, then, presents a Shakespeare

From *Studies in English Literature, 1500–1900,* 30, no. 2 (Spring 1990): 315–33. © 1990 by Rice University.

who finds racial and cultural difference insignificant and who assimilates his Moor into the "human" condition.[6]

Critics impressed by the importance of Othello's Moorishness have tended to respond in two quite different ways. Some, like Albert Gerard and Laurence Lerner, have argued that Othello is fundamentally savage. For Gerard, "Othello's negroid physiognomy is simply the emblem of a difference that reaches down to the deepest levels of personality.... Othello is, in actual fact, what Iago says he is, a 'barbarian'."[7] I Laurence Lerner calls *Othello* "the story of a barbarian who (the pity of it) relapses" and concludes that Shakespeare "suffered from colour prejudice."[8] For such critics the play is a study of a character whose innate savagery is disguised by a thin veneer of civilization and Christianity.

A more persuasive and influential response to Othello's Moorishness has been to contrast Shakespeare's treatment of race with that of his contemporaries. Both G.K. Hunter and Eldred Jones, in particular, have argued that Shakespeare invokes the negative Elizabethan stereotypes of Africans only to discredit them. According to Hunter, the play "manipulates our sympathies, supposing that we will have brought to the theatre a set of careless assumptions about 'Moors'. It assumes also that we will find it easy to abandon these as the play brings them into focus and identifies them with Iago, draws its elaborate distinction between the external appearance of devilishness and the inner reality."[9] Jones praises Shakespeare for his "complete humanization of a type character."[10] Despite their emphasis on the issue of race, both Jones and Hunter ultimately take a position very similar to that held by the critics who transcend it altogether. The same can be said of Richard Marienstras's insightful treatment of Othello's alienation and of Martin Orkin's recent and very useful account of racism within the play and within its critical and theatrical traditions.[11] Once such critics conclude that Othello is not a stereotype, he tends to lose his individuality as a Moor and to become a representative of humanity.

Although I agree broadly with the arguments of Jones and Hunter, it seems to me important to appreciate the particularity of Shakespeare's portrait and its resistance both to negative stereotyping and abstract universalizing. There is little question that in choosing Othello for his protagonist Shakespeare sought to create a realistic portrait of a Moor. The protagonist in his source, Cinthio's *Gli Hecatommithi*, is a mere stereotype, noteworthy in Venice only for being black, jealous, and vengeful. Shakespeare's protagonist is not only richly complicated but individualized and set apart from Venetian society in almost every respect—in his blackness, his past, his bearing, and, above all, his language, with its unusual rhythms, grandeur, and exoticism. As Lois Whitney has shown, moreover, many of Othello's specific attributes probably derive from Shakespeare's reading of Leo Africanus, whose *Geographical Historie of Africa*, translated by John Pory, was published in London in 1600.[12] Whitney shows that Pory's description of Leo's life is remarkably like Othello's. He too was a Moor of noble descent, an inveterate wanderer in exotic lands, a convert to Christianity; he too was once sold into slavery and redeemed. Leo's descriptions of the Moors, in addition, emphasize many of the attributes that critics have noted in Othello: simplicity, credulity, pride, proneness to extreme jealousy and anger, and courage in war.

If Shakespeare depended upon Leo Africanus for such details, he must have been much more interested in "racial psychology" than critics such as Bradley or Heilman suggest. His interest, of course, was not anthropological in the modern sense. As Whitney makes clear, he seems to have constructed not a member of a particular society but a composite "African," a synthesis of details drawn from Leo's descriptions of both "tawny" and "black" Moors. In this, he was doubtless encouraged by the looseness of Leo's own terminology, which blurs distinctions among the various groups he describes. Although such synthesizing may be anthropologically suspect, in an Elizabethan context it represents a progressive movement away from medieval stereotypes to recorded experience. Leo's varied and balanced view of the people of Africa made possible a composite far more complex and balanced than that provided by the familiar negative stereotype. While not ethnographically accurate, such thinking frees one to imagine authentic cultural difference.

If we consider the "African" attributes that Shakespeare probably took from Leo Africanus, we can see in the characterization of Othello complex gestures towards cultural differentiation. Othello's "African" qualities are presented from two sides. Iago calls Othello a "credulous fool" (IV.i.45), for example, but he also alludes to his "free and open nature" (I.iii.399).[13] Othello's pride appears at times as vanity, at times as rightful self-respect. His passionate nature leads to murderous violence, but it also contains deep love and tenderness. His courage serves him well in war but is ill-adapted to the complexities of peace.[14] Othello's reactions to the stress created by Iago do bring to the surface what seem to be latent or repressed aspects of his "Moorishness": his uncontrollable passion, for example, his superstitious interpretation of the handkerchief, or his ritualistic attempt to make the murder of Desdemona a sacrifice. But neither his character nor the cause of the tragedy can be reduced to some innate savage impulse. Shakespeare's portrayal of Othello takes important steps towards cultural concreteness but does not end in psychological determinism. Othello is neither Everyman nor an inhuman savage.

In responding to Othello, then, it is important to recognize both the concreteness and complexity of his "Africanness." Paradoxically, however, Othello's "Africanness" is crucial to his tragedy not because of what he is, innately or culturally, but because of how he is perceived, by others and by himself. In this sense, *Othello*, like Faulkner's *Light in August*, is a tragedy of perception.

To develop this point, as I shall do for the remainder of this essay, it might help to begin with Tzvetan Todorov's recent book, *The Conquest of America*.[15] Todorov argues that, from the time of Columbus, the early Spanish explorers and missionaries tended to view the New World Indians in one of two ways: either as essentially the same as Europeans and therefore worthy of assimilation; or as essentially different and inferior, worthy of enslavement and destruction. According to Todorov, the Spaniards could not imagine that the Indians might be equally human but culturally different, neither inferior nor in need of assimilation. Failing to recognize the cultural integrity of the Indians, the Spaniards could only project upon them their own values. For them, the Indians were either not fully human, or, if human, merely latent Spaniards, awaiting Christianity and civilization.

Todorov's book is highly speculative and betrays some of the limitations of a non-specialist in the field.[16] Nonetheless, it offers an extremely suggestive paradigm of early colonial attempts to rationalize contact with the "other." Todorov's description of the two opposing ways of defining and ultimately oppressing the "other," moreover, provides a remarkably useful framework for Shakespeare's tragedy. As we shall see, both the Venetians and Othello himself tend to view Othello from one or the other of Todorov's poles. He is either assimilated into Europe or expelled from humanity.

To understand Othello's predicament, one must appreciate not only his "Africanness" but his position as a black man in Venetian society; he is the Moor of Venice.[17] The fact of Othello's alienation is the play's most striking visual effect. One can imagine something of the original impact upon Shakespeare's audience by viewing the Longleat drawing of a scene from *Titus Andronicus*, reproduced in the Riverside edition (Plate 9), in which Aaron the Moor, by virtue of his intense blackness and physical position, stands alone. Othello's blackness is not only a mark of his physical alienation but a symbol, to which every character in the play, himself included, must respond. The potential impact of his physical appearance upon audiences is suggested by Charles Lamb's frank admission that although he could find Othello admirable in the reading he was only repelled by the figure of a *"coal-black Moor"* on stage; he concluded that the play should be read, not seen.[18] According to Margaret Webster, modern audiences were stunned more constructively by the first appearance of Paul Robeson in the role: "Here was a great man, a man of simplicity and strength; here also was a black man. We believed that he could command the armies of Venice; we knew that he would always be alien to its society."[19]

The most dramatic reactions to Othello's blackness within the play are those of Iago and Roderigo in the opening scene. Their overt and vicious racism provides the background for Othello's first appearance. For Iago Othello is "an old black ram" (I.i.88), "the devil" (I.i.91), and a "Barbary horse" (I.i.111); the consummation of his marriage is a making of "the beast with two backs" (I.i.115–16). Roderigo, who shares Iago's disgust, speaks of Desdemona's "gross revolt" (I.i.134) and the "gross clasps of a lascivious Moor" (I.i.126). As Jones and Hunter have shown, these characters evoke, in a few choice epithets, the reigning stereotype of the African on the Elizabethan stage. Othello is black, and his blackness connotes ugliness, treachery, lust, bestiality, and the demonic. This poisonous image of the black man, as we shall see, later informs Othello's judgment of himself. Although Iago's notorious artistry is usually linked to his capacity to shape a plot, it extends as well to characterization, for the Othello he in many ways creates comes to see himself as his own stereotype.

Although he lacks Iago's sardonic wit, Brabantio shares his imagery of blackness, for his rage at Othello expresses the same racism Iago and Roderigo had incited in the streets of Venice. Brabantio has often entertained Othello and, with Desdemona, listened to his tales. Yet the discovery that his daughter has married the Moor releases in him violent feelings of fear, hatred, and disgust. He accuses Othello of being a "foul thief," of being "damned," of arousing Desdemona's love by witchcraft (I.ii.62), of working against her by "practices of cunning hell" (I.iii.102), of being a bond-slave and pagan (I.ii.99). At the root of his amazement and outrage is physical revulsion; he cannot believe that his daughter would "run from her guardage to the sooty bosom / Of such a thing as thou—to fear, not to delight!" (I.ii.70–71). This sense of Othello as a revolting object, a "thing," recurs with tragic irony at the end of the play, when Lodovico turns away from the corpses of Othello and Desdemona on the marriage bed and orders, "The object poisons sight, / Let it be hid" (V.ii.364–65). The tragic culmination of Othello's repulsiveness is a sight that must be hidden.

Emilia is an even subtler study in latent racist feeling than Brabantio. Up to the point of the murder, she never alludes to Othello's race; nor is her relationship to him in any way remarkable. She serves her lady, commiserates with her when her marriage turns sour, defends her against Othello's attacks, and generalizes her frustration with him into cynical comments about all men. When Othello confronts her with his murder of Desdemona, however, she explodes with suppressed racial hatred:

> *Othello.* She's like a liar gone to burning hell:
> 'Twas I that killed her.

Emilia. O, the more angel she,
And you the blacker devil!
    (V.ii.129–31)

Even though the emotion of the moment centers upon the fact of the murder, what Emilia reveals about herself in the use of the word "blacker" is
startling. Her cynical attitude towards men has apparently masked a revulsion against Othello's blackness. Having exposed his evil, Othello becomes
for her a "blacker devil," the phrase revealing that in her imagination he
has always been a black devil. He also becomes Desdemona's "most filthy
bargain" (V.ii.157), a creature "as ignorant as dirt" (V.ii.164). As she learns
more about Iago's responsibility for the crime, Emilia becomes less violent
in her outrage—Othello becomes more fool than devil—but she dies with
no change in these feelings of abhorrence and contempt. Her savage and
reductive outburst of racist feeling at this crucial moment in the play enables
audiences to vent and, ideally, to exorcise their own latent hostility, as well
as their suspicions that Othello would eventually conform to type. Emilia's
violent reductivism may enhance an audience's awareness, even at this point
in the play, of Othello's humanity.

Desdemona loves Othello and dies defending him against the charge
of her own murder. Yet she is perhaps the subtlest victim of Venetian racism. Brabantio ascribes her love to witchcraft because he cannot believe that
she could otherwise overcome the horror of Othello's blackness—"and she,
in spite of nature, / Of years, of country, credit, every thing, / To fall in love
with what she fear'd to look on!" (I.iii.96–98). Brabantio's imputation of fear
in Desdemona may be in part a projection of his own emotion, but Othello
himself later confirms her reaction when he agrees with Iago's assertion that
she "seem'd to shake and fear your looks" (III.iii.207). Desdemona too provides implicit confirmation when she tells the Duke "I saw Othello's visage
in his mind" (I.iii.252). This implicit denial of physical attraction shows that
Desdemona tries to separate Othello's essential humanity from his appearance, but it also shows that she is sensitive to and disquieted by the insinuations that there must be something unnatural in such a love. She does not
say that she found Othello's blackness beautiful but that she saw his visage
in his mind.

More significant than this, however, is the sense of cultural estrangement that is woven into the love itself. Othello's exoticism is deeply attractive to Desdemona—she loves him for the adventures he has passed—but it
also contributes to her undoing. This sense of estrangement helps to explain
what to many critics has seemed a paradox in Desdemona's behavior: the
contrast between her independence and aggressiveness in Venice and her

helplessness and passivity in Cyprus. She is secure among Venetians, insecure and uneasy in her marriage to a man she does not fully understand. Although Iago is wrong in ascribing to her the licentiousness that he calls the Venetian "disposition," she responds to Othello's jealousy with the tragically inappropriate reflexes of a Venetian lady. She attempts to win favor by coyness and indirection—teasing Othello about Cassio, equivocating about the lost handkerchief, asking Emilia to make the bed with their wedding sheets. Such gestures are intensely ironic not just because they tend to work against her but because they reflect her lack of understanding of Othello. In her struggle to comprehend, she turns not to him for explanation but to fellow Venetians—to Emilia, who responds only with cynicism, and to Iago, who responds with hypocritical sympathy. Perhaps the subtlest and most pathetic indication of Desdemona's estrangement comes when she answers Emilia's rhetorical question—"Is he not jealous?"—with, "Who, he? I think the sun where he was born / Drew all such humors from him" (III.iv.29–30). Audiences need not have read Leo Africanus to note the pathetic irony in this, for the linkage between hot climates and hot passions was an Elizabethan cliché. The cultural gap between Othello and Desdemona confirms John Bayley's observation that the play is "a tragedy of incomprehension, not at the level of intrigue but at the very deepest level of human dealings."[20]

Perhaps the most pervasive sign of Othello's alienation is to be found in the use or, more precisely, the avoidance of Othello's name. The Folio title, *Othello: the Moor of Venice*, presents two alternatives: the one implying assimilation, the other alienation. Within the play, broadly speaking, characters can be divided by their preference for one or the other: the more racist the character, the less the inclination to use Othello's name. Iago refers to Othello by name only five times; he calls him "the Moor" more than twenty times. Roderigo never refers to Othello by name, calling him "the Moor" twice, "the thicklips" once. Brabantio too never uses Othello's name, nor does Emilia; the former calls him "the Moor" three times, the latter, eight. Among these characters the naming of Othello becomes an exercise in reducing the individual to a class, the person to an object. Othello is a "thing" long before the image of his body and Desdemona's "poisons sight."

Characters without overt racial hostility tend to use Othello's name more often, and when they call him "the Moor," as they almost all do, they tone down the label's negative connotations by means of positive adjectives, as in Montano's "the noble Moor" (II.iii.138). Montano uses the name twice, the epithet three times. Cassio uses the name once, the epithet once. Desdemona refers to Othello only once by name, four times by epithet, softening it twice in the phrases "the Moor, my lord" (I.iii.189) and "my noble Moor" (III. iv.26). The only character in the play who restricts himself to Othello's name is the Duke, who does so twice in the "trial scene," for obviously political reasons: he almost ignores Brabantio's entrance; so intent is he upon securing "valiant" Othello's assistance in the present emergency. That even the play's sympathetic characters tend to label Othello "the Moor" betrays the pervasiveness of his alienation. Iago's malicious "I hate the Moor" (I.iii.366) is a far cry from Desdemona's loving, "the Moor, my lord." But even her phrase implies an awareness of difference that estranges. Throughout the play, the naming of Othello keeps an audience subtly conscious of the impossibility of Othello's complete assimilation and gives to his numerous self-references, as in "That's he that was Othello" (V.ii.284), a special weight.

Racial tension of some kind thus affects Othello's relationship with every character in the play, and it operates within the boundaries suggested by Todorov, ranging from Iago's blatant racism to Desdemona's naive and uncertain assimilationism. The central question is how such tension affects Othello. Perhaps one should start with an effect it might have but does not. One possible response to racial antagonism is an aggressive assertion of one's own identity. Shylock never apologizes for his Jewishness but matches his Christian enemies insult for insult. Aaron the Moor in *Titus Andronicus* draws subversive power from a total commitment to his own blackness; in protecting his black child, he challenges Tamora's sons with an assertion of the superiority of black to white—"Coal-black is better than another hue, / In that it scorns to bear another hue" (IV.ii.99–100). Othello never defends his blackness; nor does he defend the religion or culture that lies behind him. The most rootless of Shakespeare's tragic heroes, he has no geographical or cultural anchor to his being. He is not only a convert but has been, from the age of seven, a wanderer; in Roderigo's sarcastic phrase, he is an "extravagant and wheeling stranger / Of here and every where" (I.i.136–37).

Given the lack of information available to Elizabethans on African cultures, even in Leo Africanus, Shakespeare might have had Othello's rootlessness virtually forced upon him; representing a homeless wanderer perhaps offered him a way of dramatizing alienation without the necessity of creating a credible cultural background. If so, Shakespeare turned this ethnographic defect into an imaginative virtue, for Othello's very lack of a cultural identity becomes a powerful ingredient in his tragedy. Othello's alienation goes much deeper than Shylock's, for he is estranged not only from Venetian society but, as a "wheeling stranger," from his own. Perhaps because of this Othello defines his identity from the outside, drawing upon images created by Venetian society—images which, as we have seen, reproduce Todorov's dichotomies. Throughout the play, Othello sees himself either as an exotic Venetian, a convert in the fullest sense, capable of complete assimilation, or he sees himself as a barbarian, worthy of destruction. His failure to break free of this constricting framework, to achieve a true sense of personal identity, is one of the play's most powerful sources of tragic feeling.

Such a claim may seem paradoxical for a character whom critics often accuse of pride and whose first appearance seems to demonstrate a magisterial self-confidence. Othello's first action in the play is to brush aside Iago's warning of Brabantio's challenge to the marriage. "My parts, my title, and my perfect soul, / Shall manifest me rightly" (I.ii.31–32), he claims. He asserts that his own social status is worthy of Desdemona—"I fetch my life and being / From men of royal siege" (I.ii.21–22)—and that his past services to the state will guarantee his security: "My services, which I have done the signiory, / Shall out-tongue his [Brabantio's] complaints" (I.ii.18–19). Here and throughout the play Othello's language is often rhetorically inflated; Shakespeare even calls attention to this quality in Iago's mocking allusion to Othello's "bumbast circumstance" (I.i.13). The inner cause of this language is not pride, however, as moralistic critics contend, but insecurity of the kind the Player Queen reveals when Hamlet accuses her of protesting too much. Challenged by Brabantio, Othello surely knows that he has crossed a dangerous line; he has, after all, eloped. In asserting so grandly his imperviousness to attack, Othello is not proud and foolishly complacent but, as later events confirm, somewhat naive and secretly insecure.

When his marriage is challenged, Othello rests his defense upon his abilities, his rank, his virtue, and his service to the state. As the attitudes of Iago, Roderigo, and Brabantio make clear, however, none of these is relevant to the most fundamental threat he poses, that of miscegenation, embodied in Iago's nightmarish image of the "beast with two backs." Brabantio calls attention to the disparities in years, social status, and religion that separate Othello from Desdemona, but his anguish centers on the unnaturalness of the marriage; what obsesses him is Othello's "sooty bosom," his status as a "thing." Othello has no defense against such unreasoning hatred, and it is no surprise that he does not recognize overtly the possibility of its existence. The threat of miscegenation is the play's hidden nightmare, and it cannot be overcome by arguments about virtue or service to the state.

Nor is it. What saves Othello's marriage, the "trial scene" makes clear, is not Othello's "perfect soul" but political expediency. Preoccupied as he is by fears of a Turkish attack, the Duke greets Othello effusively, scarcely noticing Brabantio's presence. Upon hearing Brabantio's complaint, he promises him the "bloody book of law" (I.iii.67), but as soon as he discovers that Othello is the accused, he urges moderation and acceptance of the marriage. He accepts the stories of Othello and Desdemona without demur, and once Brabantio capitulates, he pushes on to the military threat that is uppermost in his mind. Brabantio's anger is not mollified; nor are his charges of unnaturalness answered, merely suppressed. The threat of Othello's blackness cannot be submerged entirely, however, for it surfaces in Desdemona's need to rationalize her attraction—"I saw Othello's visage in his mind" (I.iii.252)—and in the Duke's attempt to placate Brabantio: "If virtue no delighted beauty lack, / Your son-in-law is far more fair than black" (I.iii.289–90). Although the "trial scene" ostensibly vindicates Othello, it actually reveals his vulnerability. The threat represented by Othello's blackness is not extinguished by the Turkish invasion, as Brabantio's parting words make clear: "Look to her, Moor, if thou hast eyes to see, / She has deceiv'd her father, and may thee" (I.iii.292–93).

The implications of the "trial scene" extend throughout the play. Iago carries forward Brabantio's attack upon Othello, with better success, and once the Turkish threat is removed, Othello is left vulnerable both within and without, prey to the complex interaction of psychological and social forces that occasion his downfall. The longstanding critical controversy surrounding the character of Othello, with its tendency to polarize responses into sentimental defenses or moralistic attacks, has done justice neither to the protagonist nor to the play as a whole. If I can do so without adding to this critical reductivism, I should like to focus on a single element in the unfolding of Othello's tragedy which the critical debate has tended to obscure and which does much to explain Othello's tendency towards self-dramatization, his susceptibility to Iago, his fury at Desdemona, and his final attempts at self-justification. This is his anxiety about his blackness.

Othello is often accused of self-dramatization, and at some level the charge is difficult to deny. His account of his courtship before the Duke is certainly dramatic and, despite his disclaimer, rhetorically effective. As he himself admits, moreover, he has used the same skills upon Desdemona, first provoking in her the desire to hear his stories, drawing from her "a prayer of earnest heart / That I would all my pilgrimage dilate" (I.iii.152–53), and then pretending to "consent" (I.ii.155) to the very request he had contrived. In his courting as well as in his defense before the Duke, Othello is rhetorically manipulative.

To see this behavior as self-dramatizing, however, and especially to moralize it as a symptom of pride, is to ignore its underlying cause. In the case of his courtship, Othello's alienation forces him to woo Desdemona indirectly, and only after she has hinted at her attraction. More importantly, what we tend to call self-dramatization has almost nothing of self in it. Othello tells Desdemona stories. Such tales were the stock in trade of all travellers, and Shakespeare later mocks them in *Antony and Cleopatra*, when Enobarbus regales his fellow Romans with the wonders of Egypt. Through these tales Othello reveals little about himself except, by implication, his rootlessness:

he has been a warrior and wanderer since his "boyish days." Desdemona falls in love not with Othello's self but with his adventures: "She lov'd me for the dangers I had pass'd" (I.iii.167). What she responds to is more properly called self-creation than self-dramatization, for through his stories Othello attempts to shape an image of himself that will win acceptance in Venice and, by his own admission, awaken Desdemona's love. Paradoxically, this image does not dramatize difference but identity; it reduces alienation to adventures. Othello presents himself not as an African but as an exotic Venetian. As Stephen Greenblatt has argued, Othello's "identity depends upon a constant performance . . . of his 'story,' a loss of his own origins, an embrace and perpetual reiteration of the norms of another culture."[21]

This kind of self-creation does not represent conscious deception on Othello's part but a belief in the possibility of assimilation; the self he shapes for his audience is that to which he aspires. He is a Christian convert, and the Christian doctrine of the equality of all human souls opens the way to such assimilation. Behind this aspiration, however, lies anxiety—the anxiety of the convert, who struggles to see himself as a member of a community from which he has been alienated. It is this insecurity that Iago exploits to set Othello's downfall in motion.

In Act III scene iii, Iago begins his temptations. He first awakens Othello's suspicions of Cassio, then warns him against the dangers of jealousy. As in Act I scene ii, when Iago had warned him against Brabantio, Othello attempts to brush aside the warning, expressing his faith in Desdemona's virtue and his own worth. His defense of himself, however, merely exposes his inner fears: "Nor from mine own weak merits will I draw / The smallest fear or doubt of her revolt, / For she had eyes, and chose me" (III.iii.187–89). Coming after Brabantio's contemptuous reference to his "sooty bosom," the Duke's allusion to his blackness, and Desdemona's "I saw Othello's visage in his mind," this reliance upon Desdemona's eyes is unnervingly ironic. Desdemona chose Othello not because of but in spite of her eyes, sublimating spiritually the visage Brabantio says she feared to look upon. Othello's allusion to Desdemona's eyes conveys the inner truth of a Freudian slip: he seizes for his defense a subject of deep anxiety.

Iago senses this anxiety, for he turns immediately to the matter of Othello's alienation. He first establishes his own credentials as an insider, privy to the ways of Venetian women: "I know our country disposition well: / In Venice they do let [God] see the pranks / They dare not show their husbands" (III.iii.201–203). Then he reminds Othello of Brabantio's parting threat, that one betrayal would lead to another: "She did deceive her father, marrying you, / And when she seem'd to shake and fear your looks, / She lov'd them most" (III.iii.206–208). Othello's admission, "And so she did," marks the erosion of his faith in Desdemona's eyes, for he allows that her reaction to his visage might have actually signalled her potential for betrayal.

As Othello begins to rationalize this possibility—"And yet how nature erring from itself" (III.iii.227)—Iago interrupts him and, with unusual intensity, twists his words so that they allude to the unnaturalness of the marriage:

> Ay, there's the point; as (to be bold with you)
> Not to affect many proposed matches
> Of her own clime, complexion, and degree,
> Whereto we see in all things nature tends—
> Foh, one may smell in such, a will most rank,
> Foul disproportions, thoughts unnatural.
>   (III.iii.228–33)

Iago immediately backs away from this line of thought, for he sees he has touched a nerve in Othello. That he is nearly trapped by his own rhetoric suggests that he himself is moved, carried away by some inner loathing of black sexuality. Whatever his motives, his words remain with Othello, for his insinuation that Desdemona is not only deceptive but sexually perverse, titillated by an unnatural love, later haunts Othello's imagination.

This first phase of Iago's temptation ends with a soliloquy, in which Othello, now deeply suspicious, attempts to find a motive for Desdemona's infidelity. The speech is masterfully evasive:

> Haply, for I am black,
> And have not those soft parts of conversation
> That chamberers have, or for I am declin'd
> Into the vale of years (yet that's not much),
> She's gone. I am abus'd, and my relief
> Must be to loathe her. O curse of marriage!
> That we can call these delicate creatures ours,
> And not their appetites! I had rather be a toad
> And live upon the vapor of a dungeon
> Than keep a corner in the thing I love
> For others' uses. Yet 'tis the plague [of] great ones,
> Prerogativ'd are they less than the base;
> 'Tis destiny unshunnable, like death.
> Even then this forked plague is fated to us
> When we do quicken.
>   (III.iii.263–77)

In these lines Othello struggles to evade the deepest source of his anxiety. His first thought is of his blackness. And well it should be. His blackness is the cause of Brabantio's opposition to his marriage, it affects the consciousness of everyone around him, and it has just been pressed upon him by Iago's insinuations of Desdemona's unnaturalness. That he goes on to trivialize this impediment, equating it syntactically with his inadequacies in the "soft parts of conversation" or in years, is deeply irrational. He cannot probe the real cause of his anxiety because to do so would be utterly destructive, leaving him with only two options: to embrace his blackness and hurl its beauty and power in the face of his enemies, as does Aaron in *Titus Andronicus*, or to internalize their image of him and yield to self-loathing. Either choice would proclaim his complete alienation. Instead, he places himself within another heroic fiction, this one as fatalistic as the truth but self-vindicating. If cuckolding is the destiny of great ones, then Othello is not alienated but assimilable: his betrayal becomes not the mark of an outcast but of a noble Venetian.

Having been convinced of Desdemona's treachery, Othello projects his self-loathing upon her. In his diseased imagination she becomes, paradoxically, the stereotype of the Moor: cunning, "black," sexually depraved, and diabolic. He calls her at various times a "slave" (III.iii.442), a "lewd minx" (III.iii.476), a "fair devil" (III.iii.479), and a "subtile whore" (IV.ii.21). This transformation of white virgin into "fair devil" is doubly ironic: not only does Desdemona become the opposite of herself; she becomes the image of disgusting sensuality that Iago had conjured up of Othello in the first scene of the play. Infected by Iago's imagery of licentiousness, Othello converts Desdemona into his own alter-ego, subjecting her to the same abuse that Roderigo and Iago had hurled against him in the streets of Venice. Othello's sexual disgust is thus not merely a "universal" symptom of repressed sexuality, as has often been argued, but is deeply implicated in the specific question of race.[22]

Othello finds Desdemona's betrayal horrifying not only because she corrupts herself but because her "blackness" confirms his: "[Her] name, that was as fresh / As Dian's visage, is now begrim'd and black / As mine own face" (III.iii.386–88). In part, his grief is expressed in fear and rage at the prospect of his lost reputation; the Folio text even replaces "Her name" with "My name" in the above quotation. At its deepest level, however, his anguish derives from his identification of himself, through love, with Desdemona. What he cannot endure, finally, is the loss or perversion of this love:

> But there, where I have garner'd up my heart,
> Where either I must live or bear no life;
> The fountain from the which my current runs

Or else dries up: to be discarded thence!
Or keep it as a cestern for foul toads
To knot and gender in!
    (IV.ii.57–62)

Desdemona is the pure source of Othello's being: his current runs from her fountain. He cannot dissociate himself from her corruption, therefore, for he takes his life from her. The ultimate horror for Othello is that this pure fountain should become a dark and loathsome place, full of repulsive, bestial sensuality. The knotting toads bring to mind Iago's repulsive image of the beast with two backs, the very nightmare of black sensuality that haunts the imagination of Venice and that Othello has tried to repress.

In the murder scene, what Othello tries to kill is thus in some sense his own blackness. By taking upon himself the role of justice, he attempts to fulfill his obligation as defender of the state, suppressor of those dark and passionate forces that threaten to undermine it. To maintain this role, he must struggle against his own passion, in his eyes the sign of his susceptibility to the evil Desdemona has committed. Hence he recoils from the loving sensuality her image evokes, a sensuality that might have saved her, and, when angered by her refusal to confess, he tries to stifle the rage that eventually turns his "sacrifice" (V.ii.65) into a murder. The deepest terror of this scene arises not from Othello's violent passion, as it would have if Shakespeare had chosen to dramatize the reversion of a savage to type, but from his steely efforts to suppress his emotion in the interests of a higher law.

The final moments of the play show Othello attempting to absorb the meaning of his terrible deed. His first response is a familiar evasiveness: "Who can control his fate?" (V.ii.265). But this effort to absorb his evil into a heroic "Venetian" self cannot be sustained. Prompted by the sight of the dead Desdemona, he confronts directly the horror of his responsibility and condemns himself to a black and burning hell: "O cursed, cursed slave! / Whip me, ye devils, / From the possession of this heavenly sight!" (V.ii.276–78). His immediate reaction to the murder thus reflects his divided image of himself: he is either doomed like all great men or destroyed by his own blackness.

Othello's final speech attempts to repair this inner division, to assert the emotional truth of the two contradictory self-images that have haunted him throughout the play. In a paradox that can only be resolved in death, Othello becomes imaginatively both the "Venetian" hero, doing service to the state by killing a treacherous Turk, and the treacherous infidel himself: "I took by th' throat the circumcised dog, / And smote him—thus" (V.ii.355–56). This is Othello's final narrative self-creation, but it no more captures an essential self than any of his earlier stories.[23] Neither singly nor together do these images of a "Venetian" hero or "Turkish" savage portray the truth of Othello as a man. Even in his own imagination he cannot see himself as both different and human. He attempts to transcend the constricting framework of assimilation or inferiority not by breaking free of it but by asserting, in death, that its opposite extremes are both true. This gesture cannot be called one of self-recognition, moreover, because both selves are artificial constructs, imposed upon Othello by his own internalizing of the Venetian mentality. Hence the pathos and terror at the heart of his final speech derive ultimately from the fact that Othello is to the end all narrative, and narrative directed from outside. Othello dies in a story he tells, but it is framed by assumptions that deny him an authentic self.

Othello's alienation, then, is central to the play. It is important not merely because Shakespeare portrays Othello as a Moor or because racial tension and anxiety pervade the atmosphere of Venetian society, affecting Othello's relationship with every character and increasing his susceptibility to Iago's appeal; it is important because Othello himself, in his aspirations towards assimilation and anxieties about his blackness, internalizes a false dichotomy that can only dehumanize him. A rootless wanderer, Othello defines himself in Venetian terms, as an exotic European or a brutal savage, or, in the final paradox of his death, as both. In Todorov's terms, he tries to unite the opposing images of his own oppression.

I have suggested that in representing Othello's "Africanness" without resorting to negative stereotyping of racial difference or to abstract universalizing of the human essence, Shakespeare stretched the mental framework of the age, thrusting upon audiences a more sympathetic understanding of the alien than was customarily available. Shakespeare's most penetrating insight into the nature of alienation, however, does not arise from his characterization of Othello as a Moor, which is inevitably deficient in cultural depth and resonance, but in the way in which the racial atmosphere that Othello breathes determines his own responses to his tragic predicament. The most disastrous consequence of racial alienation for Othello is not the hostility or estrangement of the Venetians but his own acceptance of the framework within which they define him. In his incapacity to break free of this mental construct, to affirm his own identity, as do Shylock and Aaron, Othello becomes a double victim of the early colonial imagination, an alien to others and himself.

NOTES

1. A.C. Bradley, *Shakespearean Tragedy* (1904; rpt. London: Macmillan, 1941), p. 187.

2. Robert Heilman, *Magic in the Web* (Lexington: Univ. Press of Kentucky, 1956), p. 139.

3. Harold Clarke Goddard, *Alphabet of the Imagination*, ed. Eleanor Goddard Worthen and Margaret Goddard Holt (Atlantic Highlands, NJ: Humanities Press, 1974), p. 81.

4. Jane Adamson, *"Othello" as Tragedy* (Cambridge: Cambridge Univ. Press, 1980), pp. 7–8.

5. F.R. Leavis, "Diabolic Intellect and the Noble Hero," in *The Common Pursuit* (London: Chatto and Windus, 1952); T.S. Eliot, "Shakespeare and the Stoicism of Seneca," in *Selected Essays* (London: Faber and Faber, 1951).

6. For an illuminating recent exception, which aligns Othello's marginality with Desdemona's, see Karen Newman, "'And wash the Ethiop white': femininity and the monstrous in *Othello*," in Jean E. Howard and Marion F. O'Connor, eds., *Shakespeare Reproduced* (New York: Methuen, 1987). I should also except many members of two seminars I organized in 1988–89: one for graduate students at the University of Victoria, the other for colleagues at the annual meeting of the Shakespeare Association of America. My thanks to both groups for ideas that I know I have assimilated but cannot with any confidence now attribute to individuals.

7. Albert Gerard, "'Egregiously an Ass': The Dark Side of the Moor. A View of Othello's Mind," in *Aspects of "Othello,"* ed. Kenneth Muir and Philip Edwards (Cambridge: Cambridge Univ. Press, 1977), p. 13.

8. Laurence Lerner, "The Machiavel and the Moor," *EIC* 9 (1959): 360.

9. G.K. Hunter, "Othello and Colour Prejudice," *Proceedings of the British Academy* 53 (London: Oxford Univ. Press, 1967): 152.

10. Eldred Jones, *Othello's Countrymen* (London: Oxford Univ. Press, 1965), p. 109.

11. Richard Marienstras, *New Perspectives on the Shakespearean World*, trans. Janet Lloyd (Cambridge: Cambridge Univ. Press, 1985); Martin Orkin, "Othello and the 'plain face' of Racism," *SQ* 38 (1987): 166–88.

12. Lois Whitney, "Did Shakespeare Know *Leo Africanus*?" *PMLA* 37 (1922): 470–83.

13. All citations are to *The Riverside Shakespeare*, ed. G. Blakemore Evans (Boston: Houghton Mifflin, 1974).

14. Shakespeare's complex handling of Othello's "Moorish" characteristics is analyzed by K.W. Evans in "The Racial Factor in *Othello*," *ShStud* 5 (1969): 124–40. Evans argues that "the same Moorish traits that precipitate his [Othello's] downfall later redeem him" (p. 139).

15. Tzvetan Todorov, *The Conquest of America*, trans. Richard Howard (New York: Harper and Row, 1982).

16. See the critical review by Roberto Gonzalez-Echevarria, "America Conquered," *YR* 74 (1984–85): 281–90. Despite its limitations, Todorov's book remains a stimulating and even moving attempt to confront historically a central problem of our time.

17. Like most contemporary critics, including Eldred Jones and G.K. Hunter, I find that the weight of evidence favors a black over a tawny Othello. Since Shakespeare portrays a composite figure, however, the alternative interpretation remains possible. Norman Sanders provides a useful survey of the problem in the introduction to his edition of the play (Cambridge: Cambridge Univ. Press, 1984), pp. 10–14. For reviews of the theatrical tradition, see Carol Jones Carlisle,

Shakespeare from the Greenroom (Chapel Hill: Univ. of North Carolina Press, 1969), pp. 188–97, and two articles by Ruth Cowhig: "Actors, Black and Tawny, in the Role of Othello—and their Critics," *ThR* 4 (1978–79): 133–46, and "The Importance of Othello's Race," *JCL* 12 (1977–78): 153–61.

18. *The Works of Charles and Mary Lamb*, ed. E.V. Lucas, 7 vols. (London: Methuen, 1903), 1:108.

19. Margaret Webster, *Shakespeare Without Tears* (1942; rpt. Cleveland: World Publishing, 1955), p. 236. For a verbal study of the role of color in the play, see Doris Adler, "The Rhetoric of Black and White in *Othello*," *SQ* 25 (1974): 248–57.

20. John Bayley, *The Characters of Love* (London: Constable, 1960), p. 146.

21. Stephen Greenblatt, *Renaissance Self-Fashioning* (Chicago: Univ. of Chicago Press, 1980), p. 245. Greenblatt's essay focuses not on racial norms but on Iago's manipulation of Othello's belief in the repressive Christian doctrine of sexuality.

22. See, for example, the essay by Edward A. Snow, "Sexual Anxiety and the Male Order of Things in *Othello*," *ELR* 10 (1980): 384–412; although he recognizes the importance of Othello's blackness (pp. 400–401), Snow emphasizes the universality of the portrayal. For a useful and sympathetic review of related approaches, see Carol Thomas Neely, *Broken Nuptials in Shakespeare's Plays* (New Haven: Yale Univ. Press, 1985), pp. 107–108.

23. In a stimulating recent study, *The Properties of "Othello"* (Amherst: Univ. of Massachusetts Press, 1989), James L. Calderwood says of this final speech: "Instead of a core-self discoverable at the center of his being, Othello's 'I am' seems a kind of internal repertory company, a 'we are'" (p. 103).

THOMAS MOISAN

Repetition and Interrogation in Othello: "What needs this Iterance?" or, "Can anything be made of this?"

Introduction

And first of all others your figure that worketh by iteration or repetition of one word or clause doth much alter and affect the eare and also the mynde of the hearer, and therefore is counted a very braue figure both with the Poets and rhetoriciens. . . .

There is a kind of figuratiue speech when we aske many questions and looke for none answere, speaking indeed by interrogation, which we might as well say by affirmation.

—George Puttenham

The ears of men are not only delighted with store and exchange of divers words but feel great delight in repetition of the same. . . .

Interrogation is but a warm proposition, and therefore oftentimes serves more fitly than a bare affirmation, which were but too gentle and harmless a speech. . . . It is very fit for a speech to many and indiscreet hearers . . . and then it may well be frequented and iterated.

—John Hoskins

To the ears of a Puttenham or a Hoskins Shakespeare's *Othello* would not have sounded out of tune. For it is a play that has been frequently cited, and celebrated, for, in Bernard Shaw's phrase, "the splendor of its word-music,"[1]

From Othello: *New Perspectives*, edited by Virginia Mason Vaughan and Kent Cartwright, pp. 48–73. © 1991 by Associated University Presses.

for memorable resonances created and impressed, and reimpressed, upon the ear by an opulent array of what Puttenham calls "auricular figures."[2] Conspicuous among these are the figures described above, interrogation and repetition, or what Othello at one point in his most critical and enlightening exchange with Emilia near the end of the play (5.2.150) terms "iterance." Much of what is said in *Othello* seems to get said a number of times and is often repeated in the form of questions, questions not infrequently answered by their own reiterated echoes. Hence, with Othello we may ask, "What needs this iterance?" What purpose is served, what effect achieved by the numerous and recurrent questions uttered in the play? For all that they may contribute to its acoustical architecture, what role do repetition and interrogation in *Othello* play in its definition, and the audience's experience of it, as tragic theater?

Or, rather, what "roles"? For in what is to follow I would propose that the figures of repetition and interrogation in *Othello* "operate" in a diversity of ways and with a polyphony of resonance that complicate our experience of the play and underscore the complexity that its students, at least since the time of Rymer, have found in it. Instrumental in giving formal shape to *Othello* as an argument and fable, underscoring the premises of its plot and the predicates of its actions, the play of repetition and questioning simultaneously evokes a dissonance that challenges our understanding of what the play enacts and, more to the point, challenges our ability to know and make judgments about what we have experienced. This challenge has been most perceptible, perhaps, in the notorious penumbrae that invest the issues of character and motive in the play, in the ever recurrent questions it has inspired concerning character motivelessly malignant and character all too readily corrupted. Yet the workings of repetition and questioning in *Othello* seem to have a deeper and subversively reflexive force as well, giving voice to an ambivalence within the play about the very medium of its expression: exemplifying the manipulative power of rhetoric, they at times suggest a rhetoric that eludes the control of those who would manipulate it; employed ostensibly to underscore a reference and seek elucidation, they often appear to underscore nothing so much as the power of language to obscure or suppress reference, and help to enunciate what Gayle Greene has called the play's "refusal to elucidate."[3]

At the same time, the repetition and questioning we encounter at the verbal surface of *Othello* are but the audible signatures of that deeper recursiveness and "demand for narrative" which, as Patricia Parker has reminded us recently, are central impulses in the play, impulses dramatized in its opening moments and in its closing words.[4] By the same token, however, the dissonances we detect in the operations of repetition and questioning alert us to the tensions which that recursiveness and "demand for narrative" occasion. For in the rhetorical world of *Othello* narration seems ever to entail variation, repetition with a "difference"—or *différance*—while the insistent demand for narrative seems persistently part of an ambivalent response to what has already been narrated, a response in part incredulous and resistant to what has been heard, but ultimately willing to hear more. "Tush, never tell me," Roderigo tells Iago in the opening line of the play, and waits to be told again, and again, how Iago hates the Moor. "She wish'd she had not heard it," Othello recalls Desdemona saying after she had heard his "story," a demurral attended by a request that Othello takes as grounds for a reprise (1.3.162–66).

A central activity of contemporary criticism, Jonathan Culler has observed, has been to discover in a text its appetency for "self-reference," a "self-reference that ultimately brings out the inability of any discourse to account for itself."[5] Culler's remark comes to mind here because to a considerable degree the activity, and preoccupations, to which it alludes are reflected in the issues my essay raises, the strategy it pursues, the vocabulary it employs, and—with some qualification—the argument it constructs. To examine the play of repetition and interrogation in *Othello* is, I would maintain, to encounter a rhetoric at once reflexive and subversive, and suggestive of a discourse commenting upon itself and turning what it says and enacts either literally into questions or into something questionable, something that evades accountability. In the echo chamber *Othello* comes at times to resemble, the action of the play gets distilled into catechetical *examens* of individual phrases and words which in their reverberations ultimately remain unelucidated, leaving unresolved the very issues to which they are instrumental in calling attention. Yet far from expressing an inability "to account for itself," what I believe the operations of "iterance" and interrogation ultimately enable us to experience in *Othello* is theater proclaiming with no little self-assurance its power to create spectacle and hold attention, no matter how inscrutable its protagonist, no matter how fluid—or flimsy—the narrative premises of the main action. Indeed, in that recursiveness and demand for narrative we hear in the play of its repetition and interrogation, *Othello* engages us intertextually in the kinds of narratives, and narrativity, from which it derives its fable, only to underscore its distance and difference from those narratives, only to assert its power to improvise, creating and revising its script as it goes along, a power that it incarnates in, and ultimately arrays against, the arch improviser of the play, Iago.

I

At the verbal surface of *Othello*, the many instances of repetition and interrogation one encounters seem very much the accouterments of mimetic
fidelity, with the impression of rhetorical eloquence they impart to the
play a measure of its thematic elegance. Investing the play with that "formality" of style G. Wilson Knight so admired,[6] figures of repetition and
questioning help to frame it as a formal discourse, or, as Marion Trousdale
has analyzed it, as a rhetorical *res*, as an illusion to be perpetrated and
argument to be mounted and persuasively sustained.[7] To hear Othello, for
example, refer again and again to "honest" Iago is, again and again, to hear
"amplified"—as Shakespeare's contemporaries understood the term[8]—the
deceit of Iago and the credulity of Othello. To gauge the enormity of Iago's
duplicity, we need but sense the surprise implicit in Emilia's reiterated question, "My husband?" when Othello insists to her that Iago knew all about
Desdemona's alleged infidelity: "Thy husband knew it all" (5.2.136–52).
And to be reminded of how widely Othello's suspicion of Desdemona misses
the mark, we need but listen to Desdemona ask Emilia repeatedly whether
a woman would ever" do such a deed" as Othello has accused her of, "for all
the world," only to turn the words of her question into an emphatic denial:
"Beshrew me, if I would do such a wrong / For the whole world" (4.3.61–79).
Examples abound the cumulative effect of which is to shape and italicize
what would appear to be the central premises of the tragedy: the curiously
grand yet precarious credulity of Othello, the abused and misprised virtue
of Desdemona, the perfidy of "honest, honest" Iago.

In fact, rather than ask what the repetition and interrogation tell us, we
might wonder why we need to be told it so often, why we need, to take one
of the most blatant examples, to have the magnitude of Iago's duplicity—and
others' gullibility—impressed upon us so insistently by the word *honest* and its
cognates no fewer than, to go by William Empson's count, fifty-two times.[9]
Here, though, we sense something of the reflexive, and subversive, force in
the play of repetition and interrogation in *Othello*. For, as has often been
remarked, the proliferation of references to "honesty" in *Othello*—as a term
for the bluntness with which Iago colors his speech, or for the moral probity
he is erroneously perceived to possess, or for the sexual fidelity Desdemona
is erroneously perceived to lack, or for any of the fifty-seven varieties of the
word Empson has so finely sifted—brings nothing to our attention as much
as it does the multivalency, and semantic slipperiness, both in the word *honest* itself and in the language of the play as a whole. Parker has addressed
this multivalency with especial acuteness by exploring the sundry and com-
plementary significations of the word "dilations," in the phrase, "close dilations" (3.3.123). Enumerating the meanings attached to the word, *dilate*, in

Shakespeare's time, "to unfold" or "amplify," "to delay," and "to accuse," Parker argues that to understand the "close dilations" of *Othello* is not to choose any one preferred connotation of *dilation*, but to read the term for its totality of reference and as "a kind of semantic crossroads or freighted term suggestive of all three of those resonances—amplification, accusation, delay—which are so much a part of the unfolding of this particular tragedy."[10] Still, the more appreciative we grow of the "multivalency" of the language in *Othello* in general, the more keenly we may feel the "ambiguity" of that language in particular instances, a feeling that the operations of repetition and interrogation greatly help to intensify. There is irony in hearing Iago referred to as "honest," an irony that increases with the reiteration of the reference. Yet the irony lies in our repeated recognition, not simply of a discrepancy between what Iago is and how he is perceived and described, but of a dissonance between the word and the reality it has failed to represent. To hear Iago repeatedly called "honest" is to hear the language of the play repeatedly advertise its own unreliability and the tenuousness of its relationship to "truth."

At the same time, however, in the echoing refrains of "honest, honest Iago" the language of Othello may be signaling, not only its unreliability—literally, its irresponsibility—but its rhetorical power as well, its power to shape illusions and theatrical facsimiles of reality. Trousdale, for one, has argued that through Iago in particular Shakespeare shows "not how evil rhetorical method is, but how effective in the most unpromising of situations such rhetorical method can be."[11] Implicit in this comment is the suggestion that Shakespeare's challenge in *Othello* is but one remove from Iago's. If Iago's is to bring about, in almost no time at all, the subversion of the noble Othello's love for the virtuous Desdemona through nothing more substantial than the power of language, so Shakespeare's is to bring all of this off *and* to remind us that he is bringing it off by employing a rhetoric that calls attention to its own power by repeatedly insisting upon what it has contrived.

We hear this rhetorical self-advertisement in the reiteration that highlights, as we have noted, the central premises of the play: the credulity of Othello, the virtue of Desdemona, their love, his jealousy, and ever, of course, the "marvelous" malignancy and skill of Iago.[12] We also hear it, though, in the repetition of a number of rhetorical questions that punctuate the play as so many pieces of ecphrasis. "Is he not jealous?" asks Emilia about Othello (3.4.29), only to answer her question by repeating it when Othello gives Desdemona her first hint that he might, indeed, be subject to that emotion (3.4.99). "Is this the noble Moor whom our full Senate / Call all in all sufficient? Is this the nature / Whom passion could not shake?" asks Lodovico after one of Othello's least "sufficient," most passionate displays, "whose solid virtue / The shot of accident nor dart of chance / Could neither graze nor pierce?" (4.1.264–68). "I will catechize the world for him," the Clown remarks in response to Desdemona's request that he find Cassio, "that is, / make questions, and by them answer" (3.4.16–17).

In no instance does interrogation in *Othello* seem more rhetorical and more self-referential than in the recurrence of the seemingly inconsequential and exclamatory question, "Is't possible?," a "question" to be taken, one presumes, not as a genuine solicitation for information or clarification, but as a rhetorical interjection—an interrogative translation, perhaps, of *mirabile dictu!*, or forerunner of "That's incredible!" Expressive of incredulity in varying degrees of sincerity, the question "Is't possible?" challenges the plausibility of the proceedings to which it responds only to underscore their marvelousness and their dramatic truth, only to call attention to the dramatic pass to which matters have been brought by Iago's machinations. Yes, it is possible that Cassio was drawn into an extremely compromising brawl with someone and for some reason entirely unknown to him (2.3.284–87); and that Othello's suspicions move so far so fast that the mere thought of them convinces him that his "occupation's gone" (3.3.347–58); and that Othello's obsession with his jealousy is such that he endows that errant handkerchief with magical powers—"weaving" various stories about its history—the more significant to make its disappearance (3.4.55–75); and that, Othello's disbelief notwithstanding, Desdemona is neither a "strumpet" nor a "whore" (4.2.70–87). In its reiteration the question, "Is't possible?" functions as a commentary on the action of the play, and, as much as it asks anything of anyone onstage, it demands the audience's acknowledgment that these "incredible" developments have really come off. "Is't possible?" we hear ourselves being asked, to which we feel expected to answer yes.

Do "we," though? Or do the very configurations of language that ask the audience to ratify the experience of the play permit it to question that experience at the same time? Some years ago John Shaw charted the recurrence in *Othello* of yet another seemingly inconsequential question, "What is the matter?" To listen repeatedly to this altogether ordinary query, Shaw argued, is ultimately to grow more aware of how little most characters at most points of the play know, but also to grow less assured that we in the audience know at a given moment "what the matter is," or, even, what "matter" may mean.[13] Similarly, however "rhetorical" we may take a question to be, its very formulation as a question entails the conversion of a statement or assertion of fact into something hypothetical. The more we are asked, "Is't possible?" the more we may feel invited, not only to affirm the possibility of what has happened onstage, but to affirm it as mere possibility. Reiterated in the repetition of "Is't possible?" are both the insistent appeal the play is making for our credence, but also the insistent reminder that in *Othello* we find a fictional enterprise where what "is" is only as certain as what "may be," and where what "may be" demands our continued assent for its validation. "I have told thee often, and I retell thee again and again," Iago admonishes his not entirely credulous dupe, Roderigo, "I hate the Moor" (1.3.364–66). Even as Iago's reiterated appeals to Roderigo's trust elicit repeated doubts, so the credence the play repeatedly seeks from the audience may have the effect of engendering the very disbelief it would have the audience suspend. In short, the more we are asked, "Is't possible?" the more we may wonder whether we must or can say yes.

II

In its fullest resonance, the question, "Is't possible?" echoes the action of *Othello* as a whole. For *Othello* is very much a drama of and *about* hypothetical shreds and patches, of surmises and questions concerning character and conduct which in being voiced and rehearsed yield further surmises and questions that turn unexamined assumptions about character and conduct into threatening nebulae. At no point does the question of what is possible reverberate more destructively, of course, than in the celebrated "seduction" scene of act 3, in which the insinuations of Iago turn the loving and trusting Othello into the "green-ey'd monster" of hateful jealousy. To comment on a scene that has been so frequently discussed is to risk a redundancy especially embarrassing in an essay on repetition, but I turn to it here because it demonstrates so richly the doubleness, the impulses mimetic and subversive, embodied in the play of repetition and interrogation throughout *Othello*. Instrumental, on the one hand, in the rhetorical procedure through which Iago "poisons" the character of Othello, the tropes of repetition and questioning in the "seduction" scene have the underlying effect of reducing Othello's character, and character itself, to enigmas, to things inscrutable; exemplifying a language cunningly manipulated and misused, the reflexive pulsations of question and repetition in the scene suggest a discourse calling attention to its own power, its power to elude the control of those who would manipulate it and to confuse "what is real" with "what is possible."

In the unfolding of the "seduction" scene, figures of repetition and interrogation are most immediately conspicuous for the contribution they make to that syntax of indirection in which Iago ensnares Othello. A half-completed, half-retracted remark here and question there seem all that Iago requires to arouse Othello's curiosity and direct his attention to the possibility of Desdemona's infidelity and Cassio's dishonesty, a possibility Iago makes appear all the more luridly real by conveying the impression that he would rather drop the matter, so that, as Trousdale has put it, "Othello must literally drag the facts out of him."[14] For a choice reprise of Iago's method, we need but consider that proto-Pinteresque exchange that ensues when Othello, prompted by Iago's leading questions, recalls that, yes, Cassio did know of Othello's love for Desdemona before they were married, "and," in fact, "went between us very oft":

> *Iago.* Indeed?
> *Oth.* Indeed? ay, indeed! Discern'st thou aught in that? Is he not
> honest?
> *Iago.* Honest, my lord?
> *Oth.* Honest? ay, honest.
> *Iago.* My lord, for aught I know.
> *Oth.* What dost thou think?
> *Iago.* Think, my lord?
> *Oth.* Think, my lord? By heaven, thou echo'st me,
> As if there were some monster in thy thought
> Too hideous to be shown. Thou dost mean something.
>   (3.3.101–8)

It is a measure of Iago's rhetorical acumen that in what Puttenham calls "redoubling" the last word of Othello's question, "honest,"[15] Iago turns the question back upon Othello and compels him to ponder its multiple significations. Again, as with the reiterated question, "Is't possible?", the mere reference to Cassio's honesty as a question—whatever answer Othello thought he was eliciting—makes Cassio's honesty something questionable and turns Othello's likely supposition that Cassio is honest into the possibility that he may be, from which cannot be excluded the possibility that he may not be, a possibility that Iago's interrogative echoing of "honest" enhances simply by not dispelling it.

The ease with which Iago triumphs in the "seduction" scene, and the rapidity with which Othello succumbs, have been crucial to the distinctions critics have drawn between the characters of Othello and Iago, distinctions which, in turn, have often been associated with the ostensible differences in the ways in which the two characters use and conceive of language, differences in their elocutionary styles, in the degrees of self-consciousness they bring to their speech, indeed, in the relationship they see between their words and their "selves." As Greene has noted, for example, perceptions of Othello have consistently fused, or confused, grandiloquence and inner grandeur, as Othello's "splendid, mouth-filling phrases win our allegiance and admiration" and lead us to take his eloquence as the "expression of that character's nobility."[16] More important, Othello's eloquence and attitude toward language have been taken as metaphors of his integrity and what might genuinely be called his self-possession, a sense of self predicated in Othello's belief in an absolute correspondence between the outer and the inner man, between what he says and does and what he is, a sense of wholeness reflected in the conviction he confides to Iago that "My parts, my title, and my perfect soul / Shall manifest me rightly" (1.2.31–32).[17] A character so deeply convinced of the correspondence between his own words and the truth may well be especially vulnerable to the rhetoric of an Iago, whose sense of self, inscribed in that frequently cited negation, "I am not what I am" (1.1.65), is clearly not burdened by any similar conviction. Madeleine Doran has argued that the poetically graceful, declarative pronouncements we associate with Othello's speech are more than an accident of style; they are the idiom of Othello's self, an idiom inimical and unequal to the conditional syntax with which Iago shapes the dialogue of the "seduction" scene. "Othello cannot entertain *ifs*," Doran observes; unable to cope with the uncertainty of "what is possible," Othello can only replace the certitude of his unquestioning trust of Desdemona with the certitude of her infidelity.[18]

Such distinctions, and the essentialist reading of character in which they are rooted, would very much seem to be challenged by the operations of repetition and interrogation both in the "seduction" scene and in the play as a whole. The often stichomythic and catechetical exchanges through which Iago "works" upon Othello turn the two into rhetorical mirrors of each other in which distinctions of character are effaced, with the result, not so much of transforming the "noble" Othello into a clone of the "ignoble" Iago—though Othello's ultimate behavior might suggest that—but of revealing the character of Othello to be as much of an enigma, his motivations as far beyond accountability, as are the character and motivations of his adversary.

For one thing, Iago's ability to lead Othello on in the "seduction" scene depends heavily upon Othello's ability to follow, upon, not Othello's rhetorical innocence, but his sophistication, his ability to "read" the cues transmitted by Iago's repetition and questioning as a Puttenham or Hoskins would have them read, that is, as cues, as signifiers of some deeper, perhaps darker, meaning.[19] One senses that Othello and Iago may be communicants in the same rhetorical idiom in that exchange I cited just above, where, from Iago's first "indeed?" Othello's "victimization" is triggered by Othello's ability to read Iago's words closely, scrutinizing them rather as if he were interpreting a text, offering a commentary on both the verbal and nonverbal inflections of Iago's remarks:

> And when I told thee he was of my counsel
> In my whole course of wooing, thou criedst,
> "Indeed!"
> And didst contract and purse thy brow together,

As if thou then hadst shut up in thy brain
Some horrible conceit. If thou dost love me,
Show me thy thought.
    (3.3.111–16)

As Portia remarks of her unfortunate suitors in *The Merchant of Venice* (2.9.81), Othello displays just enough rhetorical wisdom here by his wit to lose: he takes Iago's "Indeed" to be very much what Puttenham calls the figure of "*Synechdoche*" or "*Quicke conceit*," a "single word" in which a "quicke wit" will discern some "intendment or large meaning . . . as by the halfe to vnderstand the whole," and he construes Iago's behavior in general as, in Puttenham's terminology, a figure of *Noema* or "*close conceit*," "whereof," Puttenham explains, "we do not so easily conceiue the meaning, but as it were by coniecture, because it is wittie and subtle or darke,"[20] in Othello's words, "[s]ome horrible conceit."

Nor, it must be recalled, is that "horrible conceit" the exclusive property of Iago. Indeed, it can be argued that what Othello "drags out" of Iago, what he seeks to hear from Iago, are not "the facts" Iago has invented, but the voiced confirmation of Othello's own "exsufflicate and blown surmises." "[T]hou echo'st me," Othello complains, "As if there were some monster in thy thought / Too hideous to be shown," an echoing that at once conceals the monster in Iago's thought only to reveal the monster Othello himself has conceived. "Give thy worst of thoughts / The worst of words" (132–33), Othello will subsequently demand of Iago, to which might be appended the translation, "give *my* worst of thoughts *thy* worst of words."

"Characters," Jonathan Goldberg has insisted, "exist within texts; their interiors are texts,"[21] an argument brought forcibly to mind by the rebounding words and echoing questions of the "seduction" scene, which seem less to reflect, or represent, the motivations, the "interiors" of character than to prescribe and conscribe them. Othello becomes suspicious of Cassio and Desdemona, it can be argued, because it is rhetorically possible to conceive of such a suspicion; the rhetorical canniness Othello displays in "reading" Iago's words enables him to make the case, or "cause," of this suspicion, and the formulation of the "cause" suffices for its substance. In the process, what might have appeared to be the *données* of Othello's character are effaced: the "free and open" nature Iago had ascribed to him (1.3.399), indeed, even his love for Desdemona. That Othello loves Desdemona initially would seem unquestionable; he proclaims that love quite unequivocally, after all, during a lull in the "seduction" scene, just before Iago renews his attack. Yet he expresses his love for Desdemona by casting it as part of an antithesis, as a condition coexistent with its negation:

Excellent wretch! Perdition catch my soul
But I do love thee! and when I love thee not,
Chaos is come again.
      (3.3.90–92)

The reiterated sonorities of "love thee" and "love thee not" testify to the felicitous sound of Othello's speech, but one consequence of Othello's penchant for euphony here is, once again, the eradication of the distinction between fact and possibility, with what we might have taken to be the fact that Othello loves his "[e]xcellent wretch" sharing equal rhetorical billing with the chance that he may come not to love her, a chance worded very much as if it were an eventuality. When Chaos is imaginable in this way, Chaos can most surely be come again.

Here it might be objected that the analysis to this point both wrongly ignores the instrumental role accorded Iago in hastening Chaos's arrival and blurs a critical distinction between Iago's designs and their effects upon Othello. Put simply, Iago is in control and Othello is not; Iago knows what he is doing with language; Othello appears not to know what language is doing to him. Still, to scrutinze the "inner workings" of Iago's character, to assay, with many others, what Coleridge dubbed Iago's "motiveless malignity," and to note what Stephen Greenblatt has described as the improvisational properties of Iago's machinations[22] is to grow increasingly dubious of the nature or degree of that control. "I know not if't be true," Iago observes, in private, of the rumor about Othello that "twixt my sheets / Was done my office; But I, for mere suspicion in that kind, / Will do as if for surety" (1.3.387–90). Scan Iago's notoriously unhelpful autobiographical pronouncements, or as Alessandro Serpieri terms them, his *énonciations*,[23] and one will find an ego-centrifugal "self" whose "deepest" impulses are sublimated and conscriped within reiterative formulas: the tautologous stipulation that "Were I the Moor, I would not be Iago" (1.1.57), the self-denying assertion that "I am not what I am" (1.1.65). In Iago's speech duplication is the linguistic inflection of the duplicity that is his character, a "doubleness" self-canceling rather than self-affirming, concealing his real self from others only to reveal that self to be, in Greenblatt's words, "absolute vacancy" (p. 236). Doubly corrosive, then, is the echoing that leads Othello to hear himself in Iago's words, which even as it renders questionable the inherent nobility of Othello's self, makes it conceivable that at the core of that self lies a vacancy no less absolute than Iago's.[24]

III

So far, at least, it might be argued that what has been observed about the effects of repetition and interrogation in *Othello* is simply consistent with the rhetorical dicta of a Puttenham or Hoskins or other commentators of the period, who envisioned such figures as instruments of an orator's or poet's intentions and extensions of his control.[25] That Shakespeare has Iago make use of repetition and interrogation to mirror Othello's thoughts in such a way as to render questionable what had been presumed would seem nothing more than an exemplary demonstration of the adroit indirection and manipulation that Puttenham describes above in that "kinde of figuratiue speach when we aske many questions and looke for none answere, speaking indeed by interrogation, which we might as well say by affirmation,"[26] or that the rhetorically astute Falstaff has in mind when he upbraids Hal for employing "damnable iteration" to twist Falstaff's words into jokes at Falstaff's expense. Yet, as the dynamics of the "seduction" scene suggest, the self-referential play of questioning and repetition in *Othello* simultaneously evokes as a possibility the power of language to elude control and divorce itself from clear and clearly retrievable referents, rendering motives ever ulterior or elliptical and turning emotions and convictions of identity into mere traces of feeling and hypotheses of self-definition.[27]

Such is the effect of the repetition and questioning through much of the interaction of Iago and Othello, and one finds an especially vivid example in the piece of *catechesis* one happens upon in the opening moments of act 4:

> *Iago.* Will you think so?
> *Oth.* Think so, Iago?
> *Iago.* What,
> To kiss in private?
> *Oth.* An unauthorized kiss.
> *Iago.* Or to be naked with her friend in bed,
> An hour, or more, not meaning any harm?
> *Oth.* Naked in bed, Iago, and not mean harm?

In his analysis of the "seduction" scene, Serpieri has commented on the use Iago makes of such deictic remarks as "I like not that" (3.3.35) to leave "the precise sense suspended" and excite a "demand" in Othello for "explication of the meaning, that is for a semantic disambiguation" (p. 141). In the opening of act 4 we find both an echo and an elaboration of this pattern, with Iago once again making use of deixis, though not so much to suspend the "precise sense" of something Othello has said, as to render it dubious, questioning it to turn it into something warranting justification and, shortly thereafter, rejection. Here, however, dramatic form and Iago are in clear collusion. For the assertion literally in question is submerged in the interval between Othello's peremptory exit from the previous scene and the start of this one, submerged only to be refracted and metonymized at the verbal surface in the bits and pieces of Iago's—and Othello's—prurient exempla: "To kiss in private," "An unauthorized kiss," "to be naked with her friend in bed, / An hour, or more." Moreover, in repeating Iago's opening question in elliptical, subjectless form, "Think so, Iago?", Othello implicitly dissociates himself from whatever it was to which Iago—and the trace word "so"—had been referring. When, as the exchange develops, we surmise that what has been questioned and undermined here is the possibility that had been raised—presumably, but not "unquestionably," by Othello—that Desdemona did "not mean harm," we can appreciate how erosive the force of language has been in this instance. For in effacing the original statement in which the possibility of Desdemona's innocence had been advanced, the play of repetition and questioning in the exchange also suppresses the connective tissue of emotion and thought that had made that possibility at least conceivable. To be sure, the exchange can be read as still more evidence of Iago's rhetorical agility; yet the suppressive and reflexive force of interrogation and reiteration here effectively asserts the power of language to create and re-create its own contexts of reference even as it obliterates the contexts from which it had proceeded.

Nor is it only in the interaction of Iago and Othello that this power is trumpeted. One hears it as well in the recurrent transformation of persons and propositions into metonyms, in words or labels which in being echoed in reiterative and interrogative configurations might seem intended to divert attention from what they ostensibly represent.[28] Nowhere is this more dramatically evident than at the moment in act 5 in which Othello contemplates the sleeping Desdemona and weighs the action he is about to take against her:

> It is the cause, it is the cause, my soul!
> Let me not name it to you, you chaste stars,
> It is the cause.
>   (5.2.1–3)

It is one of the speeches Bradley cites as evidence of Othello's "poetic" nature,[29] and at least a part of its poetic and emotional resonance lies in the eloquent reiteration of the "cause." What has been called in passing Othello's "logically needless" insistence upon the "cause"[30] might well be explained as evidence of a conflict within Othello between his love for Desdemona and the "cause" which has been ordained, and to which he is impelled, by Justice. Yet to offer this hypothesis is to overlook how much the sense, or reference, here is elliptical, and how much the effect of the reiterated "cause" is to divert the audience, and Othello himself, from identifying what "it" is. In fact, far from attesting to Othello's love for Desdemona, the repetition of "cause" might just as readily inscribe an attempt by Othello to absolve himself from having to acknowledge and reexamine the conviction that has determined her fate, the more assuredly to pass on to her execution. That "it" refers to the issue of Desdemona's infidelity one might infer from Othello's reluctance to mention "it" to the "chaste stars" who happen to be present in the bedroom, though, again, their very presence provides a convenient pretext for Othello not to name, or, perhaps, think, of the "it" for which Desdemona is shortly to be dispatched. Instead, the antecedent of "it" gets subsumed within the multiple and undiscriminated significations of "cause"—as "agency," "principle," and "argument"—in a passage that reads like an odd variation on praeterition, one in which the matter to be passed over actually gets passed over!

In turn, the same metonymic process that suppresses the antecedent of "it" and "cause" in this speech works upon the presence and very identity of Desdemona as well. "Put out the light," Othello instructs himself, "and then put out the light" (7). In repeating the words, Othello turns the self-instruction into a self-referential trope, and what begins as the preparative to the killing of Desdemona turns into a brief exercise in explication and a process of transfiguration, with Desdemona undergoing a depersonification to become "Thou cunning'st pattern of excelling nature" (11), even as the candle, whose light put out can be "relumed," is personified as "thou flaming minister" (8). With Desdemona at once raised and reduced to an image, to but an exquisite "pattern" of perfection, Othello effectively suppresses Desdemona's identity, acknowledging that suppression only after he has smothered her, when Emilia's knock at the door brings back to him the word and with it the wife he has extinguished:

> If she come in, she'll sure speak to my wife.
> My wife, my wife! what wife? I have no wife.
>   (96–97)

Indeed, the recognition into which Othello is jolted here serves not only to alert us to what has transpired in this scene, but to underscore the connubial disfigurement Desdemona has sustained throughout the play by being represented either as Othello's "wife-about-to-be" or his "wife-about-to-be-destroyed." Epitomized in Othello's repetition and questioning and final negation of the word *wife* is an effect produced by iteration and interrogation throughout the play, and that is, not simply to leave the complexities of character and relationships shadowy, but to illuminate them as shadows.

At the same time, the divorce of language and reference evoked by the subversive and suppressive play of repetition and questioning in Desdemona's murder scene is allegorized in the various tautological configurations and allusions to "words" that recur throughout *Othello*. The frequent use of reiterative devices, such as the *diaphora* and *ploce* that Iago employs in his self-nondefinitions, creates an aural image of language as some self-contained, self-referential system, powerful and destructive, not in spite of its literal "irresponsibility," but because of it. "[W]ords are words," the aggrieved Brabantio replies to the Duke's platitudinous *sententiae* of consolation. "I never yet did hear / That the bruis'd heart was pierced through the ear"(1.3.218–19), a proposition which, as Greene has commented, much of what actually happens in the play would seem to refute (p. 270). In turn, *paranomasia*, the pun, emerges as the figurative emblem of this studied insistence of language upon its "disconnectedness." If this disconnectedness is at first comically underscored in the exchange between Desdemona and the Clown in which the latter "answers" Desdemona's question, "Do you know, sirrah, where Lieutenant Cassio lies?," by teasing out of thought the divers significations of the word "lie" (3.4.1–13), its destructive force is more lugubriously reaffirmed in that reprise on "lie" in the very next scene, where, amid the echoing possibilities of lying "with," lying "on," and belying her, Othello falls from sense to, as James Calderwood has put it, "the edges of the sublinguistic" (p. 297): "Pish!" (4.1.35–43). "Can any thing be made of this?," Desdemona asks (3.4.10); "Is't possible?," Othello demands (4.1.42): questions to which the rhetoric of the moment seems to impel the successive answers, "No," and "Yes."

Again, answers to such questions in *Othello* seem never to be quite as univocal as might at first be supposed, and here one must be careful not to confuse what the language of the play proclaims and what it actually achieves. For the recurrent imbrication of words in doubling, self-referential tropes serves not so much to secure the divorce of language from a referential function as to create the sense that everything in the play is to be heard and seen through a tension created by dual and dissonant foci of reference, the one encased in rhetorical discourse, the other in a veritably shadowy realm that lies beyond the world of rhetoric and that rhetoric cannot reach, and of which the words themselves that rhetoric employs *may* be but chimeras. Such is the tension Othello at once acknowledges and challenges en route to his verbal and physical collapse when he protests that "Nature / would not invest herself in such shadowing passion / without some instruction. It is not words that shakes / me thus" (4.1.39–42), with what Kittredge calls Othello's "incoherent madness"[31] but a theatrical reflex of his inability to locate coherence, to ascertain if there is a coherence between the "shadowy passion" of his words and some ulterior "instruction." Such is the tension Desdemona feels when she tells Othello that "I understand a fury in your words, / But not the words," when Othello's rhetorical power subsumes both his rage at her infidelity and the need to confront her in an elaborate parody of a brothel transaction (4.2.23–33). And finally, it is the tension born of this dual perspective that is metonymically underscored through the interaction of figures of repetition and interrogation calling into question the meaning, identity, and very being of the words designating the fundamental relationships in the play. Even as Othello formally voids his "wife" some moments after destroying the person who bore that title, so Desdemona must ask Emilia, "Who is thy lord?" only to conclude, "I have none" (4.2.101–2), and even as Emilia herself, in that exquisitely protracted moment of *anagnorisis*,[32] will repeatedly incarnate everything she cannot understand, or accept, in Othello's account of Desdemona's infidelity in just two words: "My husband?" "I say thy husband," Othello reiteratively insists. "[D]ost understand the word?" (5.2.141–153).

IV

Even as Emilia's repeated question, "My husband?", very much vexes Othello in his attempt to give an account and justification of his "cause," so it also brings emphatically into juxtaposition, or collision, two significant elements of our experience of *Othello*, on the one hand, the dissonances and instability of the "word" that we encounter on the verbal surface of the play, and on the other, the underlying recursiveness and demand for narrative that inform the structure of the play. The most audible registers of this recursiveness and narrativity, figures of reiteration and interrogation, alert us in their subversive and self-referential play to the narrative discontinuities *Othello* embodies, redefining the play for us as a set of revisionary texts and enabling us to hear in its repeated calls for narrative a repeated questioning, as in Emilia's interrogation of Othello, of the narratives it presents. Indeed, that the call for and the questioning of narrative are inseparable is underscored in the opening line of the play, where Roderigo's rejection of whatever it was that Iago had most recently said, "Tush, never tell me!", ensures its being resaid, though clearly resaid with a difference calculated to gain its acceptance and Roderigo's credence. Opening as it does, *Othello* casts itself from the start in a rhetorical posture curiously identical to that of its designated villain, while establishing an equally curious—and somewhat demeaning—mutuality of interests between its audience and one of its villain's designated dupes. If unlike Roderigo "we" as audience do not enter the play on a note of hostility and outright rejection, we are quickly associated with him in our need to hear rehearsed the grounds for whatever it is that Iago is contriving. Trousdale has made the Renaissance rhetorical predilection for *copia* through variation central to her discussion of Shakespeare's dramaturgical strategies in *Othello* and other plays,[33] and the use to which Iago puts "varying" in reessaying, or reassailing, Roderigo well exemplifies the power of this method when skillfully applied. In Iago's practice, however, "varying," repetition with a difference, comes so much to resemble Derridean *différance* in the violence of its revisions and displacement of antecedents as to seem a travesty and transgression of the very method it exemplifies.[34] If Iago's singular variation on varying is most conspicuously on display in his repeated voicings of his motives, it is epitomized in his hortatory remarks to Roderigo near the end of act 1, where the forcible reiteration of "put money in thy purse" ironically italicizes the disparate character of the particulars Iago has forcibly yoked together to make the case for the imminent dissolution of Othello's and Desdemona's relationship (1.3.339–72). Again, the audience may find its own response personified in Roderigo, who, repeatedly questioning Iago's account of things, is repeatedly a witness to and participant in the ever more elaborate spectacle of Iago's rhetorical improvisation.

Nor, of course, is it in the language of Iago alone that this spectacle is to be beheld. It takes no more than the first twenty lines of Othello's first appearance in the play, after all, to sense the degree to which Othello equates himself with the telling of the story of himself, with the narrative voicing of his deeds: alerted by the" solicitous Iago that Brabantio is likely to take action because of the elopement of Desdemona, Othello is confident both that the "services which I have done the signiory / Shall out-tongue his complaints" (1.2.18–19), and that his own "demerits / May speak, unbonneted, to as proud a fortune / As this that I have reach'd" (22–24). So too, because for Othello one's self and one's resume are so closely linked, there are a recursiveness and reflexivity intrinsic to Othello's very sense of being, so that, as Calderwood has remarked, Othello's "self-defense" before the Venetian Senate parses as "a voice telling about himself telling about himself" (p. 294).

Yet as storytelling is inherently rhetorical, so the story that Othello equates with his life is indissociable from a rhetorical agenda. Well aware of the curiosity the recitation of his story repeatedly arouses in both Desdemona *and* Brabantio, Othello recalls taking that curiosity as the "hint" to relate his story again and again (1.3.142, 166). At the same time one would expect Othello, rhetorically attuned to the interests of his auditors, to be rhetorically sensitive to the strategies required to shape and reshape his narrative to keep its reiteration "still" (i.e., repeatedly) interesting, repeatedly responsive to the questions that his account repeatedly engenders (1.3.128–29) and that call for further narration. So it is that one finds evidence of "varying" in Othello's story—varying which, given the identification of Othello's story with his "self," amounts to a genuine self-differentiation. One hears such varying in

the discrepancies of Othello's successive descriptions of that errant handkerchief, which Othello will ultimately say was "an antique token" given to his
mother by his father (5.2.216–17), but which he earlier had "woven" into a
talisman given his mother by an Egyptian charmer (3.4.55–68), as if in an
attempt, not only to intimidate Desdemona with its importance but, again,
to invest it with a significance that would exacerbate his suspicion that Desdemona had given it away. And, to be sure, one finds evidence of "varying"
in the surprise one feels at Desdemona's recollection of the role Cassio had
played in Othello's courtship (3.2.70–73), a detail that had managed not to
find its way into the account of his wooing that Othello had earlier given
to the Senators.[35] To the degree, then, to which Othello's "story" draws our
attention to the narrativity of the play, it also helps to inscribe the play as a
discourse ever revising itself and improvising its own text, and calls to mind
G. Wilson Knight's intuitive perception of *Othello* as a work of "outstanding
differences."[36]

 To the degree, however, to which *Othello* calls attention to itself as a narrative, it also, and literally, contextualizes itself among the narrative sources
that provide the nutrients of its fable and the models for its characters. One
vein of the writings to which *Othello* is heir has, of course, been well explored
by Geoffrey Bullough, who has gone far in compiling the many details of
plot and characterization that connect *Othello*, not only to its likely immediate source in Cinthio's *Gli Hecatommithi*, but to the store of Italian *novelle*
so popular in the latter decades of the sixteenth century—those stories of
domestic tragedy and sensationalist love cum violence so excoriated by
Ascham as the "merry books" and "enchantments of Circe brought out of
Italy to mar men's manners in England."[37] Yet another vein, however, has
been discussed in recent studies by Rosalind Johnson and Karen Newman,
and comprises the various travel accounts of Africa that at once appealed
to and stimulated Shakespeare's contemporaries' sense of the exotic, among
them *The History and Descryption of Africa* (1526, trans. 1600) by Al-Hassan
Ibn-Mohammed Al-Wezaz Al-Fasi, or, as he was more often called in the
West, Leo Africanus.[38]

 To situate *Othello* among these writings is to sharpen and complicate
one's sense of its recursiveness. Reprising and affiliating itself with scenarios
and characters already and often rehearsed for its audience in other works,
Othello also proves recursive in the degree to which the incidence of reiteration we encounter in its language and structure is but an echo of and allusion
to the recursiveness to be heard in its sources and analogues. In listening to
Othello tell about telling about the story of himself, one may, for example, be
reminded both of the repeated accounts Leo Africanus delivered about himself as he made his way, sometimes captive, through the numerous cultures

of the Mediterranean region, and of the many marvels and strange travails which Leo, like Othello, endured and re-presents as the record of his life. Yet what most audibly connects Othello and Leo is the frequentative, reiterative character of their accounts and exploits. "I maruell much how euer he should haue escaped so manie thousands of imminent dangers," Leo's English translator, John Pory, remarks, recording his admiration at—if not for—his subject's repeated feats of survival in a set of interrogative variations on "Is't possible?". "I maruel much more, how euer he escaped them. For how many desolate cold mountaines, and huge, drie, and barren deserts passed he? How often was he in hazard to haue beene captiued, or to haue had his throte cut by the prouling Arabians, and wilde Mores? And how hardly manie times escaped he the Lyons greedie mouth, and the deuouring iawes of the Crocodile?" (p. 6).

So too, the ecphrastic, exclamatory questions that punctuate *Othello*, such as Emilia's "Is he not jealious?", would seem to have their antecedents in the recurrent efforts of the *novella* writers and translators to fit the often lurid spectacles they are presenting into at least a facsimile of a moral frame. So it is that the narrator in Geoffrey Fenton's translation of Bandello's story of "The Albanian Captain" opens the tale by asking "how he can be acquitted from an humour of a frantic man, who, without any cause of offence in the world, commits cruel execution upon his innocent wife, no less fair and furnished in all perfections than chaste and virtuous without comparison?"[39] Later, just in case the answer to that question may have eluded his reader, Fenton asks an easier "follow-up": "What life were like to the married man's state, or pleasures semblable to the joys of the bed, if either the one or the other might be dispensed withal from the fury of frantic jealousy?"[40] "Is not this man jealious?"

Yet even as *Othello* offers a repetition of the details and conventions of its narrative sources, its repetition is, again, one with a "difference." At the outset of "The Albanian Captain" Fenton promises to "expose" to his readers "a miserable accident, happening in our time, which shall serve as a bloody scaffold or theatre, wherein are presented such as play no parts but in mortal and furious tragedies."[41] *Othello* enacts the "accident" and provides the "Scaffold or theatre," but, as has been seen, it undermines the very sort of questions that a Fenton would use as moral framing devices, eschews narrative continuity, and in doing so asserts its self-sufficiency as a theatrical spectacle. Indeed, the tension we encounter at the verbal surface of *Othello*, the sense the play of repetition and interrogation conveys of a duality of focus, is a signature of a dissonance the play orchestrates between the particularity of its action, its "accident," and the paradigms and revisions inscribed in the stories and discourses that have nurtured it. The most conspicuous—and most frequently noted—trace of this dissonance is the dual time scheme, through which the play makes just enough reference to actions that demand a frequentative and extensive duration of time to recall, on the one hand, the temporal spaciousness and illusion of temporal verisimilitude inhabiting the fictional world of its sources, and on the other, the temporal economy of the world of the stage.[42] In the juxtaposition of the two temporal orders, the audience is confronted with an incongruity that cannot be explained, or explained away, and with a vivid image of the right claimed by theater to improvise the unfolding of its spectacle by its own laws.

The uneasy antiphony the play negotiates between its narrativity and its theatricality receives its final and fullest voicing in the play of repetition and interrogation with which *Othello* concludes. Like the final moments in other Shakespearean tragedies the ending of *Othello* invites its audience to empathize with those onstage seeking to make sense of the spectacle they have witnessed, even as it ultimately leaves the effort unrewarded, or, at least, incomplete. The audience may, at any rate, hear its own desire for clarification articulated in Lodovico's question:

> O thou Othello, that was once so good,
> Fall'n in the practice of a damned slave,
> What shall be said to thee?
>   (5.2.291–93)

At once ecphrastic and censorious, Lodovico's question in its very framing would appear to prescribe its answer and obviate further questions. For once the premise is accepted that Othello was "once so good" but had "Fall'n in the practice of a damned slave," what more need or can be said? Here one detects an attempt on the part of the play to circumscribe and finalize itself in morally lucid and reassuring terms, with Othello the culpable dupe whose "fault" must "be known / To the Venetian state" (336–37). When Othello subsequently stabs himself Lodovico punctuates the act as a "bloody period" (356), at once a tribute to the periodic eloquence—and length—of Othello's closing "word or two" (338–56), but also a compensatory attempt to declare the case resolved, with no further adjudication required than to dole out suitably grim punishment to the insolently silent Iago, to whom now falls the sole responsibility for "the tragic loading of this bed; / This is thy work" (363–64). When Lodovico then closes the play with the declaration that he "will straight abroad, and to the state / This heavy act with heavy heart relate" (370–71), one fully expects that his account will include a reiteration of the moralistic and self-answering question he had moments before uttered, a question bound to do little to elucidate the tragedy of Othello, but just the sort of reassuring question that one could imagine oneself encountering in the kinds of sensationalized fiction that provide the sources for plays like *Othello*.

Contributing to the sense that all has not been resolved, and leaving an impression of dissonance in what it does not say, is the silence of Iago, a silence that, among other things, suggests a resistance of the play as theater to being inscribed in the kind of account Lodovico will "relate."[43] In the articulation of his will to remain silent, however, Iago offers a recapitulation and epitome of the subversive roles repetition and interrogation have performed throughout the play:

> Demand me nothing; what you know, you know:
> From this time forth I never will speak word.
> (303–4)

So familiarly tautological in style, Iago's nonresponse to a question that had not yet been directly posed ensures the questioning it ostensibly would preempt. Denying Othello's question, it turns back upon and locates in Othello himself the literal responsibility for its answer. Italicizing what "we" know, it intensifies our sense of not knowing and our sense of language in the play as a domain impervious to the demands of reference.

Above all, the silence that ensues offers itself as the improvisationally resourceful Iago's ultimate *coup de théâtre*, a gesture which asserts the distinction between what theater enacts and what others may say about what has been enacted, and which, coupled with Othello's act of suicide, transforms the theatrical action into something self-consuming, self-immolating. At the same time, a gesture that asserts the particularity of what has been transacted onstage, Iago's very silence is an articulate repetition of the silence that envelops the tragic stage throughout Shakespeare's time. In the silence assumed by Iago and Othello, a silence assumed against the background noise of Lodovico's final words and promised report, one hears the self-enforced silence of the tongueless Hieronimo and the "silence" that for Hamlet was all "the rest."

NOTES

Sources for the epigraphs are as follows: George Puttenham, *The Arte of English Poesie*, ed. Edward Arber (Westminster: A. Constable and Co., 1895), pp. 208, 220; John Hoskins, *Directions for Speech and Style*, ed. Hoyt H. Hudson (Princeton: Princeton University Press, 1935), pp. 32–33.

1. George Bernard Shaw, "*Othello*: Pure Melodrama," in *A Casebook on "Othello*," ed. Leonard F. Dean (New York: Thomas Y. Crowell Co., 1961), p. 135. Shaw's sense of the musicality of *Othello* had already found expression, of course, in

the collaboration of Verdi and his librettist, Boito, and would receive fuller elaboration in G. Wilson Knight, "The Othello Music," in *The Wheel of Fire: Interpretations of Shakespearean Tragedy, with Three New Essays* (London: Methuen; 1949), pp. 97–119.

2. Puttenham, *Arte of English Poesie*, p. 173.

3. Gayle Greene, "'But Words Are Words': Shakespeare's Sense of Language in *Othello*," *Etudes Anglaises* 34 (1981): 281.

4. Patricia Parker, "Shakespeare and Rhetoric: 'dilation' and 'delation' in *Othello*," in *Shakespeare and the Question of Theory*, ed. Parker and Geoffrey Hartman (New York: Methuen, 1985), pp. 55ff.

5. Jonathan Culler, *On Deconstruction: Theory and Criticism after Structuralism* (London: Routledge and Kegan Paul, 1983), p. 201.

6. Knight, *Wheel of Fire*, pp. 97–98.

7. Marion Trousdale, *Shakespeare and the Rhetoricians* (London: Scolar Press, 1982), pp. 162–68.

8. See Hoskins, *Directions for Speech*, pp. 17, 29, and Puttenham, *Arte of English Poesie*, pp. 230–31; see also the discussions in Parker, "Shakespeare and Rhetoric," pp. 54–59, and Rosemond Tuve, *Elizabethan and Metaphysical Imagery: Renaissance Poetic and Twentieth Century Critics* (Chicago: University of Chicago Press, 1947), pp. 146–54.

9. William Empson, *The Structure of Complex Words* (Norfolk, Conn.: James Laughlin, 1951), p. 218.

10. Parker, "Shakespeare and Rhetoric," p. 56.

11. Trousdale, *Shakespeare and the Rhetoricians*, pp. 162–63.

12. One is reminded of the reaction of the audience to the machinations of the Ensign against the Moor and Disdemona in the principal source of *Othello*, the story of the Moorish Captain and his Venetian wife in Giraldi Cinthio's Gli *Hecatommithi*, translated by Geoffrey Bullough in his *Narrative and Dramatic Sources of Shakespeare*, vol. 7 (London: Routledge and Kegan Paul, 1973). At the conclusion of the tale the narrator observes that "It appeared marvellous to everybody that such malignity could have been discovered in a human heart," p. 252.

13. John Shaw, "'What Is the Matter?' in *Othello*," *Shakespeare Quarterly* 17 (1966): 157–61.

14. Trousdale, *Shakespeare and the Rhetoricians*, p. 165.

15. Puttenham, *Arte of English Poesie*, p. 210.

16. Greene, "'But Words Are Words,'" p. 271.

17. See Knight, *Wheel of Fire*, p. 105; D. A. Traversi, "Othello," in *Shakespeare: The Tragedies*, ed. Clifford Leech (Chicago: University of Chicago Press, 1965), p. 171; and James L. Calderwood, "Speech and Self in *Othello*," *Shakespeare Quarterly* 38 (1987): 294–95.

18. Madeleine Doran, "Iago's 'if': An Essay on the Syntax of *Othello*," in *The Drama of the Renaissance: Essays for Leicester Bradner*, ed. Elmer M. Blistein (Providence: Brown University Press, 1970), pp. 69–72. See also Wolfgang Clemen, *The Development of Shakespeare's Imagery* (London: Methuen & Co., 1977), pp. 119–32; Norman Rabkin, *Shakespeare and the Common Understanding* (New York: Free Press, 1967), pp. 67–73; and Greene, pp. 270–82.

19. Othello's sensitivity to rhetorical cues is evident from the account he gives the Senators of how Desdemona came to be in love with him, or, rather, how she

came to love him "for the dangers I had passed." Twice in his speech he uses the word "hint" in a rhetorically suggestive context, saying first that it was his "hint" and his "process" to talk to Brabantio of his exotic exploits and travails (1.3.142), while adding later that when he perceived Desdemona's interest in his story he took that as his "hint" to speak (166). Indeed, Othello prefaces his address to the Senators with what, given his eloquence, sounds suspiciously like a rhetorically canny "modesty topos," when he announces, "Rude am I in my speech, / And little bless'd with the soft phrase of peace." Interestingly, one finds a similar disclaimer in the prefatory remarks of a figure who has at times been thought of as the inspiration for Othello, Leo Africanus, who appeals to his reader to accept his account of Africa "albeit not adorned with fine words, and artificiall eloquence," a rhetorically prudent but not overwhelmingly sincere note to be struck by someone described by his translator as having been "euen from his tender yeeres trained up at the Vniuersitie of Fez, in Grammar, Poetrie, Rhetorick, Historie, Cabala, Astronomie, and other ingenuous sciences. . . ." See John Pory's translation of Leo Africanus, *The History and Description of Africa* (1600), ed. Robert Brown (London: Hakluyt Society, 1896), vol. 1, pp. 5, 188.

20. Puttenham, *Arte of English Poesie*, p. 238.

21. Jonathan Goldberg, *Voice Terminal Echo: Postmodernism and English Renaissance Texts* (New York: Methuen, 1986), p. 3.

22. Stephan Greenblatt, *Renaissance Self-Fashioning from More to Shakespeare* (Chicago: University of Chicago Press, 1980), pp. 232–34.

23. Alessandro Serpieri, "Reading the Signs: Towards a Semiotics of Shakespearean Drama," trans. Keir Elam, in *Alternative Shakespeares*, ed. John Drakakis (London: Methuen, 1985), p. 139.

24. Serpieri (ibid., p. 142) has suggested an underlying equivalence between Othello and Iago in the degree to which both are "imprisoned" in the antithetical "rhetorical modes" that Serpieri takes to be the defining idioms of their beings, Iago in "negation," Othello in "hyperbolic affirmation." In *Shakespeare: Seven Tragedies: The Dramatist's Manipulation of Response* (London: Macmillan, 1976), pp. 77–100, E. A. J. Honigmann has established a bond between Othello and Iago in the degree to which the personalities and behavior of both are shaped by "secret motives" that are kept inaccessible to the audience throughout the play.

25. Puttenham, for example (*Art of English Poesie*, p. 207), commends the use of auricular figures as a strategy enabling the author to manipulate and capture the mind of his reader by appealing to the reader's ear: "Therefore the well tuning of your words and clauses to the delight of the eare, maketh your information no lesse plausible to the minde than to the eare: no though you filled them with never so much sence and sententiousnese."

26. Puttenham, *Arte of English Poesie*, p. 220.

27. It is this power that is implicated in Plato's suspicion that the use of rhetoric was indissociable from its abuse, a suspicion voiced most stridently, perhaps, in Socrates' analysis of the "art" of rhetoric in Plato's *Gorgias*, trans. W. R. M. Lamb (London: William Heinemann, 1925), pp. 313–21. And it is this power that Shakespeare most memorably italicizes in that scene in *Julius Caesar* in which the Plebeians, incensed by the rhetorical "mischief" of Marc Anthony's rhetoric (3.2.259), mistake Cinna the poet for Cinna the conspirator and demand that he be torn apart because "his name's Cinna. Pluck / but his name out of his heart, and turn him going" (3.3.33–34).

28. Tuve (*Elizabethan and Metaphysical Imagery*, pp. 129–30) has argued that figures of metonymy and synecdoche work by reducing what they represent and name, giving delight in the degree to which we as readers acknowledge the aptness of their designations. For Renaissance rhetoricians, Tuve observes, "Metonymy is . . . praised for serving to variety, brevity, and signification." As Tuve's discussion would suggest, then, for the writer of the Renaissance metonyms are a kind of rhetorical shorthand that permits us to acknowledge and admire their "aptness" without having to articulate the lines of connection between the figures themselves and whatever it is for which they are designations.

29. A. C. Bradley, *Shakespearean Tragedy: Lectures on "Hamlet," "Othello," "King Lear," "Macbeth"* (London: Macmillan and Co., 1904), p. 188.

30. Albert Cook, "Milton's Abstract Music," in *Milton: Modern Essays in Criticism*, ed. Arthur E. Barker (London: Oxford University Press, 1965), p. 398.

31. See Kittredge's note to 4.1.35–43, in *The Kittredge Shakespeare: Othello*, rev. Irving Ribner (New York: John Wiley & Sons, 1966), p. 94.

32. Harley Granville-Barker, *Prefaces to Shakespeare* (Princeton: Princeton University Press, 1947), 2:130, likened each of the replies Emilia's reiterated question fetches from Othello to "the tearing of a screen from before that closed mind." Doubtless it was Emilia's mind to which Granville-Barker was referring, but the effect of the exchange is to give us a glimpse of two minds locked into two very different illusions of reality.

33. Trousdale, *Shakespeare and the Rhetoricians*, pp. 38–64.

34. In his notorious coinage, *différance*, Jacques Derrida deliberately conflates the notions of "difference" and "deferral" in order to underscore the full dynamics of the "differentiation" he sees inherent in the play of language. For Derrida an utterance always bears the suggestion, not only of "nonidentity," of "distinction" or "inequality," but also of temporal "deferral," "the possible that is presently impossible." See Derrida's delineation of the term in *"Difference,"* in *Speech and Phenomena And Other Essays on Husserl's Theory of Signs*, trans. David B. Allison (Evanston, Ill.: Northwestern University Press, 1973), pp. 129–30.

35. Empson (*Structure of Complex Words*, p. 222) feels that the disclosure of Cassio's role in the courtship serves the dramatic purpose of giving Iago yet one more pretext for his jealousy of Cassio and his hatred of Othello: "Iago feels he has been snubbed, as too coarse to be trusted in such a matter, and he takes immediate advantage of his discomposure."

36. Knight, *Wheel of Fire*, p. 104.

37. Bullough, *Narrative and Dramatic Sources*, pp. 193ff; Roger Ascham, *The Schoolmaster*, ed. Lawrence V. Ryan (Charlottesville: University Press of Virginia, 1967), pp. 67–68.

38. Rosalind Johnson, "African Presence in Shakespearean Drama: parallels between *Othello* and the Historical Leo Africanus," in *African Presence in Early Europe, Journal of African Civilizations* 7 (1985): 267–87; Karen Newman, "And wash the Ethiop white": Femininity and the Monstrous in *Othello*," in *Shakespeare Reproduced: The Text in History and Ideology*, ed. Jean E. Howard and Marion F. O'Connor (London: Methuen, 1987), pp. 143–62.

39. *Bandello: Tragical Tales*, trans. Geoffrey Fenton (1567), introd. Robert Langston Douglas (London: George Routledge and Sons, 1923), p. 187.

40. Ibid., p. 200.

41. Ibid., p. 188.

42. To take but one example, the reference by Desdemona to the fact that Cassio has known of Othello and Desdemona's courtship and had even spoken on behalf of Othello bears an intrusive force in the play, not only because it complicates the audience's perception of the relationship of the three characters and creates the possibility of a triangle where none had existed before, but also because it disrupts the audience's sense of time, creating the illusion of a frequent activity extending over some nebulously long duration of time either before the play begins or even, and more unsettlingly, after the play has begun. The allusion to Cassio's implication in the relationship of Othello and Desdemona is, however, an echo of a detail from Cinthio that fits much more naturally into the capacious temporality of prose fiction. "In the same company there was also a Corporal who was very dear to the Moor. This man went frequently to the Moor's house and often dined with him and his wife. The Lady, knowing him so well liked by her husband, gave him proofs of the greatest kindness, and this was much appreciated by the Moor," in Bullough, *Narrative and Dramatic Sources*, 7:243.

43. It is, perhaps, the moment in the play at which one feels most keenly the coincidence of Derrida's contention in "Border Lines: Living On," trans. James Hulbert, in *Deconstruction and Criticism*, ed. Harold Bloom et al. (New York: Seabury Press, 1979), pp. 104–5, that "all organized narration is 'a matter for the police,' even before its genre (mystery novel, cop story) has been determined." See Parker's reference to Derrida's remark, "Shakespeare and Rhetoric," p. 69.

MAYNARD MACK

"Speak of Me as I Am": Othello

I

There is probably no play of Shakespeare's about which at the present time the interpretations of critics differ so radically and at so many points as about *Othello*.[63]

This is partly owing to extraneous factors that have nothing to do with the play. One such, of course, is the nature of criticism, colored as it always is and must be by the pressures of a particular culture and time as well as the biases, experiences, and values of the individual practitioner. A notably perplexing addition to this traditional fountain of discrepancy has emerged in recent years with the formation of group ideologies ... which annex the distortions of a program to the already myopic character of the personal lens. And further, at least in the United States, there is the circumstance that most literary criticism including Shakespeare criticism is carried on in college and university faculties, where, for advancement if one is young and notoriety if one is not, it has become more expedient to voice new opinions than to improve on old ones—"And give to dust that is a little gilt More laud than gilt o'er-dusted" (*Troilus and Cressida*, 3.3.177).

This having been said, it remains true that over the years much in Othello itself has invited and continues to invite disagreement. Historically, the critical record shows that playgoers and readers alike have been troubled,

From *Everybody's Shakespeare: Reflections Chiefly on the Tragedies*, pp. 129–49, 267–71. © 1993 by Maynard Mack.

when not shocked or outraged, by the union of a black man with a white woman. That a beautiful Venetian girl should fall in love with "a veritable negro"[64] seemed to many implausible, in fact "monstrous." The words are Coleridge's, but the sentiment was widely shared and, on the nineteenth-century stage, was increasingly taken into account by "orientalizing" the hero, making him appear to be what one of that century's best-known actor-directors declared he emphatically was: "not a negro" but "a stately Arab."[65] Perhaps nothing manifests more clearly the dependence of critical opinion on more general climates of opinion than the realization that an Arab Othello in the 1990s would be fully as likely to meet with audience condescension as any African chief.

Today, haunted as we are by our unfinished history of racial and ethnic intolerance, and possibly to a far greater extent than the conscious mind understands by ancient taboos against sexual unions outside the bounds of cult, caste, tribe, or race (each of which, after all, is only xenophobia writ large), it becomes difficult to find an angle of vision that does not appropriate *Othello* to some sociological or political cause. Add to this the vast ranges of untrammeled speculation that open when one applies twentieth-century psychosexual lore to fictitious personages in an early seventeenth-century play, and the opportunities for dissension, not to say confusion, proliferate like rabbits.

No assumption should be made that the interpretation of *Othello* attempted in the ensuing pages is imagined by its author to be the "right" one or the "best." Like all the views advanced in this book, it carries its own existentially personal baggage. What it undertakes merely is to look at the play without invoking either the older inhibitions about miscegenation that have exercised so many in the past and still exercise too many, or the newer psychoanalytic suppositions (questionable enough when applied to living persons, as the quarrels among the several schools show), whose tendency when superimposed on the contrived creations of dramatic artifice is to dissolve necessary distinctions between reality and stage. My aim, in short, is to bear in mind, first, that the currents of thought and feeling swirling through the play are fed by a *Renaissance* sensibility and, second, that the play unfolds itself for audiences in the theater and readers in the study not by topics but speech by speech and scene by scene—far less an occasion for consulting-room theories of repression and psychoses than a vehicle of situations, movements, gestures, colors, sounds, and acts and words that break the heart.

2

A striking feature of Hamlet's world, it may be recalled, is mystery. Not only his own, which he is not about to have plucked out either by himself or others, but the larger mysteries on which he broods and among which, like the rest of us, he has to learn to live and act.

It is obvious that Othello's world differs sharply. Mystery may be operative in the motivation of Iago—"Will you, I pray, demand that demi-devil Why he hath thus ensnared my soul and body?" (5.2.301)—though one suspects he refuses to reply because his creator has no answer (on these matters, who has?) and certainly does not wish to remove from him the implication so carefully nurtured throughout the play and in the impassioned question just cited that he connects with something beyond understanding, like the witches in *Macbeth*.

In any event, what comes to us most forcefully from the stage in *Othello* is not mystery but the agony of loss, loss all the more tragic, in some instances, for not being inevitable. Brabantio loses (in every sense) his much-loved only child and eventually dies of grief. Cassio in a drunken moment loses his soldier's discipline, then his lieutenancy and his cherished comradeship with Othello. Othello, in turn, losing under Iago's tuition his ability to distinguish the individual woman he married from the standard cynical stereotype, abandons with it all pride in his profession together with the self-command that made him the man he was. And Desdemona, through no real fault of her own, loses the magical handkerchief.

Magical in *my* view, though I know how far opinions differ on this point, as a way of asking us to recognize that the love these lovers share before Iago's corruption sets in does indeed have magic in its web, contains a "work" (3.3.296) that a relationship like Cassio's and Bianca's can never match or "take out," commands a power that sets it as far above the commonplace as Desdemona is in the radiant generosity and innocence that makes her vulnerable, as Othello is in the "free and open nature" (1.3.393) that makes *him* vulnerable, and in the courage and determination to do justice on himself that earns the closing accolade: "For he was great of heart" (5.2.361).

To my mind, it is precisely the loss of a love as rare and magical as the fabled handkerchief by a pair of lovers whose vulnerabilities are inseparable from their beauties that tears at the feelings throughout this play and brings to any audience listening to Othello's comparison of himself to "the base Indian"[66] (5.2.347) who threw a pearl away richer than all his tribe—not knowing what he had or what it was worth—a shock of self-recognition.

Supporting and extending the sense of irretrievable loss that the play conveys is a succession of poignant retrospectives opening on what we realize, though the speakers may not, was a securer or freer or happier or at least less perplexing condition than the one now being experienced. Othello, recounting before the Senate the toils and hazards of his past life to refute charges of witchcraft in his wooing that could cost his life, evokes for us, if not for himself, the "unhousèd free condition" (1.2.26) he has put behind him for the love of Desdemona. Even Iago is allowed his brief memory of a stay in "sweet England" (2.3.83), where the natives were "most potent in potting" (2.3.72), and he no doubt held his own with the best.

The most moving retrospectives come later. Desdemona, preparing for bed on the night that will be her last, remembers her mother's maid "called Barbary":

> She was in love, and he she loved proved mad
> And did forsake her. She had a song of "Willow;"
> An old thing 'twas; but it expressed her fortune,
> And she died singing it. That song to-night
> Will not go from my mind. (4.3.25)

Here time present, in which Desdemona speaks and sings, and time future, in which we know she (like Barbary) is to die from an absolute fidelity to her intuition of what love is and means, recede even as we watch into a lost time past, when Desdemona had a mother and all love's agonies and complexities could be comprehended in a song. A song, moreover, bringing to her consciousness the sheltered world in which she grew up, now balanced beside the world she chose. In that other world, her husband might have been a Venetian gentleman, someone like Lodovico perhaps—"a proper man," she confides to Emilia—such a man as surely would never strike his wife in public or humiliate her in private as a common prostitute? But the song itself refuses to take sides. And as she sings, she seems to be understanding that there is no world worth living in without love, and no love worth having that is immune to pain—if not from the particular wounds she has met with, then by others. Surely one of the key epiphanic moments in all drama, the song serves to remind us that Shakespeare's own song of "Willow," about the tragedies and treacheries of love, is the play before our eyes.

The last remembrance of things past belongs to Othello. As he stabs himself, he recalls a moment "in Aleppo once" (5.2.352), when at the risk of his life (for the fate of any Christian who assaulted a native in Aleppo was immediate death) he struck down a Turk who had struck a Venetian and traduced the state. He has been that Turk in his treatment of Desdemona, and he now punishes his deed by executing himself. But he also knows that on that occasion as on so many others he has put his life on the line for Venice. Let the record then stand as it really is, tragically mixed: "Speak of me as I am" (5.2.342). It is a caveat not to be ignored as we turn to the first scenes.

3

Scene I, we all remember, takes place on a dark street in Venice. So dark in most modern stagings that at first we are only conscious of clashing voices, one saying impatiently, "Tush, never tell me!," the other replying, "'Sblood, but you'll not hear me!" Though we will perhaps not notice at the time, it may occur to us later that this "'Sblood" (for "God's Blood"), like the "Zounds" (for "God's Wounds") that explodes twice from these lips in the next few minutes, is calculated to tell us something about this speaker, whose first word initiates a program of profaning, trivializing, and vulgarizing that will end only when the play ends.

Meantime, this same speaker, whose name it now develops is Iago, has been assuring his companion of his hatred for someone he calls "the Moor" (1.1.40). The Moor, it seems, ignoring Iago's rightful claim, has appointed as his lieutenant a West-Point type named Cassio, whose soldiership is "Mere prattle without practice" (1.3.26). If we are inclined for a moment to feel some sympathy for Iago's resentment, it is soon qualified by the *non sequitur* of his argument. He craves the profit of what he calls the "old gradation, where each second Stood heir to the first" (1.1.37). Yet he has only scorn for the kind of investment that made the old gradation feasible. Not for him the loyalties that bind Kent to Lear, Enobarbus to Antony, or, in this play, Emilia to Desdemona and Cassio to Othello. No. "Whip me such honest knaves." "For, sir, It is as sure as you are Roderigo, . . . not I for love and duty But seeming so for my peculiar end" (1.1.55). Here again, an alacrity in defaming, not only the particular trust that in the soldier's trade is as indispensable as armor but the very bonds that make civil society possible, should later give us pause.

But only later. For suddenly the two voices get down to business and we learn what that matter is for which Roderigo has been reproaching his companion. The Moor, it seems, has run off with the daughter of a Venetian senator, Brabantio, at whose house they are about to raise an outcry. Once convinced by what they say, Brabantio and his household swarm into the street with torches. The scene is visually unforgettable. And is meant to be, for it will be many times repeated: one torch, or many torches, or perhaps only a single taper, moving in the darkness of our ignorance of each other. A darkness, we increasingly understand, not confined to the stage. What do we know, really (no matter how intimately we live with them), about that man or woman sitting beside us in the next chair?

Just now, however, as we listen to his plans evolve, the darkness seems chiefly to be Iago's element. In the darkness of this Venetian street, he moves to disrupt Othello's marriage if he can. Later, in the darkness of a street in Cyprus, he will close his trap on Cassio, involving him in a scuffle that will cost him his lieutenancy. Still later, in that dark island outpost, he will set Roderigo to ambush Cassio, and so (he hopes) be rid of both. Simultaneously, in a darkness that he has insinuated into Othello's mind, Desdemona will be strangled. So when we see Othello make that fateful entry into their bedroom bearing a pitifully small light, we are to bear in mind this opening moment when, for all his torches, Brabantio quite misunderstands what has long been before his eyes. It is not Othello only who proves vulnerable to Iago's darkness, but, in some degree, everyone in the play.

4

Scene 2 brings us further evidence about Iago. If the manuscript of the play, it has often been remarked, had been lost except for the first scene, the only Othello we would know would be the stereotypical white man's version of the black man that Iago and Roderigo contemptuously describe: "the thicklips" (1.1.66), "an old black ram" (1.1.88), "a Barbary horse" (I.I.III), "the gross clasps of a lascivious Moor" (1.1.125). This Othello is a Muslim, for that was a primary meaning of Moor in Shakespeare's time. He is also "an extravagant and wheeling stranger" (1.1.135), meaning a rootless alien with no settled home. He is as well a typical blowhard soldier, a *miles gloriosus*, "Horribly stuffed" says Iago, "with epithets of war" (1.1.14). And he is apparently some sort of sexual satyr, since that is what Iago's grosser insults imply. His black skin, moreover, links him with lechery and especially with the devil. "A Moor, Of all that bears man's shape, likest a divell," writes Shakespeare's contemporary Thomas Heywood.[67] If you don't stop this elopement, Iago advises Brabantio, "the devil will make a grandsire of you" (1.1.91).

To all this, you will recall, the second scene brings a startling change. Our satyr, it turns out, has eloped with Desdemona not because (as in Iago's book and many since) a black man is always in rut, but because he loves her and, as we are soon to learn, she loves him. Our braggart soldier and rootless alien, we now discover, is a prince, who when he knows "that boasting is an honor" (1.2.20) will let it be told that he descends from "men of royal siege" (1.2.22). As for our Muslim, he is in point of fact a Christian, one of Christendom's champions in the defense of Europe against "the general enemy Ottoman" (1.3.49). Cyprus, every Elizabethan knew, had long been a bastion in that defense. It was only thirty-odd years since the sultan's armies had been thrown back from the walls of Vienna.

Here is an about-face indeed. And we may reasonably guess that such an entire reversal of perspective, not found in the other tragedies, is purposeful. One requirement, clearly, was to prepare *Othello*'s first audiences for a figure as unassimilable as Othello is to many of the stereotypes of Moorishness present in the culture and regularly purveyed on the contemporary stage—by Shakespeare's own Aaron, for instance, in *Titus Andronicus*. As all rhetoricians know, and all debate teams, to show complete familiarity with a popular opinion and even what at first may be taken for a degree of sympathy with it is the most politic way to gain a hearing for another view. It is also the likeliest way to give that other view maximum dramatic impact when disclosed, as we have just seen happening in Scene 2.

But perhaps the greatest single gain from the reversal was that it required an audience to discover how easily it could be led into mistaken judgments, especially judgments that had been found congenial, and especially when packaged by a skilled manipulator of lies and truths. For a few moments, we in the theater are placed in a situation interestingly parallel to that in which Othello will soon find himself. As we are invited (with alarming success, theater history shows) to buy into the stereotype of the brutal Moor, Othello will be invited to buy into the stereotype of the promiscuous Venetian wife who lets only God see the pranks she dare not show her husband. The crucial difference is that the play immediately sets us right, while not till its end will Othello's knowledge equal ours. When it does, he will respond to Iago as we do.

Or at least, as the play asks us to do. Hazlitt gets it right, it seems to me, when he says that Iago's fascination for us combines equal parts of admiration and horror.[68] Admiration for his cunning, his resourceful opportunism, his street-smart confidences, his public charm. Horror at the envious fury raging inside that cool exterior which drives him to shrivel with his caustic cynicism and destroy with his murderous indifference anyone and anything with qualities beyond his grasp. His reaction to Cassio—"He hath a daily beauty in his life That makes me ugly" (5.1.19)—says it all.

Yet our disposition recently on both stage and page has been to downplay the horror, ignore the implication of his many references to one whom Macbeth calls "the common enemy of man" (3.1.69), and present an ingratiating stage manager comically engaged in exploding an "exsufflicate" or stuffed-shirt Othello. Possibly this distortion reflects the uneasiness, not to say downright discomfort, that in the age of Freud we tend to bring to the contemplation of whatever looks to be heroic or magnificent or grand.[69] Or possibly it springs from the current fashionable conviction in academic circles that all relationships are power relationships and the customary fidelities of the married state merely masks to hide a greedy capitalist enclosure of private property. Whatever its source, it has diminished our empathy with the play's hero and made more acceptable to us than they should be all those hard-bitten "truths," as it flatters us to call them, all those faint-hearted scepticisms and incredulities, by which like Iago we cut what makes us ugly down to an unthreatening size.

What should be noticed in particular is that, essentially, Shakespeare invented Iago;[70] set him down in his *dramatis personae* with the single epithet "a villain"; and devoted most of the play's lines and scenes to showing in detail the cunning, malignancy, and cruelty of his nature, including the cowardice of his murder of his wife. It seems to me therefore impossible to believe, as some recent critics would have us do, that the root causes of Othello's ruin are to be sought in some profound moral or psychological deficiency peculiar to *him*. He shows, to be sure, the degree of inexperience that follows naturally from his being a new husband, a soldier who has spent his entire previous life in the field, an outsider unacquainted with Venetian ways, and a man whose straightforward nature assumes the like in others. These are failings that a skilled manipulator can exploit, and their exploitation is precisely what we watch with sinking hearts. But once we go beyond this to postulate a deep and deadly fault in Othello's inmost being we come up against the implausible conclusion that one of the most experienced of dramatists has badly bungled his play. For what he has created in Iago, in that case, is a master intriguer and corrupter with no function proportionate to his stature, if what he exists to do has already been done for him by a self-doomed victim. A master intriguer, moreover, whose repeated assertion of diabolical power may well remind his theater audience of an earlier occasion when envy and a plausible exterior destroyed a pair of innocents.

5

This same scene has much to say about Othello, the nature of whose tragedy it begins to define. Fresh from alarming Brabantio, Iago now seeks to alarm his master by recounting Brabantio's abuse. Othello remains composed: "'Tis better as it is" (1.2.6). Then an armed group appears with torches. Iago urges Othello to withdraw, claiming it is "the raisèd father and his friends" (1.2.29), and no doubt hoping that withdrawal will be taken as a sign of guilt. Othello remains composed: "Not I; I must be found" (1.2.30). A second armed group appears. This time it *is* Brabantio and his party, and there is the flash of drawn steel. Othello remains composed: "Keep up your bright swords," (1.2.59) he says, with the professional soldier's amusement at the department-store glitter of civilian weapons, "for the dew will rust them." Brabantio then assails Othello with every insult in the white man's book. What girl, he asks, least of all my daughter, would "Run from her guardage to the sooty bosom Of such a thing as thou?" (1.2.70). Othello remains composed: "Hold your hands, Both you of my inclining and the rest. Were it my cue to fight, I should have known it Without a prompter" (1.2.81).

These repeated upsurgings of violence against calm establish what I take to be the play's fundamental dramatic rhythm. Calm—sleep, in fact—invaded by uproar and violent language at Brabantio's house. Calm resisting and quelling violence in the three encounters just described. Calm unruffled before the Senate, easily blowing away Brabantio's violent charges. Calm of fulfilled happiness in the central scenes, attacked and gradually possessed by forms of violence it has no art to cope with. Finally at the play's close, calm retrieved and reasserted at great cost. All these confrontations are vivid in our experience when we see *Othello* in the theater and should, I think, warn us that the core of tragedy is to be looked for here where it is found in Shakespeare's other tragedies of this period. Compressed to six words, the inmost shape of tragedy in all these plays—its common denominator—is the shape that Hamlet gives it unwittingly in his first soliloquy: "That it should come to this" (1.2.137).

That, in other words, a young idealistic student should become, even against his will, an intriguer and killer, as Hamlet does. Or that a great king should be reduced to beggary and madness, and by his own daughters, as Lear is. Or that a man gifted with a moral imagination so intense that even the anticipation of murder can make his hair stand on end should reach a condition so benumbed, so supped full with horrors, that to go back is as tedious as "go o'er," as happens to Macbeth. Or that the greatest soldier of the ancient world, once the king of courtesy, should be reduced to having his rival's emissary whipped, as in the case of Antony. Or that an earlier famous soldier should be so mastered by self-will and pride as to defect to the national enemy and war against his kin—the story of Coriolanus.

Here is where tragedy normally resides in Shakespeare's mature work, and I see no evidence that it resides elsewhere in Othello. There would be nothing tragic, in the senses of tragic that apply to drama, in the commission of a murder by one who was in fact a barbarian—that is melodrama. Or about the anguish of a lover naturally inclined to jealousy—that is one of the oldest of comic themes, touched on already in *The Merry Wives*. What seems to me tragic in *Othello* is precisely that its hero is not a barbarian and, as he himself tells us, not easily jealous—in short, that it is possible for a human being who is what Othello is repeatedly shown to be at the play's beginning to become what he has become by its end: his command of himself and others shattered, his mind fouled, his occupation gone, his embrace of love changed to the embrace of murder. Or, as Lodovico the Venetian ambassador puts it, in words that only an ideologue could ignore, "Oh thou Othello, that wert once so good, Fall'n in the practice of a damnèd slave. What shall be said to thee?" (5.2.291).

If tragedy, as Aristotle thought, has to do with terror, Othello's being brought to kill the thing he loves is terror, for it can happen to us, and does, as many a newspaper headline will remind us. And if pity too is part of the tragic experience, here is pity in its intensest form, for we know it to be a law of life in our world that what is beautiful is always vulnerable and what is precious can cause the greatest pain.

6

I have dwelt considerably on these opening scenes, since in the theater we cannot ignore them any more than we can ignore the climax to which they point: the great moment on the sea-wall when Othello and Desdemona are reunited.

By this time, there has been considerable suspense as we watch Othello escorted to the Senate House under guard, his personal fate uncertain till the story of his wooing wins the Senators as securely as the story of his life won Desdemona. More suspense as we wait for Desdemona to appear, followed by a shock of surprise as we learn how mature and spirited she is and how little her father knew her: "A maiden never bold; Of spirit so still and quiet that her motion Blushed at herself" (1.3.94). Or should we say perhaps instead that what she discovered when she "saw Othello's visage in his mind" released something in her own that was waiting to be released, as when the sleeping princess wakes to the kiss of the wandering prince?

Then falls the first of many hardships. The Duke declares Othello must away tonight. "Tonight, my lord?" says Desdemona, with what feelings we can guess.[71] "This night," comes the firm reply. After which Othello has four words: "With all my heart" (1.3.278).

Much has been made of these words. And if we believe that Othello is a sexual cripple, or has a narcissistic incapacity to love any but himself, or is emotionally underdeveloped because of some problem in achieving separation from his mother during infancy, or, conversely, is a man so passionate he dreads his powerful sexuality (four popular theories of recent years), we will expect the actor to speak the four words briskly and on the upbeat, as if his martial ego were straining like a sled-dog to release him from this pickle.

But if we believe otherwise and see in Othello one version of the warrior-lover figure so congenial to the Renaissance imagination, the occasion will be treated very differently. After the Duke's ultimatum, several seconds of painful silence ensue while Othello gazes longingly, even despairingly, at his new wife, as she at him, and then says with a sigh in his voice and a tone that conveys his disappointment along with his recognition that in the soldier's trade orders are orders: "With all my heart." It is one of the most telling moments in the play and, performed as suggested here, only confirms the depth of their affection, together with the persistent theme of loss.

When next we see the lovers, they come like mythic figures from the sea. The great storm is winding down, having first destroyed the Turkish fleet; and the perils of the Cyprus voyage (seas, winds, "guttered rocks, and congregated sands" [2.1.69])—moved by beauty—so Cassio's courtly gallantries would persuade us—have let "go safely by The divine Desdemona" (2.1.72). This is tall talk. Tall talk that like so much else in this tragic play (as earlier in *Romeo and Juliet*, later in *Antony and Cleopatra*) weaves into it some of the colorings of romance: that genre of writing, as Henry James once pointed out, in which experience is "liberated, . . . disengaged, disembroiled, disencumbered, exempt from the conditions that we usually know to attach to it . . . and drag upon it."[72] Romance colorings leap out again as Cassio utters his prayer for the lovers' safety, enfolding their reunion in the ancient myth that human sexual consummation brings fruition to all other things:

> Great Jove, Othello guard,
> And swell his sail with thine own pow'rful breath,
> That he may bless this bay with his tall ship,
> Make love's quick pants in Desdemona's arms,
> Give renewed fire to our extincted spirits,
> And bring all Cyprus comfort! (2.1.77)

As he speaks, Desdemona enters, wearing a traveling gown of purest white (or so it was in one production I recall), high on the crest of the abutment that defends the city from the sea. For a thrilling instant, her radiance transforms all that lies about her. Then she descends, Cassio painting her once again in great brush strokes of legend, as if it were the homecoming of some divinity. (Should we perhaps remember here that Cyprus is the ancient home of Aphrodite?) "O behold!" he cries,

> The riches of the ship is come on shore!
> You men of Cyprus, let her have your knees.
> Hail to thee, lady! and the grace of heaven,
> Before, behind thee, and on every hand,
> Enwheel thee round! (2.1.82)

And then, quite suddenly, another voice is heard, sharp and mocking. "Sir," says this voice to Cassio, who has saluted Emilia with a kiss, "Would she give you so much of her lips As of her tongue she oft bestows on me, You'ld have enough" (2.1.100). Romance may disencumber all it pleases from those conditions "that we usually know to attach to it," but in tragic life their "drag" will still be felt.

At Othello's entry, the pattern recurs. He stands at the top of the sea-wall where Desdemona stood before, and she goes up to his side. His robe of state is red, and with it folded about them both she is visibly his "fair warrior" (2.1.180)—so he calls her—and for that moment they command the scene, lost in a joy that those below (significantly) look up to. "If it were now to die" (2.1.187), Othello says, voicing the Renaissance lover's sense of an achieved perfection already containing all that life can offer, but fused with the tragic hero's intimation of some doom possibly yet hanging in the stars:

> If it were now to die,
> 'Twere now to be most happy; for I fear
> My soul hath her content so absolute
> That not another comfort like to this
> Succeeds in unknown fate. (2.1.187)

May "this, and this," he adds, kissing her, "the greatest discords be That e'er our hearts shall make." But then, from down below, reserved this time for our ears alone, comes the interrupting challenge of a man in black: "O you are well tuned now! But I'll set down the pegs that make this music, As honest as I am" (2.1.197).

7

Iago's untuning of their "music"—plainly a glancing allusion on Shakespeare's part to the belief that when the universe sprang from Chaos to become a Harmony in which the compelling force was Eros (the same belief that underlies Othello's exclamation at Desdemona's beauty, "Perdition catch my soul, But I do love thee, and when I love thee not, Chaos is come again" (3.3.90)—occupies the so-called "temptation scene" of the third act. We come to this from two earlier temptations. In the first, Roderigo's tentative resistance to the maxim that love is "merely a lust of the blood and a permission of the will" (1.3.333) succumbs so completely to Iago's corrosive references to the wedding night of Othello and Desdemona—"when she is sated with his body, she will find the error of her choice" (1.3.347)—that he revises his ambitions from a not very seriously intended suicide to "enjoying" her (1.3.354). In the second, having been tested along this same fault-line and found impregnable (2.3.15), Cassio incautiously accepts Iago's invitation to a night of good fellowship and drink, and so becomes an easy mark for the street brawl that loses him his lieutenancy.

Othello's temptation is the culmination of these. The brilliance of its adaptation of complex psychological materials to the conditions of theater deserves a monograph. One can only say here that the scene *plays* best when the director establishes a distinctive area or symbolic object at either end of the stage. One is to be suggestive of Desdemona—perhaps a pair of virginals or a lute, since we know she "sings, plays, and dances" (3.3.185) (A lute will have the advantage of making more explicit the image of strings "well tuned.") The other area or object should be a reminder of Cassio—a chair, say, or couch, on which still lies (preferably) an offering of flowers, but possibly a hat or cloak or some other possession easily identified as his, left behind in his hasty retreat. During the course of the scene, Iago will drive Othello, with many rebounds, from the area of the lute to the area of the hat or nosegay. At this spot, having roared out his wish that Cassio had "forty thousand lives" (3.3.442), Othello kneels with Iago in their mutual oath of revenge.

All this has to do with the scene onstage, where few audiences have ever been in doubt about its power and persuasiveness. On the other hand, the scene *reads* better if we bear in mind Santayana's remark about poetry in general. "Poetry is not at its best," he writes, "when it depicts a further possible experience, but when it initiates us, by feigning something that as an experience is impossible, into the meaning of the experience we have actually had."[73] So we are asked here to let clock time fade into emotional time (the play's much-discussed "double-time scheme" facilitates this), in order that the playwright may crowd into one intense theatrical experience the mysterious evolution of states of feeling that can, and do if spread over days or weeks in the real world, lead human beings from confidence to perplexity to doubt to surrender to breakdown.

"Mysterious" is the crucial term; for though Shakespeare gives us here on the side of realism a notable succession of psychological advances and retreats, he seems to have known as well as we do that these are all finally "signals" alerting us to psychological events, not the events themselves, which even in our therapies today remain graspable only by metaphor. And he knew also as a practicing playwright that creatures sitting at a play in his time did not expect (nor probably could he have provided) elaborate verisimilitudes of intellection at work. Often he is content to signal psychic change simply by absenting his hero from the stage, as with Hamlet and Lear, and as with Othello in mid-scene here. But elsewhere in this scene he goes all out to give his indicators of mental process the maximum illusion of reality. Edmund in *King Lear* deceives Gloucester into thinking Edgar is about to kill him in something less than ninety seconds of playing time. Here, by contrast, Iago's silences, evasions, and insinuations prior to Othello's first exit make up a plausible quarter-hour sequence establishing just those conditions of perplexity and doubt that the street brawl has already shown us Othello's forthright nature cannot endure.[74]

8

Soon after this, we witness the heart-breaking consequences of Iago's triumph. Othello—"the nature Whom passion could not shake, whose solid virtue The shot of accident, nor dart of chance, Could neither graze nor pierce" (4.1.257)—erupts in anger at Desdemona for having mislaid the handkerchief that in some occult way represents love's "magic." In full view of the embassy just arrived from Venice, he strikes her in the face; and, his mind having been turned into a brothel, proceeds to turn his home into one, greeting Emilia as a procuress and Desdemona as a woman for sale.

When next we see him for any length of time, he is in their bedroom contemplating her beauty by the candle in his hand. We have reached this scene after another street brawl, with the usual outcries, the usual flash of steel, the usual torches pitted vainly against the several sorts of darkness that surround all action in this play. But now for a moment we have calm, this time judicial calm—"It is the cause, it is the cause, my soul"—until Desdemona in her innocence insists on not playing the role of guilty wife that Othello's perverted script demands. What rouses him again to anger is noteworthy. When at the news of Cassio's death she bursts into tears and cries out, "Alas, he is betrayed and I undone!" (5.2.76), she looks and speaks like the guilty woman he believes her to be. She means only that Cassio has been falsely accused, and now there is no witness left to confirm her innocence. But to Othello she seems to be saying, "Cassio is exposed, and now I am done for." Taking her tears as further confirmation, he kills her.

Much of the rest of the play is devoted to exposing the details of Iago's plot (5.2.181), Othello's role becoming largely that of suffering auditor. But when Lodovico says at last, "Bring [him] away," Othello interposes. "Soft you! a word or two before you go" (5.2.338). He draws from the bed the great red robe of state in which he entered Cyprus as commander and in which he entered Desdemona's bedroom as officer of state to carry out an execution, flinging it now across his shoulders as if he were preparing for another of his life's journeys, this one his last. But he knows he will not be going. If the scene in their bedroom was, as he now understands, a blind miscarriage of truth and justice, this is to be his reaffirmation of both. He will have nothing extenuated, but nothing set down in malice either: "Speak of me as I am." Much of the preceding tragic action, we have by now come to realize, consists in a losing contest between those six words and six others that were burned on our attention in the first scene: "I am not what I am."

Here, as elsewhere, Shakespeare conveys a vivid sense of Othello's personality in his speech. Nothing could be simpler or more direct than "Speak of me as I am," or "'Tis better as it is," or "Not I. I must be found," or "Soft you, a word or two before you go." This is the Othello whose language has been shaped and seasoned by a life in action, whose forthright idiom expresses nobly the "free and open nature"—acknowledged so scornfully by Iago—"That thinks men honest that but seem to be so" (1.3.394). But there is another stratum in Othello's language, as in his person. He is an outsider and speaks as one; a traveler with a haunting past; a Mauretanian prince whose every gesture in the early scenes has the dignity of Saladin; and (as always) he is the larger-than-life Shakespearean hero, brushed in this instance with the glamor that Africa's rumored kingdoms once held for Western eyes. The natural language of this stratum, as in African and Middle Eastern poetry generally, is opulent and grand; and in this farewell, as at other moments earlier, his imagination roams freely through time and space to give his pain of loss the widest possible definition:

> Then must you speak
> Of one that loved not wisely, but too well;
> Of one not easily jealous, but, being wrought,
> Perplexed in the extreme; of one whose hand,
> Like the base Indian, threw a pearl away
> Richer than all his tribe; of one whose subdued eyes,
> Albeit unusèd to the melting mood,
> Drop tears as fast as the Arabian trees
> Their med'cinable gum. Set you down this.
> And say besides that in Aleppo once,
> Where a malignant and a turbaned Turk
> Beat a Venetian, and traduced the state,
> I took by th' throat the circumcisèd dog,
> And smote him thus. (5.2.343)

Driving the dagger home, he moves painfully to the bed where Desdemona lies and, as his last words tell us, dies "upon a kiss."

9

"A tragedy without meaning," says Granville-Barker of this close; and others have echoed him since.[75] Certainly, as in *Hamlet*, there is much of death before us on the stage. Moreover—what is uniquely painful in this play— these dead have higher claims on our sympathy than Claudius, Gertrude, and Laertes. Whatever their frailties, these were essentially good people of great integrity (Roderigo would be the exception but his body is not on the stage) brought down in considerable part by the envious ego of "some eternal villain," as Emilia calls him before she knows his name, "Some busy and insinuating rogue, Some cogging, cozening slave" (4.2.131).

Still, one wonders. Is there not more to it than Granville-Barker allows? The Orson Welles film of *Othello*, despite many faults, caught in its opening frames, it seemed to me, a poignant question rather than a verdict. These showed the upturned dead faces of Othello and Desdemona lying side by side on their funeral cortege as it moved slowly down the Cyprian fortifications, silhouetted against the sky and sea.[76] They were beautiful faces, at peace now, the black skin glowing beside the white, the white radiant beside the black, together here in death as in the play we saw them first, when Desdemona stepped to Othello's side to assure the Senators of her love.

The dazzling contrast of those still faces conveyed superbly (when one paused to reflect) the leap of faith that all love is—"And when I love thee not, Chaos is come again"—together with a thrilling sense that what was about to be put at risk in the play to follow was the immemorial human dream of creating a world in which (as in Renaissance cosmologies) polar opposites are held in harmony by love: black and white, male and female, warrior and "moth of peace," together with all those other contraries that it was believed perfection called for. "As with the bow and the lyre," Heraclitus had said, "so with the world: it is the tension of opposing forces that makes the structure one."[77]

The very idea of such a dream is laughable to Iago, as it is to all of us in our Iago moods, and for a time is made to seem so to Othello. Yet we see it forming again from the ruins of his life as he learns the truth about Desdemona and crawls to her side to die "upon a kiss." The words by this time are charged. They have in them the accents of the Elizabethan love poets in their struggle to affirm love's authority over death. And they bring with them—unavoidably, I believe, in a play so studded with patterns of iteration—the two earlier moments when we have seen these lovers kiss. One was on the sea-wall, where he greeted her with words that show unmistakably with what values Shakespeare is associating them: "O my fair warrior," an all but exact translation, as Rosalie Colie long ago pointed out, of Petrarch's address to Laura: "O dolce mia guerriera;"[78] and where Shakespeare also gives him, to describe his joy, the traditional sonnet figure of the laboring bark come home to harbor and heaven in the beloved's arms:

> O my soul's joy!
> If after every tempest come such calms,
> May the winds blow till they have wakened death!
> And let the laboring bark climb hills of seas
> Olympus-high, and duck again as low
> As hell's from heaven. (2.1.182)

The other moment occurs in their bedroom when he kisses her before he kills her. The scene is bitterly ironic when set against the earlier scene, and the irony is only deepened by his entering (as we have seen so many in this play do, quite unaware how dark the surrounding darkness is) "with a light"—says the quarto stage direction—which he then compares to the light that shines in Desdemona as she sleeps. (Can it be an accident that from this moment on she is always seen by him as having an inner radiance: the rose, the alabaster, the one entire and perfect chyrsolite, the pearl richer than all his tribe?) "Put out the light," he says, referring to the taper in his hand,

> and then put out the light:
> If I quench thee, thou flaming minister,
> I can again thy former light restore,
> Should I repent me; but once put out thy light,
> Thou cunning'st pattern of excelling nature,
> I know not where is that Promethean heat
> That can thy light relume. (5.2.7)

And then he quenches both. The taper first, for even by its flickering fire the figure before him can never be other than Desdemona, the lovely individual woman he married and of whom he once exclaimed, "If she be false, 0, then heaven mocks itself! I'll not believe't" (3.3.278). But now, given over to Iago's darker outlook on sexuality, he can abstract her into the generalized category of disloyal wife and commit her to a generalized fate.

Much of the horror of this scene for spectators in the theater lies in its seeming to mark the irreparable defeat of something greatly precious that Desdemona's whole being has asserted and Iago's whole being has denied. Yet it is against our sense of defeat at this point that we are invited to witness at the play's end Othello's reinstatement of the commitment he had made at the beginning. "My life upon her faith!" (1.3.294), he had told Brabantio then. Now he makes that promise good.

> I kissed thee ere I killed thee; no way but this,
> Killing myself, to die upon a kiss.

I believe these lines ask us to understand that though he now does justice on himself to punish his injustice to Desdemona, it is love, not justice, that he declares for at the last. What Iago's philosophy seeks throughout the play to discredit as merely paper money, backed by nothing but a lust of the blood and a permission of the will, three suffering human beings—Desdemona first and next Emilia and now Othello—have stepped forward to redeem with gold.

NOTES

63. Though it is possible to find many intervening shades of opinion, the two major schools of thought (on this play as on several others) are irreconcilable. One

holds that Othello is a man essentially noble who is brought to ruin by the incongruity of his virtues with the circumstances in which for the tragic purposes of the drama he has been placed. In the background of this view lies the assumption that dramatic characters are created for particular dramatic ends and have no existence otherwise or elsewhere. The opposing view is that Othello is a man deeply flawed who is destroyed by his own inner defects or even vices, fed by a massive egotism attributable variously to the effects of a patriarchal culture, psychological woundings from his early childhood, the erotophobia of contemporary Puritanism, or twentieth century identifications of love and power. Here the assumption is that dramatic characters, once created, have an existence in the real world that renders them as liable to medical or political diagnosis as any man or woman encountered in the street.

The first Othello, sometimes called by those who see him differently "the sentimentalist's Othello," is by and large the Othello of nearly four centuries of theater history, and his career *there* has been brilliantly traced by Marvin Rosenberg in *The Masks of Othello* (University of California Press, 1961).

The other Othello is a comparatively new figure of the last four decades, deriving from the habits of an intensely verbal academic culture which is at the same time in many quarters heavily committed to one or other of the current group ideologies. How far it is possible deconstructively to develop an interesting Othello unimaginable historically and altogether incommunicable onstage may be profitably examined in Martin Elliot's *Shakespeare's Invention of Othello* (New York, 1988).

64. *Coleridge's Shakespearean Criticism*, 2 vols., (Harvard UP, 1930), I: 47.

65. Herbert Beerbohm Tree's comment in a letter to his wife explaining his choice of make-up for his performance of *Othello* in 1912. (Herbert *Beerbohm Tree. Some Memories of Him and His Art Collected by Max Beerbohm* [London, 1920], 148.) Regardless of make-up, if the reviewer of that performance for the *Daily Telegraph* may be trusted, Tree's interpretation caught much in the play that is now frequently overlooked or disdained. "This Othello speaks as having authority, and not as the scribes. He has the habit of command and great affairs. He is past the passions of youth, as indeed he says. He has not much of the days of gallantry. He speaks of Desdemona with great tenderness. He treats her with gentlest affection. He is plainly all in love with her, but not after a young man's fashion of love. Through the long battle with Iago, the slow irresistible onset of doubt was finely played" (*Ibid.*, 147).

66. The quarto reading, in favor of which I part here and elsewhere from the inferior folio reading "Judean."

67. Thomas Heywood, *The Fair Maid of the West*, ed. R. K. Turner, Jr. (Lincoln: University of Nebraska Press, 1967), Pt. 2: I.I.329.

68. *Complete Works*, ed. P. P. Howe, 14 vols. (London, 1967), 4: 14–17, 200–09.

69. As far back as 1940, a famous essay by Joseph Wood Krutch in his *The Modern Temper* traces our century's shrinking from the idea of heroism and with it the disappearance of tragedy as Shakespeare knew it. See also, more recently, George Steiner, *The Death of Tragedy* (New York, 1961).

70. Iago's counterpart in Shakespeare's source (the seventh tale of the third decade in Giraldi Cinthio's collection: *Hecatommithi* [1565]) has no name but "the Ensign," as Othello has no name but "*The Moor*," and shares little beyond villainy with the Iago that Shakespeare conceived.

71. I adopt here the reading of the quartos, as does Robert Heilman in his *Wit and Witchcraft in Othello* (Lexington: University of Kentucky Press, 1961), 140 ff. The folio text has no interposition by Desdemona. There, a "Senator," not the Duke, instructs Othello that he must away tonight, and Othello replies, as in the quarto, "With all my heart" (1.3. 278). Considering what we have seen already of Desdemona's courage, her defiance of protocol in eloping, and her frank concern right now about "the rites for why I love him" (1.3. 257), I find it impossible to imagine her standing in submissive silence while her new husband receives an order to leave her on her wedding night.

Heilman cites Othello's four words in support of his belief that Othello is immature about matters sexual and happy to be despatched on the Cyprus mission. It is a belief difficult to share in view of the commanding stature given Othello throughout the play and the preconceptions of Jacobean audiences about the sexuality of Moors. If Othello is a sexual cripple, much in the passion he later turns against Desdemona and in the erotic fury of the act with which he murders her, becomes inexplicable.

As evidence of Othello's lack of interest in the "rites" of which his new wife wishes not to be "bereft" (1.3. 257), some cite his lines in support of her plea to be allowed to accompany him to the wars (1.3. 260). There he assures the Senators that he seconds her request "Not to comply with heat—the young affects In me defunct" (1.3. 263)—and that they need not fear he will "scant" (1.3. 267) his responsibilities as their officer. "No," he adds, "when light-winged toys Of feathered Cupid" (1.3. 268) so dull my faculties that pleasure interferes with duty, "Let housewives make a skillet of my helm" (1.3. 272), and let all ill fortunes overtake me.

It is difficult to imagine a high service officer of mature years making any very different reply to his civilian superiors even today, and one notices, lurking in the background as he speaks, the traditional Renaissance topos of Mars feminized by Venus, lying languidly by while her Cupids—in Othello's version, the housewives—try on or sport with the pieces of his armor. Othello's message is that nothing of the sort will ever happen to *him*.

72. Preface to *The American*, vol. 2 (New York Edition, 1907).

73. George Santayana, *Interpretations of Poetry and Religion* (New York: Harper Torchbooks, 1957), 284.

74. Throughout this scene, as I see it, we are as much in the presence of a stage convention as we are in the Edmund–Gloucester episode mentioned above, or the radical conversion of Lady Anne from loathing to love in *Richard III*, or, to turn to another playwright, the fall of Mrs. Frankford in *A Woman Killed with Kindness*. It is also useful to recall that Renaissance drama, like Greek drama, is normally more concerned with actions and their effects than with speculation about their sources, and that when such speculation does appear it is quite unlike our own, being on the one hand more formulaic and on the other allowing greater scope to the inexplicable (See *Hamlet*, I.4: "some vicious mole of nature," "the o'ergrowth of some complexion," "some habit that too much o'erleavens," "the dram of evil," etc.).

75. Harley Granville-Barker, *Prefaces to Shakespeare*, 2 vols. (Princeton: Princeton UP, 1951), 2: 114.

76. The content of this scene is discussed further in Lorne M. Buchman's *Still In Movement: Shakespeare on Screen* (New York: Oxford University Press, 1991), 127. (For the Buchman reference I am indebted to Stephen M. Buhler.)

77. Diels, *Fragmente der Vorsokratiker*, I: 169 (frag. 80).

78. *Canzoniere*, No. 21.

T. H. HOWARD-HILL

U and Non-U:
Class and Discourse Level in Othello[1]

In general, a play is a collection of speech acts accompanied by gestures and actions. The priority of the speech acts is determined by the progress of the play from the playwright's pen to the stage. In the classical or neo-classical style of writing the quality of the speech acts must be appropriate to the social status of the characters as well as the genre of the play: decorum must be observed. And, of course, as Hamlet knew from his humanistic studies at Wittenberg, the players should suit the actions to the words. For *Othello*, then, Olivier was correct to demand for his Iago (as Berry reports) 'a solid, honest-to-God N.C.O'.[2] The basis of Olivier's choice was not, as Berry claims, Iago's rank as Ensign because in the Elizabethan military code his rank was only one step below Cassio's. Iago is identified as a 'non-commissioned officer' (in modern terms) by the properties of his speech acts. If this needed to be made clearer than it seems in the first scene of the play, Shakespeare provided as a contrast to Iago a gentleman and a different style of speech. The linguistic differences between Cassio and Iago are the focus of this essay.

Drama is a special kind of discourse in which speeches are directed from speaker to hearer and to an attendant audience at the same time. In drama such as Shakespeare's the speakers of the play and the listeners in the audience inhabit different linguistic milieus. M.H. Short has shown convincingly

From *Shakespeare's Universe: Renaissance Ideas and Conventions: Essays in Honour of W. R. Elton*, edited by John M. Mucciolo with the assistance of Steven J. Doloff and Edward A. Rauchut, pp. 175–86. © 1996 by T. H. Howard-Hill.

107

that the text rather than performance provides suitable material for discourse analysis, which rescues 'dramatic criticism from the variability of performance analysis on the one hand and the inadequacy of traditional textual analysis on the other'.[3] Nevertheless, while he recognizes 'the general *embedded* nature of drama, because features which, for example, mark social relations between two people at the character level become messages *about* the characters at the level of discourse which pertains between author and reader/audience' (p. 188), his analysis takes little account of the playwright's obligation to convey information to the audience, and neglects to consider that the audience may lack information that is ostensibly implicated by the dialogue that would enable them to complete the circuit of communication. The application of discourse theory to drama has, therefore, a complexly double function: to describe the properties of the utterances between characters in the play, within that special communicative context, and then, to identify the information that the audience should receive from the communicative exchange. This last function falls within the scope of the traditional literary criticism.

Moreover, since a play is an artificially constructed complex of conversations controlled by the playwright's design for the work, one may possibly identify quite readily the 'cooperative principle' that H.P. Grice suggested was involved in conversations, and note the application of the accompanying regulative conventions that he called 'maxims'.[4] I can summarize them briefly. The maxim of *quantity* (1) relates to parsimony: speeches should supply neither too little nor too much information. The maxim of *quantity* (2) requires speakers to believe that their contributions to conversations are true. The maxim of *relation* (3) requires relevance, and the maxim of *manner* (4) suggests the avoidance of prolix, obscure, ambiguous and disorderly speech. Fortunately for the sake of linguistic variety and the fictions of drama, the maxims are frequently broken. Sites of dislocation can point to significant variations in the relationships of dramatic characters, as the ensuing discussion shall reveal.

In apparently the only monograph devoted to the subject, *Shakespeare and Social Class*, Ralph Berry declares that 'class as motivation is the principle of *Othello*. In the relations between military rank and social class lie the causes of the tragedy' (p. 112). In Cinthio's story, the Moorish Captain, the Ensign and the Corporal operate on the company level and the spread of social class is not great, nor is it insisted on. The Ensign lusts after Disdemona and it is on account of his rejection that he plots against the Corporal and Disdemona. (The Moor is his confederate, not the object of his hate.) In *Othello*, as is well known, the situation is remarkably different. Although his military relations with his officers seem to be those of a captain of a company, the Moor is also the commander of the Venetian forces. His lieutenant, Cassio, besides his immediate responsibilities within the company, has capabilities as an officer that warrant his appointment from Venice to succeed Othello as the military governor of Cyprus. By enlarging the military dimension of the play, Shakespeare thickened the motivational texture of the source in a manner that makes the class relationships of the principal characters freshly significant.

Declaring that 'Rank goes with class', Berry elaborates the distinction that Iago himself draws in the opening of the play: 'this counter-caster (accountant)' Michael Cassio,

> A fellow . . .
> That never set a squadron in the field,
> Nor the division of a battle knows
> More than a spinster—unless the bookish theoric,
> Wherein the toged consuls can propose
> As masterly as he.
>   (I, i, 21–6)[5]

Iago's words can elicit surprising sympathy amongst naive readers and listeners. He voices the common antipathies between doers and thinkers, men of affairs and mere scholars, workers and bosses, common soldiers and their officers, and frontline soldiers and base staff in a speech directed to the 'silly gentleman', Roderigo. Iago's complaint is motivated by hatred and fed by envy and resentment and is therefore intrinsically unreasonable. Even in our egalitarian society it is not expected that soldiers who have fought 'At Rhodes, at Cyprus, and on other grounds, / Christen'd and heathen' (I, i, 29–30) even with distinction[6] are thereby qualified for command positions, or that staff officers should possess all the experience and military expertise of the, men under their command. To serve and to command entail different abilities and responsibilities.

If Berry is correct to assert that the causes of the tragedy lie in the relations of rank and class, then we must believe that Iago's initial and foremost motivation is to secure military promotion. Then it follows that Iago would discredit Cassia to obtain the promotion he was denied originally, or he would seek to destroy Othello to punish him for choosing Cassio in his place. Iago does indeed succeed to Cassio's place and Othello is indeed destroyed, but these events do not occur for the reasons Berry's statement suggests. It seems to me that he neglects Bradley's warning about the intrinsic unreliability of Iago's communications and ignores the circumstances that influence his speeches in Act I, i.[7] The play opens at a crucial and stressful point for Iago. He has cultivated the wealthy young gentleman, Roderigo, on the pretext that he can further his courtship of Brabantio's daughter, Desdemona. (Why he

believes that Iago has access to her the play does not explain.) Their relationship is that of Sir Toby Belch and Sir Andrew Aguecheek in *Twelfth Night*.
Indeed, the first thing that Shakespeare tells us about the two is that Iago has
had Roderigo's purse as if the strings of it were his, that is, at command (I, i,
2–3). As well, we learn later that Iago has been pocketing the gifts Roderigo
has given him to deliver to Desdemona. In short, Iago has found the gullible
Roderigo a rewarding source of undeclared income:

> Thus do I ever make my fool, my purse;
> For I mine own gain'd knowledge should profane
> If I would time expend with such a snipe
> But for my sport and profit.
>   (I, iii, 383–6)

On Desdemona's elopement with Othello this profitable arrangement seems
about to be ended.[8] Unless Iago is to forfeit it, Roderigo must be persuaded
first, to persist in his courtship of the now-married Desdemona, and second,
to continue to employ Iago as his agent. In Bertrand Evans's words,

> Seizing on Roderigo's convenient cue ... 'Thou told'st me thou
> didst hold him in thy hate,' he assures his victim that such is indeed
> the case, for has not the Moor unjustly passed him over in favour
> of the incompetent Cassio? ... Reconsidering the circumstances in
> which these protestations are made—Iago's dire need of sudden,
> dramatic speech and action if he is to keep his fish now that
> Desdemona has married—we are obliged to question the truth of
> everything spoken by the villain.[9]

In particular, we may suspect the truth of Iago's statement that 'Three great
ones of the city, / Off-capp'd to him [the Moor]' (I, i, 8–10) for his promotion because there is no other evidence in the play for the event. However,
we cannot doubt the priority of Iago's hatred of Othello to his attempt to
be promoted (if in fact that occurred at all) because Roderigo refers to an
earlier occasion when Iago 'toldst me thou didst hold him in thy hate' (I,
i, 7). Cassio's promotion is brought in to provide a circumstance that will
assure Roderigo that he hates Othello for a good reason and therefore may
be trusted to work against his commander for Roderigo's benefit.[10]

It is clear from Iago's self-serving speeches that he is deeply hostile
towards Cassio; the hostility is driven by class antagonism. Setting aside the
prior questions about Iago's chances of promotion and the expedience of his
statements to Roderigo, Shakespeare in quite few words has prepared us to

meet a Cassio who is substantially distinguished from Iago. From Iago's own words we have learned that Cassio is the kind of man who achieves high staff rank, and Iago is not.[11] Shakespeare has reversed the relative military standing of the two from his source and widened their class differences in a number of crucial passages. Noticing that 'relations between Cassio and Iago are continuingly tense', Berry maintains that Cassio knows 'perfectly well that his subordinate has in some respects a better claim to the post' (p. 113). The play gives no sign that Cassio knows anything of the kind nor would any Elizabethan suspect it. Elizabethans knew well from campaigns in Ireland, the Netherlands and at Cadiz the hazards of inexperienced gentlemen being appointed to command positions. However, that did not lead to widely experienced common soldiers being put over their social superiors but only to pleas for the appointment of more competent gentlemen: 'Rank goes with class' (Berry, p. 113) or more clearly, class governs rank.[12] Gentlemen volunteers may have been expected to trail pikes in Elizabethan armies,[13] but they remained gentlemen, with different expectations and opportunities than the likes of Bates, Williams, Bardolph, Pistol, Bullcalfe and Shadow. The play does not present, as Berry has it, a Cassio 'naturally wary and also compensatory' (p. 113) but rather, a Cassio who acts like the gentleman he is and on that count unsuspectingly gets into very deep trouble with the one character in the play whose ungentleman-like qualities are insisted on. *Othello* is not about class nor otherwise are motivations closely related to class. Nevertheless, it is the single-most important and defining aspect of the relationship between Iago and Cassio. The truth of this is revealed by examination of the language of their exchanges in the play.

Berry gets close to the point when he notes in Cassio's 'address a scarcely veiled policy of putting Iago down' (pp. 113–14) in social situations. Nevertheless, Cassio does not act from 'policy': that is Iago's forte. He acts according to his status as a gentleman: simply the thing he is makes him live. Shakespeare discloses the clear-cut difference between them in a passage that seems to have been neglected by commentators, including Berry. In Act I scene ii Iago, apparently professing ignorance of Othello's marriage, asks him about it (I, ii, 11).[14] Iago was not in Othello's confidence in the business, a situation that contrasts forcefully with what we later learn of Cassio's role. Then Cassio enters, bearing an urgent summons to attend the Duke. Othello enters the house, presumably to say farewell to Desdemona, leaving Cassio and Iago together on the stage at Cassio's first entrance. Because Othello could well have gone to the Senate immediately without attracting our attention, or occupied Cassio and Iago with other business, Shakespeare must have had some special purpose in mind for the ensuing exchange between Iago and Cassio.

> *Cas.* Ancient, what makes he here?
> *Iago.* Faith, he to-night hath boarded a land carract.
> If it prove lawful prize, he's made for ever.
> *Cas.* I do not understand.
> *Iago.* He's married.
> *Cas.* To who?
>   (I, ii, 49–52)

The first point of observation is that Cassio initiates an exchange in which he pretends not to know that Othello is married, flouting Grice's maxim of quality. He first asks what Othello is doing in that place, which may appear to be an innocent request for information. But, the question that ends the conversation ('To who') reveals rather more than a shaky grasp of verb/object agreement. At III, iii, 96 we learn that Cassio went between Desdemona and Othello in his courtship 'from first to last', and, in the historic rather than the dramatic time of the play, was Othello's confidante. We could take Cassio here to be respecting confidentiality, not knowing that at the start of the play Iago knew of the elopement and had since had it confirmed by Othello himself. However, the overall tenor of the passage and its consistency with other exchanges between Othello's two officers indicates that Cassio is purposefully reticent. In fact, because he initiated the exchange we can call this a deliberate prevarication: Cassio pretended to seek information about Othello when he was privy to Othello's actions and whereabouts all the time.[15]

However, the most significant feature of this passage is that it reveals that Cassio and Iago have a communication problem: 'I do not understand,' Cassio replies to Iago's first speech. Iago has breeched the maxim of quantity; instead of the simple 'He's married' of line 52, he shrouds his communication in metaphor, thus flouting the maxim of manner as well. Cassio's response is an almost inevitable response to Iago's failure to cooperate in their conversation. It provides Cassio's second prevarication or, if one prefers, downright lie. In fact, he responds with those words simply *because* he understands Iago. Once commentators learned that a 'carract' was 'a large trading ship' (Evans), no one found any difficulty with Iago's words. Cassio understands Iago very well but he rejects the register of the discourse and its attempt to situate Cassio within Iago's linguistic milieu. 'Unless I am mistaken,' Bradley wrote '[Iago] was not of gentle birth or breeding. . . . for all his great powers, he is vulgar' (p. 213–14). It is as a vulgarian, a charter member of the 'nudge nudge, wink wink' school of barrack-room raconteurs that Iago talks about Othello's marriage-night. Besides suggesting that the marriage is Othello's opportunistic move to better himself ('he's done all right for himself, hasn't he?'), the metaphor of a rich merchant ship taken as a prize by pirates barely conceals the suggestion of despoliation. It 'debases Othello's marriage', in Norman Sanders's words: he points out that '"Boarded" has a sexual connotation', which Iago intends to convey.[16] This language is, of course, characteristic of Iago's part throughout the play. Citing this passage, Ifor Evans remarks that 'Instead of beauty there is a continuous and emphatic imagery that renders gross and contemptible the sexual act on whose contemplation the action of the play depends.'[17] When Cassio claims not to understand Iago's communication, he rejects the offensive code employed by someone of a lower social status. Not only do gentlemen not use such language; they do not allow themselves to be addressed in such a manner. Iago simply does not know how to talk to a gentleman, and the well-born Cassio feels no obligation to accommodate himself to his vulgar colleague. We may suspect that Iago adopted that tone deliberately, as an assault on the sensibilities of a man he despises, but that is not important. The main point is that Cassio and Iago employ different speech codes based on social class, a fact that Shakespeare established in the play as early as he could.

Cassio takes the social offensive when next we see him in Iago's company, in an exchange where it is almost possible to sympathize with Iago. In Act II scene i Cassio's is the first of the ships to arrive at Cyprus, followed by Desdemona and Emilia, with Iago and Roderigo. Cassio greets Iago with unexceptional words, and then Emilia:

> Let it not gall your patience, good Iago,
> That I extend my manners; 'tis my breeding
> That gives me this bold show of courtesy.
>   (II, i, 97–8)[18]

Shakespeare confirms Cassio's social superiority to Iago by making him act like a boor. It is one thing to extend gentlemanly courtesies to the wife of a colleague of lower social class; it is another to comment on the gaping social gulf between them, as if Iago were incapable even of understanding the basis of Cassio's attention to Emilia. Then, significantly, Cassio is silent during Iago's rather clumsy foolery with Desdemona until he answers her question:

> How say you, Cassio? is he not a most profane and liberal
> counsellor?
>   *Cas.* He speaks home, madam. You may relish him more in the
> soldier than in the scholar.

This is the second time Cassio has distinguished his class superiority to Iago, the third if the opening passage (I, ii, 44–52) be counted. In fact, that is all that he has done with Iago to this point in the play. After this speech Iago is left isolated on the stage, well placed for his extended aside:

> *Iago.* He takes her by the palm; ay, well said, whisper. With
> as little a web as this will I ensnare as great a fly as Cassio. Ay,
> smile upon her, do; I will gyve thee in thy own courtship. You
> say true, 'tis so indeed. If such tricks as these strip you out of
> your lieutenantry, it had been better you had not kiss'd your three
> fingers so oft, which now again you are most apt to play the sir in.
> Very good; well kiss'd! an excellent courtesy! 'Tis so indeed ...
>   (II, i, 167–77)

Iago here is observing Cassio with Desdemona. Berry remarks that 'Behaviour appropriate to rank looks like bad acting to those of lesser station, placed as audience' (p. 115) but 'the concentrated viciousness of his commentary', as Berry describes it, draws fundamentally on Cassio's 'put down' and is merely fuelled by Cassio's further demonstration of his breeding. His 'well kiss'd' refers to the earlier occasion with Emilia as well as Cassio's present behaviour with Desdemona.[19] 'Courtesy' is a term picked out of Cassio's speech, to which he twice refers directly: ''tis so indeed'. Iago's intention announced at the conclusion of Act I, 'To get his place and to plume up [his] will / In double knavery' (I, iii, 393–4), is now invested with emotional justification: within the same scene Iago will move directly against Cassio—for Cassio's own sake, not simply as a step towards the destruction of Othello's marriage—conspiring with Roderigo to provoke Cassio to strike him and be discredited.

Iago's long speech to Roderigo at II, i, 221–47 contains his second characterization of Cassio:

> who stands so eminent in the degree of this fortune as Cassio does?
> a *knave* very voluble; no further conscionable than in putting on the
> mere form of civil and humane seeming, for the better compass of
> his salt and most hidden loose affection? Why, none, why, none—a
> slipper and subtle *knave*, a finder-out of occasion; that has an eye
> can stamp and counterfeit advantages, though true advantage never
> present itself; a devilish *knave*. Besides, the *knave* is handsome,
> young, and hath all those requisites in him that folly and green
> minds look after; a pestilent complete *knave*. . . .

So many of these lines before Iago describes Cassio's person are more appropriate for Iago himself that it is not surprising that he gives Cassio the designation that is his in the play. Iago calls Cassio 'knave' no fewer than five times in ten lines of text, a degree of repetition that must be significant. (He uses the word in *Othello* only six times.) 'Knave' had its origin in class, being often used in contrast with the word 'knight', and developed to mean 'a *base* and crafty rogue' (O.E.D.). The context indicates that craftiness is not the issue; rather, Iago is concerned to impugn the gentlemanliness that so clearly distinguishes Cassio from him. He brings Cassio to his social level first in words, only secondly in deeds.[20]

Within a short time Iago is positioned to work his plot: in Act II scene iii he and Cassio meet to set the watch. As if to emphasize the social difference between the two, as indicated by their speech, Shakespeare stages a reprise of the situation I first commented on (I, ii, 44–52). Here, however, instead of rejecting Iago's inferior linguistic codes, Cassio rephrases Iago's comments about Desdemona—who is now enjoying a second wedding-night, in Cyprus—in a different register. This is analogous to the kind of code-switching among multilingual speakers described by such linguists as Carol Myers-Scotton: speakers shift between languages as part of 'negotiations of personal rights and obligations relative to those of other participants in a talk exchange'.[21]

> [*Iago.*] Our general cast us thus early for the love of his
> Desdemona; who let us not therefore blame. He hath not yet
> made wanton the night with her; and she is food for Jove.
> *Cas.* She's a most exquisite lady.
> *Iago.* And I'll warrant her, full of game.
> *Cas.* Indeed she's a most fresh and delicate creature.
> *Iago.* What an eye she has! Methinks it sounds a parley to
> provocation.
> *Cas.* An inviting eye; and yet methinks right modest.
> *Iago.* And when she speaks, is it not an alarum to love?
> *Cas.* She is indeed perfection.
> *Iago.* Well—happiness to their sheets! . . .
>   (II, iii, 14–29)

In this stichomythic passage Iago makes four statements about Desdemona designed to draw attention to her physical attractiveness in a context of love-making. Cassio responds with four statements that translate Iago's into a different code/register. For Iago's 'sport for Jove', 'full of game', provocative 'eye' and speech, Cassio returns 'exquisite lady', 'fresh and delicate creature', 'right modest', and 'indeed perfection'. The content of this exchange again exposes the social distance between the two; the contrived parallel structure of the passage reveals that Shakespeare intended it to provide a significant element in the play.[22]

Another small exchange between Cassio and Iago deserves small attention. Because Cassio has a weak head for drink, Iago's plot succeeds: Cassio is dismissed as Othello's lieutenant. Citing his reputation as 'an honest man', Iago describes the reputation that Cassio has lost as 'an idle and most false imposition; oft got without merit, and lost without deserving' (II, iii, 268–70). Although these words are ironic when applied to the reputation for honesty Iago has cultivated, from Iago's standpoint they are literal truth. Cassio's reputation as a worthy lieutenant to Othello was indeed 'got without merit' as Iago had claimed earlier ('Preferment goes by letter and affection, / And not by old gradation,' [I, i, 36–71) and, as the contriver of Cassio's misfortunes, Iago *knows* that Cassio lost his reputation 'without deserving'. Eventually, after accepting Iago's advice, offered 'in the sincerity of love and *honest* kindness' (II, iii, 327–8), Cassio leaves: 'Good night, *honest* Iago' (334). This second of three 'honest's in 26 lines is the first occasion on which Cassio swells the chorus testifying to Iago's honesty. Iago repays him in the same language: Cassio becomes 'this *honest* fool' in Iago's concluding soliloquy. So much for honesty, and gentlemen.

At this point having discovered that necessity makes strange bedfellows, Cassio has become the third of Iago's gulls in the play. However, Iago does not yet have complete control of the situation, as he learns in Act III, iii when the focus of the spectators' attention turns to Iago with Othello. Pleading for Cassio's reinstatement in Iago's presence, Desdemona refers to Cassio's part in Othello's courtship:

> What, Michael Cassio,
> That came a-wooing with you, and so many a time,
> When I have spoke of you dispraisingly,
> Hath ta'en your part—to have so much to do
> To bring him in!
>   (III, iii, 70–3)

Shakespeare supplies only one small point of illumination of Iago's reaction to the knowledge that Cassio had deceived him in their first conversation (I, ii, 44–55). Iago himself had been duped: Cassio had known very well why Othello was at the scene of Act I, ii.

> *Iago.* My noble lord—
> *Oth.* What dost thou say, Iago?

Iago. Did Michael Cassio, when you woo'd my lady,
Know of your love?
   Oth. He did, from first to last. Why dost thou ask?
   Iago. But for a satisfaction of my thought,
No further harm.
   Oth. Why of thy thought, Iago?
   Iago. I did not think he had been acquainted with her.
   Oth. Oh yes, and went between us very oft.
   Iago. Indeed!
   Oth. Indeed? ay, indeed. Discern'st thou aught in that?
Is he not honest?

And so it goes. Desdemona's revelation of Cassio's dishonesty inspires Iago's very first speech after her departure; it, rather than her persistence in urging Cassio's reinstatement, now feeds his practice. The knowledge of Cassio's involvement in the courtship gives Iago all the ammunition he needs to pursue his design against the three principals. Because Iago is almost continuously on stage with Othello during this part of the play, there is no occasion for Shakespeare to inform us how Iago reacted to learning of Cassio's deliberate reticence. It can only have strengthened his resolve to gull the only character in the play who had gulled the guller—but in the following scenes the arch-gentleman Cassio dwindles into a pallid pawn in Iago's diabolic game. Only the unanticipated rebellion of the 'silly gentleman' Roderigo brings Iago into conflict with his social superiors. Hereafter Cassio's speeches with his ally Iago are not socially coded. But in the early half of the play Shakespeare has made the first demonstration of Iago's ability to persuade others to 'speak his language'; in the second half of the play his pupil is Othello.[23]

NOTES

1. The title refers to a classic article on the distinctive properties of upper-class British speech by Alan S.C. Ross, 'Linguistic class-indicators in present-day English', *Neuphilologische Mitteilungen*, 55 (1954), 20–56, abridged in *Noblesse Oblige*, ed. Nancy Mitford (London, 1956), pp. 11–36.

2. Ralph Berry, *Shakespeare and Social Class* (Atlantic Highlands, N.J.: Humanities Press International, 1988), p. 113.

3. M.H. Short, 'Discourse analysis and the analysis of drama', *Applied Linguistics* 11 (1981), 180–202, p. 183.

4. H.P. Grice, 'Logic and conversation', *Syntax and Semantics*, ed. Peter Cole and Jerry L. Morgan (Academic Press, 1975), pp. 41–58.

5. Shakespeare's text is quoted from G.B. Evans's New Riverside edition (Boston, Mass., 1974).

6. This speech gives the main information about Iago's military career. Even though the words are his own, it is not necessary to doubt them. He is described as

'the bold Iago' (II, i, 75), 'brave Iago' (V, i, 37) and 'a very valiant fellow' (V, i, 52), terms consistent with his function as Ensign. However, there is no certain indication that he has held any higher position than Ensign or that anyone (other than himself) in the play thinks he merits one.

    7. 'One must constantly remember not to believe a syllable that Iago utters on any subject, including himself, until one has tested his statement by comparing it with known facts and with other statements of his own or other people, and by considering whether he had in the particular circumstances any reason for telling a lie or for telling the truth', A.C. Bradley, *Shakespearean Tragedy; Lectures on Hamlet, Othello, King Lear, Macbeth* (London: Macmillan, 1904), p. 211.

    8. The play does not explain how Iago knew of the elopement. It is somewhat surprising that he does at this point in the play considering that he knew nothing of Cassio's serving as Othello's go-between. Roderigo could not have learned of Desdemona's flight from Brabantio because, as this scene shows, he was ignorant of it himself.

    9. B. Evans, *Shakespeare's Tragic Practice* (Oxford: Clarendon Press, 1979), pp. 120–1.

    10. We don't have to believe that Iago was ever a candidate for the lieutenant-ship even in his own mind. An argument designed to persuade the gullible Roderigo cannot easily withstand rational examination.

    11. Paul A. Jorgensen (*Shakespeare's Military World*, Berkeley: University of California Press, 1956) notes that 'Accelerated promotion, in an army of any period, is bound to cause resentment in anyone victimized by it' (p. 110), a view that Berry quotes in support of his argument. However, the play gives no evidence that Cassio's promotion was accelerated. He has known Othello for some time (Desdemona: 'You have known him long', III, iii, 11) and fought alongside him: (Desdemona to Othello: 'A man that all his time / Hath founded his good fortunes on your love, / Shared dangers with you', III, iv, 93–5). Only by accepting the literal truth of Iago's characterization of Cassio's military experience in Act I, ii can we believe that it was inferior to Iago's.

    12. Berry justly observes that 'Othello has rightly appointed Cassio for the very qualities he lacks—the social skills, excellent connections with the Venetian Establishment, a general worldly savoir faire' (p. 166). Having these good attributes, why should Cassio feel that he holds his position unfairly? Nothing in the text suggests he does. These qualities, too, are not those practical men-at-arms are expected to show and display Iago's lack of qualifications for the appointment.

    13. J.W. Fortescue, 'The Soldier', *Shakespeare's England* (Oxford: Clarendon Press, 1916), p. 115.

    14. The reservation comes from doubt whether 'Are you fast married' should be read as Iago's request for information he did not have before then (which I incline to believe), or as his query about the status of the marriage. The New Cambridge edition glosses 'fast' as 'firmly'. Iago then is asking Othello in effect whether he has consummated the marriage, which would make it indissoluble. However, although this interest fits some of Iago's other speeches, it doesn't seem appropriate to the circumstances of this scene.

    15. Incidentally, 'The Senate [having] sent about three several quests / To search [Othello] out' (II, ii, 46–7), Cassio's was the successful party. This suggests Cassio's prior knowledge of Othello's whereabouts.

    16. New Cambridge Shakespeare edn (Cambridge: CUP, 1984), p. 66.

17. Ifor Evans, *The Language of Shakespeare's Plays*, 2nd edn (London: Methuen, 1959), p. 150.

18. E.A.J. Honigmann, whose sensitivity to gradations of the English class speech code is greater than mine, identifies condescension in Cassio's 'good Iago'. 'Between that condescending *good Iago* and the word *Sir*, with which the ancient replies, an Elizabethan audience must have recognized a common speech barrier' (*Shakespeare's Seven Tragedies; The Dramatist's Manipulation of Response*, New York: Macmillan, 1978, p. 83). However, such monosyllables were useful for the metre and are not reliable social indicators. (Iago says 'good Cassio' at V, i, 87, in circumstances that do not suggest irony or sarcasm.) Nevertheless, a class difference may be indicated by the fact that whereas Cassio addresses Iago by his name (before they become 'friends' in Act II, iii), Iago does not use Cassio's name to his face until IV, i, 48, by which time Cassio has become his client, and he uses Cassio's rank (V, i, 56) even after he has taken his place. A context for these comments is given by Roger Brown and Albert Gilman, 'Politeness theory and Shakespeare's four major tragedies', *Language in Society* 18 (1989), 159–212, and Carol Replogle, 'Shakespeare's salutations: a study in stylistic etiquette', *Studies in Philology*, 70 (1973), 172–86, Peter J. Gillett, 'Me, U, and non-U: class connotations of two Shakespearean idioms', *Shakespeare Quarterly*, 25 (1974), 297–309, and Joan Mulholland, '"Thou" and "you" in Shakespeare: a study in the second person pronoun', *English Studies*, 48 (1967), 1–9, all reprinted in *A Reader in the Language of Shakespearean Drama*. Essays collected by Vivian Salmon and Edwina Burness (Amsterdam: J. Benjamins, 1987).

19. Iago's reference to 'her lips' (II, i, 101) shows how Cassio kissed the married Emilia in the 'bold show' of his manners. On the other hand, it hardly seems likely that the conventions of Elizabethan society permitted Cassio to lollygag around frequently kissing his general's wife on the lips. (Further, for actors to do so would give too great support to the suspicion that Desdemona and Cassio were over-friendly.) It seems from Iago's references to 'fingers' that her hands marked the limits of his liberties. Then, it would be possible for Iago and the audience to compare Cassio's treatment of married women of different social classes.

20. I do not mean that Cassio ever loses his gentility but rather, by stripping Cassio of his lieutenantry, Iago produces at least a symbolic class inversion. From the end of Act III, iii onwards, Iago—at least in terms of rank—is the gentleman.

21. Carol Myers-Scotton, 'Code switching as indexical of social negotiations', *Codeswitching: Anthropological and Sociolinguistic Perspectives*, ed. Monica Heller (Berlin: Mouton de Gruyter, 1988), pp. 151–86, p. 178. I am grateful for the advice and help my colleague provided during the writing of this paper. Code-switching among languages in plays is discussed by Esme Grobler, 'Varieties of dramatic dialogue', *South African Theatre Journal*, 4 (1990), 38–60, pp. 41–8.

22. Cassio's insistence in his drunkenness that 'the lieutenant is to be sav'd before the ancient' (II, iii, 109–10) strikes Berry as 'something Cassio has been saying all the time to Iago' (p. 114). It seems, however, that by his mention of 'the general, nor any man of quality' (106), Cassio is referring foremost to the military hierarchy (rather than to social class) and that here, by virtue of his rank, Iago is included among men 'of quality'. In brief, Cassio's modest quip here should not be read as another put-down, though of course Berry's comment that 'Shakespeare uses [Cassio] to get at Iago' (p. 114) is amply demonstrated elsewhere.

23. This point is too widely recognized to need documentation.

EDWARD PECHTER

Disconfirmation

If we try to imagine ourselves back into an early seventeenth-century Globe audience, what do [we] see at the beginning of *Othello*? Two men enter, arguing. We know they are angry—"abhor," "hate," and "despise" are spat out in the first few seconds—but not why. Presumably the black cloth hung at the rear of the stage signals a tragedy, but what's the matter—what's the subject of the play? Sometimes Shakespeare provides this information directly and immediately (*Troilus, Lear,* and *Antony*), but *Othello* is much less obliging. What is the "this" to which the first speaker refers? Who is the "him" that Iago has claimed to hate? The answers become available only gradually. "Him" turns out to refer to a military commander whom Iago resents for some perceived slight, but what is "this"? Sixty lines into the play, Roderigo refers to a triumph, "What a full fortune does the thicklips owe / If he can carry't thus!" where the "it" carried thus may seem to refer to Cassio's promotion, as though *that* is the "this" and now the "it" we have been looking for since the beginning; but with "her father" in Iago's next speech, we discover that "it" must refer to something else again: the promotion only explains why Iago hates "the thicklips" and therefore was not party to whatever "full fortune" he now possesses—the nature of which, however, we still do not know. Iago's speech here helps to shed some light on this matter, but also to obscure it:

> Call up her father,
> Rouse him, make after him, poison his delight,

From Othello *and Interpretive Traditions*, pp. 30–52, 196–202. © 1999 by the University of Iowa Press.

> Proclaim him in the streets, incense her kinsmen,
> And, though he in a fertile climate dwell,
> Plague him with flies! Though that his joy be joy
> Yet throw such changes of vexation on't
> As it may lose some colour. (1.1.66–72)

The pronouns are unstable, offering contradictory suggestions. Honigmann thinks that "him," "him," and "his" in line 67 all refer to "her father" and is skeptical about the view of "some editors" who think "the 'him' throughout is Othello." But even coming back to this speech after reading or seeing the play many times, we can't be sure whether in "his delight" and "his joy" Iago is thinking of "her father" or "the thick-lips"; and the joyful and delightful "it" on which Iago proposes to throw changes of vexation remains still to be defined.

In no other play of Shakespeare's except maybe *Hamlet* do we have to work so hard and over such a sustained period in order to determine what the play is about. "What is the matter there?" Brabantio's entering question a moment later echoes Iago at the very beginning, "If ever I did dream / Of such a matter, abhor me" (4–5) and is in turn echoed by Othello in the next scene, "What's the matter, think you?" (38). As John Shaw demonstrates, versions of this question recur like a litany throughout the action of the play. They represent the often anguished perplexity of the characters in the face of an often threatening action whose contours need to be defined. The play works hard to make it our question as well.

And to make Iago the source of our answers. The play names him right away (for Roderigo's name we are made to wait until line 55) and thus immediately gives him a special accessibility beyond physical presence ("the shorter one in the brown," or whatever). He clearly knows more than Roderigo, providing the background information to us as well as to him inside the action. Iago is the commanding figure, leading them to the position Roderigo announces they have reached ("Here is her father's house"), from which to proceed with the plan Iago has devised ("I'll call aloud"). Thanks to Iago, we have been propelled beyond discussion to the more decisive and revelatory mode of action where we might hope finally to find the clarification we seek.

In the even, we are not disappointed.

> Zounds, sir, you're robbed, for shame put on your gown!
> Your heart is burst, you have lost half your soul,
> Even now, now, very now, an old black ram
> Is tupping your white ewe! (85–88)

Here at last is the "this" we have been looking for. After so much gray indefinition, Iago gives us a sudden sharpness of focus. Passing references to "the Moor" and "the thicklips" and maybe even Iago's threat to make "his joy . . . lose some colour" emerge precipitously into a new and stunningly definite light. Roderigo's motivation is illuminated as well. Though we have to wait for a bit before he is identified as a disappointed suitor, Iago's description of interracial copulation is so appalling in its graphic specificity that it can absorb all the feelings of angry resistance and resentment we have sensed till now. The image is intensified temporally as well as pictorially. "Even now, now, very now" repeatedly thrusts the action home into the present moment of our hearing it. "Tupping" is a nasty word used of animals, a variant of "topping." The word probably sounds like "fucking" to modern audiences but must have violated the ears of Renaissance audiences as well. Iago's speech enacts the monstrous violation it describes, indecently assaulting not just Brabantio (can we avoid hearing "ewe" as "you?") but us.[1] We have been longing for knowledge, and now Iago thrusts it on us with a vengeance.

At the minimal level of being able to specify "the matter," then, we are required to enter this play under the rough guidance of Iago who, moreover, seems designed to determine not just the subject but our attitude toward it as well. Subsequent audiences come to the play knowing that Iago is not to be trusted, information picked up either from the general cultural data bank or from the dramatis personae in printed texts. Shakespeare's audience might have had some pretextual clue in the costuming equivalent to "the black wig and heavy eyebrows used by the conventional Iago" of the nineteenth-century stage (Carlisle, 222), but they saw the play before it had been assimilated into received tradition and without the advance information furnished by a play-bill. Lacking such prejudicial knowledge, what would they have understood?

Obviously Iago is self-serving in claiming he deserved Cassio's promotion, but he expresses his complaint more generally in terms of a lament for a world where old ties of loyalty have disintegrated:

> 'Tis the curse of service:
> Preferment goes by letter and affection
> And not by old gradation, where each second
> Stood heir to th'first. (34–37)

Renaissance plays are full of speeches yearning for a simpler past; their audiences seem to have been peculiarly susceptible to nostalgia, a sentimental predisposition for which there are plausible social and economic explanations.[2] In any case, by the time of *Othello*'s first performances the tone and values of Iago's speech had become part of the standard theatrical repertoire, one of McLuskie's "recurring tropes and images," a recognizable dramatic type (sometimes designated the *laudator temporis acti*, the "praiser of times past"). It can be played for laughs, as by Falstaff, but in the tragic mode it has a more or less autonomous authority, expressing the truth for the purposes of theatrical engagement. We can trust dramatic characters who talk like this, at least provisionally.

Iago's frank resentment and willful misrepresentation are unlovely qualities, but in terms again of theatrical values, even they tend to command respect, the consequence of Iago's enacting another dramatic type that achieved great prominence in the early seventeenth century. "The Malcontent," as we have come to designate this type, serves to pass harsh judgment on a thoroughly contaminated social order. At the same time, he sees no alternative but to accept his situation as a participant in this corrupt world ("Nay, there's no remedy") and protect his own interests ("In following him I follow but myself"). Like Hamlet, who maybe seen as among other things an early and probably formative version of the same dramatic type, Iago believes that "something is rotten in the state," but for strategic reasons he cannot reveal his true feelings ("I am not what I am"; compare Hamlet's "I have that within that passes show"). Like the *laudator temporis acti*, the Malcontent may be explained with relation to social and political context, but by the time of *Othello* it too had, like Iago's nostalgia for the "old gradation," assumed a more or less autonomous authority.[3] Iago is resentful, alienated, and hypocritical, but the Malcontent's position he seems to occupy is the best one available from which both to judge and to take part in the peculiarly stressful world he inhabits. Since this combination of judgment and participation is a good working description of a theatrical audience's position, small wonder that we tend to trust him.

For modern audiences the most serious obstacle to trusting Iago is his blatant racism, yet all the available evidence suggests that the original audiences would have assented easily, even automatically, to Iago's slurs about the as-yet-unnamed old ram's color. Shakespeare evidently assumes such assent in his representation of Aaron in *Titus* and Portia, the pretty much unambiguously sympathetic heroine of *The Merchant*, who insouciantly dismisses Morocco with "May all of his complexion choose me so" (2.6.79). G. K. Hunter demonstrates that "a traditional view of what Moors are like, i.e., gross, disgusting, inferior, carrying the symbol of their damnation on their skin," was normal and overt in Shakespeare's time (45). As he labors to terrify Brabantio, Iago makes systematic use of conventional ideas about black origins in acts of sexual transgression and diabolically inspired violation of the father's authority and property rights ("thieves, thieves, thieves!"; "the devil will make a grandsire of you"), resulting in the debased deformity—in Iago's inflection, the bestiality—of a sinfully contaminated progeny ("coursers for cousins and jennets for germans").[4] Such insults may have seemed exceptional to Shakespeare's audience only in their wit and verbal cleverness, the alliteration here and the slyly sarcastic pun at the very beginning ("his Moorship" for "his worship"), commanding assent reinforced by delighted if anxious laughter.

Globe audiences not only felt differently about dark skin, they must have seen something different. The play lumps together black and Moorish attributes in a way that can perplex modern audiences, who have assimilated (and in many cases more recently come to reject) the understanding of distinct racial identities from the ideas systematically deployed by scientists during the nineteenth century (the same period when, as a parallel development, the debate raged whether to play Othello as "a black African" or "a tawny Moor"). The Elizabethans were clearly able to think in terms of distinct and biologically determined identities, but such a "racialist" consciousness was a long way from full development or general dispersion. Rather, it was contained within and typically driven by "pre-racialist" assumptions of a religious nature. Skin color was not so much a thing in itself as the marker of a theological category, black is the color of the devil, evil, sin. Its significance was "moral and religious," as Julie Hankey says, "rather than racial and geographical" (ii). According to Hunter, the new knowledge derived from exploration had no effect in displacing the dominant theological mode that fundamentally structured the Elizabethans' understanding: "The vocabulary at their disposal frustrated any attempt at scientific discrimination. The world was still seen largely, in terms of vocabulary, as a network of religious names. The word 'Moor' had no clear racial status" (40); it was used indiscriminately to describe any people "in that outer circuit of non-Christian lands where the saving grace of Jerusalem is weakest in its whitening power" (41). In fact, the standard term in the Renaissance to describe a character like Othello is "Blackamoor," as in Best's "all these black Moores which are in Africa," which conflates North African and sub-Saharan racial types in just the way we don't. Richard Burbage, the original Othello, probably performed the part in blackface and Moorish costume—as a "Blackamoor"; but Renaissance audiences probably wouldn't have registered the suggestions as scientifically contradictory, perhaps partly as a result of contemporary histrionic conventions, but chiefly because they weren't used to thinking in terms of the scientific (or pseudoscientific) categories of race and geography that were being contradicted.[5]

Relatively unencumbered with a racial consciousness, the original audiences may have been more rather than less vulnerable to the play's peculiarly anxiety-producing effects. The indiscriminate mixing of black and Moorish impressions serves to endow Othello with an unstable quality that adds to and may indeed be at the heart of his terrifying strangeness. In Brabantio's incredulous question whether Desdemona would have "run from her guard-age to the sooty bosom / Of such a thing as thou? to fear, not to delight" (1.2.70–71), "thing" is a functionally imprecise word. Caliban in *The Tempest*, a "salvage and deformed slave" according to the character list in the Folio, a monstrously amorphous creature in the action, is described as a "thing of darkness" (5.1.275). "What, has this thing appear'd again to-night?" Horatio asks at the beginning of *Hamlet* (1.1.29). We do not yet know he is referring to the ghost of Hamlet Sr., and the question inspires fear precisely through the totally unconstrained suggestiveness of "thing." In the same way, Braban-tio's speech associates the indefinite with the effect of fear, both here and later in the next scene: "what she feared to look on" (99). These usages imply that the various suggestions about Othello's color might have seemed not so much contradictory to Elizabethans as emphatic, reinforcing the anxious sense of a volatile and moving target, like the ghost in *Hamlet* who cannot be fixed in a local habitation even after it is given a tentative name: "'Tis here, 'tis here, 'tis gone." As Roderigo describes him, the "lascivious Moor" is "an extravagant and wheeling stranger / Of here and everywhere" (1.1.135).

A tawny Moor, a black African, Othello is also the "turbanned Turk" of his own description at the end (5.2.351). In the opening scene, Iago refers to "the Cyprus wars, / Which *even now* stands in act" (148–149), and the emphasized words help to establish a structural analogy: as Othello invades the space of Brabantio's authority, so the Turks threaten Venice's political and economic interests. The Turkish peril seems to be playing on primal fears as well; according to the Duke, it is experienced "in fearful sense" (1.3.12), a word that echoes Brabantio's response to "such a thing" as Othello a moment earlier at the end of the preceding scene. The Turkish invasion raises the age-old specter of barbarian hordes assaulting Europe from the margins. Braban-tio evokes the idea in order to dismiss it. "What tell'st thou me of robbing? This is Venice: / My house is not a grange" (that is, not a "country house or outlying farmhouse," as Honigmann glosses "grange" in 1.1.105). By the next scene, however, Brabantio's confidence has been eroded:

> the duke himself,
> Or any of my brothers of the state,
> Cannot but feel this wrong as 'twere their own.
> For if such actions may have passage free
> Bond-slaves and pagans shall our statesmen be. (1.2.99)

Othello's action in eloping with Desdemona has in effect transformed Ven-ice from the protected and protecting center to a vulnerable outpost overrun by infidels.

If the Turks are terrifying phantoms, they are also actual personages. The threat of invasion evokes recent history; the "Turks took Cyprus from the Venetians in 1570–3 and, though heavily defeated by a Christian navy at the Battle of Lepanto (1571), henceforth dominated the eastern Mediterranean" (Honigmann, 8). These events would have been part of living memory for at least some of Shakespeare's audience, and they would have been revitalized by the presence, much commented on, of a Moorish retinue representing the King of Barbary at Elizabeth's court during 1600–1601 and by the republication on his accession in 1603 of King James's 1595 poem celebrating Lepanto.[6] Moreover, the Turkish domination in the Mediterranean was still consequential; it furnished an effective obstacle to the eastward expansion of European economic interests, providing a material reason why the English invested in the roundabout project of a western passage to the riches of the East.

But if economics helps to reinforce the fear of a demonic other, it can also account for friendlier and more familiarized images. For the Turks were themselves partners with the English in the highly profitable enterprise of the "Levant trade"; in fact the English were displacing the Venetians as the chief beneficiaries of this trade.[7] To complicate matters further, the Moors were partners for the English as well, at least potentially, in a political sense. Jack D'Amico details negotiations undertaken throughout Elizabeth's reign (the embassy of 1600–1601 was part of this) and sustained into James's, seeking to enlist Moorish support against the threats represented by continental European powers, especially France and Spain. "Relations between England and Morocco were extremely complex," D'Amico tells us, "and the opinions generated by those relations [varied] from the dangerously inscrutable alien to the exotically attractive ally" (39).

The context of religious feeling lets us most fully appreciate the intensity of contradictions during the period and their possible resonances for the play's first audiences. The threat of European invasion, which antedated the Spanish Armada of 1588 and lasted well into the seventeenth century, was consistently perceived in the context of religious disputes: a Catholic assault against Protestant England. The intensity of anti-Catholic feeling in Elizabethan and early Jacobean England is difficult to exaggerate. The specter of a Catholic invasion combined with convictions about a secret Catholic conspiracy operating inside England must have contributed to what one Tudor historian has characterized as a prevalent paranoia.[8] Since the Catholics were routinely represented as anti-Christ, the Elizabethans may well have sensed themselves positioned between two forces of invading infidels, uneasily playing off one against the other—like the Venetians in the play, using Othello to protect themselves against a danger that Othello himself symbolically represents.

This sense of ambivalent anxiety is yet further intensified by the Venetian setting. Venice serves as the center of civilized stability, as in Brabantio's speech, but the confidence of this claim may well have seemed tenuous to an English audience, from whose perspective Venice occupied an exposed position at the edge of Christian Europe. At the same time, since England occupied a comparable position at the other edge, Shakespeare's audience probably felt inclined to identify its own position with that of Venetian authority—father Brabantio and the "brothers of the state"—"feeling this wrong as 'twere their own." Like the historical realities of material commerce, the geographical facts seem to be operating inside a symbolic economy structured by deeply felt contradictions.[9] Venice worked powerfully on English imaginations during the Renaissance (and later) as an object of desire, evoking wealth, art, and Italian sophistication, but also as an object of repulsion, evoking Italianate greed and decadent sexuality.[10] This mythic Venice, something Shakespeare could count on his audiences' including with the baggage they carried into the theater, is at once where you dream of being and where you fear you already are, a "dangerously alien" and an "exotically attractive" image at the same time: D'Amico's words to describe Elizabethan feelings toward the Moors seem to fit Venice as well, and the results are "extremely complex" indeed. The conflict between Venetian and Turk defines the play's foundation, but since each of the terms reproduces the conflict in itself, the foundation tends to disintegrate. Where is the center? Where is the margin?

It is not that we cannot answer these questions (really one question with two parts), but as we are propelled by Iago through the violently shifting emotional landscape at the beginning of the play's action, each answer lasts only long enough for suggestions to emerge requiring us to change places: *here* becomes a strange and unfamiliar place, *there* turns into the position from which we find ourselves engaging with the action.[11] The negotiation of such an action need not be a fearful thing. In Montaigne's *Essays*, for instance, such volatile instability is contained within the cosmopolitan amusement of the author's controlling point of view. Like the "wise man" in the humanist adage "All the world's his soil," secure in his own self, Montaigne is at home "here and everywhere."[12] In *Othello*, though, our guide is Iago, and from his anxiety-driven and anxiety-producing perspective, the erosion of the distinction between here and everywhere else transports us violently into nowhere, an amorphously engulfing space where the constituting differences of individual identity, as between black and white, self and other, seem to be collapsing—even now, now, very now—into a monstrous undifferentiation.[13]

* * *

To judge from the immediately following scenes, *Othello* labors so consistently hard in its earliest action to absorb us into the threatened aggression of Iago's point of view only in order to disconfirm the impressions it has carefully produced. For when we meet Othello in 1.2, he is totally unlike what we have been led to expect. Iago's description of "bombast circumstance / Horribly stuffed with epithets of war" conjures up *miles gloriosus*, a ranting buffoon spun off from the Prince of Morocco in *The Merchant*. But all the aggressive self-justification at the beginning of 1.2 belongs to Iago himself; as Empson remarked, he sounds "like a ruffian in Marlowe" ("Honest in *Othello*," 234). His big talk about loyalty may be a show of passion designed to work Othello up, but even so the contrast is striking and surprising. Othello is poised and dignified. In the midst of Iago's sixteen jittery lines, complete with exaggerated physical gestures acting out his own proclaimed bravado ("Nine or ten times / I had thought t'have yerked him here"), Othello's "'Tis better as it is" stands as a stable bulwark.

We had been threatened with a disruptive "thing ... to fear," but it is Iago and then Brabantio who propel the action toward a brawl, while Othello maintains order: "Keep up your bright swords, for the dew will rust them" (59). When Kean delivered this line, according to Keats, "it was as if 'his throat had commanded where swords were as thick as reeds. From the eternal risk, he speaks as though his body were unassailable'" (Sprague, *Shakespearian Players*, 79). Irving, by contrast, "stood with his back to the audience, 'throwing up his arms in an excited manner and speaking petulantly'" (Alan Hughes, 143), but Irving's was an anomalous (and unsuccessful) rendition of the role. Readers are also impressed. "Othello's scorn is that of the professional fighter towards civilian brawlers" (Sanders, 66), but something more powerful is also at work. Along with "I must be found" a moment earlier, the "bright swords" might evoke Jesus in the Garden of Gethsemane (Honigmann provides biblical references). These resonances shouldn't be exaggerated, but they serve to provide another specific instance of the way in which Iago's suggestions ("The *devil* will make a grand-sire of you") are directly contradicted by what we see and hear.

One of these suggestions turns out to be confirmed, though in a surprising and fundamentally disconfirming way. Othello's supremely unruffled self-confidence in the face of Brabantio's expected challenge is consistent with Iago's accusatory description of "loving his own pride and purposes":

> Let him do his spite;
> My services, which I have done the signiory,
> Shall out-tongue his complaints. 'Tis yet to know—
> Which, when I know that boasting is an honour,
> I shall promulgate—I fetch my life and being
> From men of royal siege, and my demerits
> May speak unbonneted to as proud a fortune
> As this that I have reached. For know, Iago,

> But that I love the gentle Desdemona
> I would not my unhoused free condition
> Put into circumscription and confine
> For the sea's worth. (17–28)

But this speech might be characterized as *amour-propre* only in a sense emptied of any pejorative connotations. Othello manages to assert his own worth in a nonboastful way. More important than his explicit contempt for self-advertisement (for as much could be said about Coriolanus) are the apparently unintended and unconscious suggestions of an authentic modesty. "Demerits" acknowledges fallibility as it claims justification; "unbonneted" evokes a gesture of deference, removing his hat to his superiors even as he asserts his own rights. Above all, Othello is disarming in his feelings about Desdemona. He hasn't fallen in love in the usual sense of that metaphor; Othello is not Romeo, driven by an overwhelming need, still less the desperately needy suitors or petitionary courtiers of the sonnet sequences, begging for mercy. He experiences the freedom of his soldierly celibacy as a self-sufficient condition, which he trades in quite clearheadedly for something better. If this were all, Othello might indeed resemble Iago's description, loving his own pride like a self-satisfied pragmatist—a sort of high-style Pertinax Surly proposing to the Spanish Lady in *The Alchemist*, say. But the last lines of the speech defeat any such impression. Playing off a simple and direct expression of affection, "I love the gentle Desdemona," against the reiterative Latinate polysyllables and syntactic inversion by which he represents his single state, and then climaxing with the image of infinite and transcendent value (how much is the sea worth? how much more is Desdemona worth?), these beautiful lines make it clear that, whatever it means to say so, Othello is in love.

Othello's deference invites us to reconceptualize the categorical distinction between self-love and the social order, or the individual ego and the corporate order. Othello's claims for his own merit are equally claims for the fairness of "the signiory" in acknowledging his services and rewarding them appropriately. His self-confidence seems to be coterminous with a confidence in the legitimacy of Venetian political authority. And with religious authority as well:

> as truly as to heaven
> I do confess the vices of my blood
> So justly to your grave ears I'll present
> How I did thrive in this fair lady's love
> And she in mine. (1.3.124–128)

In these remarkable lines introducing his long autobiographical narrative to the Senate, Othello associates the love between him and Desdemona with guilt and sin—demerits indeed! The linkage is arresting but in the present context it works to augment the protagonist's image. By acknowledging the vices of his blood, Othello affirms an orthodox Christian and emphatically Protestant belief in original sin. *Not* to acknowledge this would constitute an arrogant claim of self-sufficiency, like Caesar's bragging just before the assassination. The words, therefore, convey an appropriate modesty, but at the same time an absolute confidence: even as he confesses to a sinful nature, he rests secure in the redemptive power of divine authority. As the "grave ears" of the Senate will perceive the merits of his demerits, so a listening heaven has already restored the defects of his spiritual nature. The Q variant of "faithful" for "truly" in the first line reinforces the theological context, as does the way in which Othello, like a good Protestant, imagines a direct relationship to heaven, unmediated by any ecclesiastical apparatus administering the sacraments. The speech clarifies Othello's statement of conviction earlier about "my perfect soul" (1.2.30) and helps to account for the fact that the statement doesn't sound as though he is in love with his own pride—quite the reverse.

Self-worth and public recognition reciprocate and mutually sustain each other for Othello, as though interchangeable and identical phenomena. A large part of his charismatic power at the beginning derives from the apparently effortless way in which his sensibility unifies categories we normally think of as distinct and even contradictory.[14] Where Iago says, "I am not what I am," Othello is what he is. This extraordinary integrity comes across most powerfully in the Senate narrative. Like all life stories, Othello's has displacement as its subject: growing up, leaving home, enslavement, liberation, religious conversion; but these potential traumas are represented (if at all) not as rupture but as continuity, the accumulation of undifferentiated experience. Hence the sense of ongoing action, things happening "oft" and "still" (meaning "always," as usual in Shakespeare), an unbroken succession of marvelous events, encountering a sequence of wonderful creatures in one romantic landscape after another. The effect has been described as "unchanging in its monotony" (Sypher, 122), but Renaissance audiences, greedily devouring reports about the exotic new worlds opening to exploration, may well have found all the "novelties" in Othello's speech the opposite of boring.

The most striking effect of continuity derives from the oddly recursive narrative. Recounting his life becomes part of the life he is recounting. His journey goes from "boyish days / To th' very moment" of the telling (1.3.133–134), and now, even now, to the very moment of his telling it again. The "antres vast and deserts idle, / Rough quarries, rocks and hills whose heads touch heaven" seem at first to belong to his life, but with "it was my hint to speak," they migrate ("here and everywhere") to the story of his life as he recounts it to Brabantio and Desdemona, and once again to the Senate and to us (141–143). "Such was my process," he says (143), referring at once to his experience and his relation of that experience, his life and his life story. At the very beginning of the "personal history" that bears his name, David Copperfield acknowledges uncertainty as to whether he will "turn out to be the hero of my own life," deferring to a text behind his own control: "These pages must show."[15] This problematic split between narrator and narrative subject, the self telling the story and the self whose story is being told, seems to be inevitable in autobiography. But Othello has somehow eluded it. He and his narrative are perfectly identical. How can we know the storyteller from the story?

The speech is a great set piece, an aria in the "*Othello* music." It is set up with the Duke's "Say it, Othello," an "unusual turn of phrase," as Honigmann points out, whose formality tends therefore to set the speech apart as well. As he introduced the speech, so the Duke has the first response to it: "I think this tale would win my daughter too." Whether speaking to Brabantio or himself, the Duke ignores Desdemona's entry: Othello's mesmerizing speech has allowed no room for other impressions.[16] At the end of the scene, the Duke is given a pithy couplet that helps to clarify the nature of his response. "If virtue no delighted beauty lack / Your son-in-law is far more fair than black" (290–291). Inevitably patronizing to modern ears, the remark must have sounded on a fundamentally different register if heard inside the theological context, powerfully present to Renaissance imaginations, that (in Hunter's description) although "all nations are Ethiopians, black in their natural sinfulness," nonetheless, "they may become white in the knowledge of the Lord" (48).

Othello, in Hunter's view, "manipulates our sympathies" in its opening movements, "supposing that we will have brought to the theatre a set of careless assumptions about 'Moors,'" on to which it then, by evoking different traditions of belief, "complicating factors which had begun to affect thought in this day," "is able to superimpose . . . new valuations" of Othello, diametrically opposed to the fear and loathing first generated by Iago (49).[17] The Duke's response here, testifying to the overwhelming power of Othello to generate affectionate admiration in those who see and hear him, squares with the declaration of the "refined and lovely young lady" at a Forrest performance: "If that is the way Moors look and talk and love, give me a Moor for a husband." Othello is not a thing to fear, but a man to love.

* * *

Desdemona provides the major confirmation—or, more precisely, disconfirmation of the beliefs originally impressed on us by the play. She enters at a crucial point in the action. Whatever the climactic quality of Othello's speech for the Duke and maybe the audience, it functions only as an interim measure, filling up the time "till she come" to provide her own evidence. Brabantio insists on Desdemona's version as the final determinant: "I pray you, hear her speak" (1.3.175).

In "The Design of Desdemona: Doubt Raised and Resolved," Ann Jennalie Cook argues that in the context "of Elizabethan courtship customs" (189), Desdemona's apparent willingness to let her own marriage be arranged behind Brabantio's back and in flat contradiction to his wishes would have seemed like a serious transgression against appropriate daughterly obedience. The social norms are perhaps less consistent than we might think, but Cook's claim is convincing, partly owing to generic signals,[18] and in larger part because it is supported by critical traditions. The sentiment attributed to Coleridge that "it would be something monstrous to conceive this beautiful Venetian girl falling in love with a veritable negro" underlies a lot of uncertainty in nineteenth-century and later response to Desdemona (Raysor, 1.42). Bradley hotly contested this view, claiming that it represented Desdemona's "love, in effect, as Brabantio regarded it, and not as Shakespeare conceived it"; but the only way Bradley could manage "to see what Shakespeare imagined" was to argue that the "later impression of Desdemona" as sweetly virtuous and self-sacrificing "must be carried back and united with the earlier," more problematic one (164–168). As we shall see in chapter 5, this is pretty much the effect of nineteenth-century theatrical performances of the part, but since this procedure of reading backward from the end inverts the process by which Shakespeare's audience processed the play's material, such critical and theatrical denial may tend only to confirm the evidence for an anxious sense of Desdemona's transgressive nature.

Cook speculates that the "unlikely alliance with a Moor might have been far less troubling than the elopement itself," but the anxieties Iago produces about Desdemona go beyond the violation of social norms (188). She is involved only passively in the image of "an old black ram ... tupping your white ewe," but with "Your daughter and the Moor are now making the beast with two backs" (1.1.114–115), Iago represents Desdemona as equally and actively cooperating in the expression of bestial passion. Roderigo's description a moment later evokes similar suggestions:

> your fair daughter
> At this odd-even and dull watch o'th'night,
> Transported with no worse nor better guard
> But with a knave of common hire, a gondolier,
> To the gross clasps of a lascivious Moor ... (120–124)

Before we fill in the gaps,[19] this elliptical speech seems to be describing
Desdemona's multiple sexual transports with (that is, attractions to) first
an unspecified common knave who then emerges into more particularized
view as a gondolier and is finally defined as the lascivious Moor.[20] The
superimposition of images metastasizes beyond the violation of social norms
to suggest a perversely promiscuous sexual appetite. These suggestions are
further reinforced by Roderigo's claim that Desdemona

>   hath made a gross revolt,
> Tying her duty, beauty, wit and fortunes
> In an extravagant and wheeling stranger
> Of here and everywhere. (132–135)

"Gross revolt" echoes the Moor's "gross clasps" just earlier; it provides a
metaphorical linkage between Othello and Desdemona beyond the literal
alliance in the dramatic action. In effect, they connect with one another in
a free space of erotic wandering, outside the constraints of stabilizing order,
to perform even now and again by the end of the next scene the specific
but unspecified deeds (for what exactly is Brabantio, referring to in "such
actions?") whose monstrous consequences will invert the hierarchical structure of patriarchal Christianity ("Bond-slaves and pagans shall our states-
men be").

Desdemona, thus, is absorbed under Iago's general direction into the
prospect of anxiety and terror embodied in Othello. Like his racism, Iago's
blatant misogyny may sound bizarre now but probably represented an entirely
unexceptional story to the play's first audience.[21] And as with Othello, the
images Iago evokes about Desdemona turn out to be either surprisingly
wrong or right only in a way that fundamentally disconfirms the expectations
Iago has set up. In response to Brabantio's request to describe "where most
you owe obedience," Desdemona responds:

>   My noble father,
> I do perceive here a divided duty.
> To you I am bound for life and education:
> My life and education both do learn me
> How to respect you; you are the lord of duty,
> I am hitherto your daughter. But here's my husband:
> And so much duty as my mother showed
> To you, preferring you before her father,
> So much I challenge that I may profess
> Due to the Moor my lord. (1.3.180–189)

In this entry speech, Desdemona confirms Brabantio's fears. She was not bewitched, was indeed "half the wooer" (176), and despite Brabantio's description of "a maiden never bold," she forcefully declares, with unequivocal emphasis in "hitherto" and "here's my husband," a transfer of affectionate loyalty from Brabantio to Othello. The transfer, however, is represented not as a violation or betrayal but an affirmation of traditional order. In moving from father to husband, Desdemona claims to be reenacting the movement of her own mother from her father to Brabantio himself. In this exchange of loyalty and duty, she nowhere affirms her own rights against the prerogatives of male authority and therefore does not seem to challenge but reinforce the structure of order on which Brabantio's own authority is based.[22]

When the focus shifts from social to sexual transgression, Desdemona's boldness is even more pronounced. In the following exchange, the Duke is responding to Othello's request for "fit disposition for my wife" while he is in Cyprus:

> *Duke.* Why, at her father's.
> *Bra.* I'll not have it so.
> *Oth.* Nor I.
> *Des.* Nor I, I would not there reside
> To put my father in impatient thoughts
> By being in his eye. Most gracious duke,
> To my unfolding lend your prosperous ear
> And let me find a charter in your voice
> T'assist my simpleness.
> *Duke.* What would you, Desdemona?
> *Des.* That I did love the Moor to live with him
> My downright violence and scorn of fortunes
> May trumpet to the world. My heart's subdued
> Even to the very quality of my lord:
> I saw Othello's visage in his mind,
> And to his honours and his valiant parts
> Did I my soul and fortunes consecrate,
> So that, dear lords, if I be left behind,
> A moth of peace, and he go to the war,
> The rites for which I love him are bereft me,
> And I a heavy interim shall support
> By his dear absence. Let me go with him. (1.3.241–260)

The context gives a full sense of Desdemona's purposiveness, especially the speech rhythms at the beginnings. "Nor I," as the third voice in the sequence, is emphatically decisive.[23] Although she defers to the Duke's authority to charter her voice, she nonetheless claims the right to choose her own fit disposition—to dispose of herself. She makes the claim on her own initiative (no one has asked for her opinion, as Brabantio did earlier, when his "Come hither, gentle mistress," suggested a reluctance on her part to enter, let alone speak to the Senate). In asserting her rights to the pleasures of Othello's company, she clearly means sexual enjoyment. The suggestions of "his valiant parts" and "the rites for which I love him," and even the metaphor by which Desdemona describes deprivation, "I a heavy interim shall support"—all these represent how consistently she imagines experience in bodily terms. Her words express a powerful sexual desire for Othello, openly declared in the public forum.

Why then does her speech tend to diminish rather than to reinforce the fears Iago has evoked? Hunter's terms to account for the disconfirmation of Iago's racism can account for his misogyny as well: the play superimposes one system of belief and feeling on another—in this instance, different ideas available in the sixteenth century about sexuality and marriage. Desdemona's speech resonates powerfully within the emergent context of "companionate marriage."[24] Her love for Othello is predicated on the desire "to live with him," to share his life in all aspects. Sex is unequivocally part of this, but so is exotic travel and the heroic romance of military affairs. So is his inner beauty: "I saw Othello's visage in his mind." Like the Duke's couplet about Othello's fairness, this line creates awkwardness for us, but adjusted to the appropriate context, it strongly confirms our conviction about Othello's "perfect soul"— and about her own, which she "did . . . consecrate" to him.

In *Table-Talk* for 27 September 1830, Coleridge indulged in some reflection about Desdemona's appeal:

> "Most women have no character at all", said Pope, and meant it for satire. Shakespeare, who knew man and woman much better, saw that it, in fact, was the perfection of woman to be characterless. Everyone wishes a Desdemona or Ophelia for a wife—creatures who, though they may not always understand you, do always feel you, and feel with you. (Foakes, *Coleridge's Criticism*, 185)

Despite the idealized sentimentality, there is something useful in emphasizing Desdemona's capacity to "feel" and "feel with." As Stanley Cavell remarks about "I saw Othello's visage in his mind," although "it is commonly felt that she means she overlooked his blackness in favor of his inner brilliance," nonetheless "what the line more naturally says is that she saw his visage as he sees it"—that is, so fully enters into Othello's existence that she experiences the world from inside his own sensibility (129). Othello himself had acknowledged this capacity in describing Desdemona's response to his story: "She wished / That heaven had made her such a man" (1.3.163–164) bespeaks a desire not just to find a man like Othello with whom to connect but to become the being that is Othello. In "my heart's subdued / Even to the very quality of my lord," Desdemona's declaration to the Senate suggests that she already has.

In the Quarto, Desdemona's heart is subdued in a more explicitly sexual phrase to Othello's "utmost pleasure," but for Edward Snow the Folio is preferable as

> a more radical expression of the ontology of sexual exchange; it stresses the active investment in Othello's masculinity that Desdemona's acquiescence to it entails. (When Juliet similarly anticipates the "manning" of her blood by Romeo, she is thinking not only of being dominated by him but of feeling her own phallic stirrings achieve mastery.) ... Q's "utmost pleasure" loses F's rich fusion of submission and self assertion. ("Sexual Anxiety," 407–408)

This description beautifully acknowledges Desdemona's powerful presence in an actively desiring selfhood where desire is explicitly though not exclusively sexual. Since Desdemona's "subdued" condition might be characterized as a literal self-abnegation or even selflessness, we can understand Coleridge's description of emptiness and lack, as though she had no self to begin with. For Coleridge, Desdemona's abundant capacity to feel and feel with is predicated on an apparently compensatory absence of intellectual character, an inability to "understand." Snow detaches us from this image of mindless affection and brings us closer to Othello's own response just after Desdemona's declaration, supporting her wish to accompany him in order "to be free and generous to her mind."

Coleridge claims to know "in fact" what all men want. The traditions of *Othello* interpretation and indeed the action itself of the play suggest that such generalizations (about men, women, blacks, Florentines, whatever) are a risky business, "dangerous conceits," as Iago says (3.3.329) Who knows what men want?[25] Snow, who implies an answer to the question very different from that of Coleridge, nonetheless winds up in basically the same position: both of them manifest a profoundly affectionate regard for Desdemona. I think this is the place the play wants us to be, or wants us to feel we ought to be (a distinction I shall turn to in a moment). However diversely edited and performed in a variety of theatrical settings to audiences interpreting according to the historically specific cultural determinants shaping response (race, class, gender, ethnicity, sexuality, nationality, etc.), the performance cues in the text as I understood it are too numerous and consistent to resist our finding ourselves by this point, despite the powerfully convincing quality of Iago's initial suggestions, in love with the gentle Desdemona.

* * *

To sum up: in its opening movements, the play aligns us with Iago's views and then, by revealing Othello's and Desdemona's stunning attractions, requires us to dissociate ourselves from him. As Hunter suggests, this process of disconfirmation is preeminently rational, assuming an open-minded audience who, in the face of negative evidence, "will find it easy to abandon" Iago's prejudiced hypotheses for more plausible ones (47). It is therefore particularly appropriate that the doubts are resolved in a meeting of the Venetian Senate, an elaborate scene where formal process endows the action with an aura of political and judicial authority. The Senate scene not only enacts disconfirmation; it focuses our attention on the process as a subject for reflection. Hence the Duke at the very beginning: "There is no composition in these news / That gives them credit." Before we know what incoherences he is talking about, we may hear in these words an echo of our own experience of contradiction in the juxtaposition of the old black ram and the noble Moor during the two preceding scenes. Then, for the next almost-fifty lines (far more than we need, as Joel Altman points out, to cover Othello's travel time [136]), we are required to watch the Senators scrupulously sifting through the conflicting reports and contradictory evidence in order eventually to reach the right conclusion ("'Tis certain then for Cyprus"). The play is going out of its way to make us conscious of the way in which belief is appropriately constituted—"to anatomize composition," in Altman's words, "specifically the way the mind composes an acceptable simulacrum of reality" (136). The passage serves to legitimate at once the Senate's interpretive procedures and our own; by the end of act 1, we should apparently be in a state of secure resolution about the noble Moor, the gentle Desdemona, and their marriage.

It hasn't quite worked out this way. This position is basically consistent with performance traditions, especially in the nineteenth century, and even the diminished Othellos of the more recent stage and film versions are generally sympathetic figures, but critical commentary, especially in our century, constitutes another story. As Arthur Kirsch demonstrates, "most of it is driven by the impulse to convict Othello of moral or psychic failure," with a similar "quest for pathology" characterizing commentary about Desdemona as well (11).[26] Kirsch thinks this is wrongheaded; he too understands the opening scenes of the play as an enactment of disconfirmation. One consequence of this situation is that Kirsch is caught in the trap Holloway recognized. The only way he has "to say anything" that might be recognized "as worth saying" is "to engage in dispute" with an inherited tradition of *Othello* commentary that is "driven by the impulse" to make negative judgments about Othello and Desdemona.

> Desdemona is not Helen or Cressida.... she is true, and ... there is no service greater than she deserves. One would suppose these to be self-evident propositions, but there are notable critics who dispute them. [Othello's big speech] should alone suggest that Desdemona is hardly an overaggressive schoolgirl. [Her] feeling for Othello is ... a sign not that she is silly or guileful, but that she has a capacity to sympathize.... We may be disposed to regard tears and the capacity for pity as cheap commodities, but Shakespeare did not.... It is nonsense to imagine that Shakespeare created [Desdemona's opening] speech for a character who was to be an unpleasant homiletic example [and] even greater nonsense to imagine that such a speech would introduce a girl incapable of "mature affection." (11–15)

All this (and more) in four pages devoted to Desdemona; still much more follows when Kirsch comes to the protagonist ("Othello's marked worship of her is an expression, not as so many critics would have it, of ... intrinsic weakness," etc. [21]). Kirsch finds himself in the unenviable position—discomforting to watch and presumably painful to occupy—of harping with increasingly irritated emphasis ("nonsense ... even greater nonsense") on denials that cannot help but repeat and therefore potentially reinforce the interpretive errors he is seeking to eliminate.

What accounts for the perversity of the interpretive tradition that has put Kirsch into this position? Kirsch holds Rymer responsible for originating the nonsensical view that Desdemona is an "unpleasant homiletic example," and this squares with Altman's point that Rymer is in general responsible for "setting the crucial question" for all subsequent *Othello* criticism. Altman's phrase suggests an analytically self-conscious process, but there are times when going back to Rymer is just something *Othello* critics do. Like the mountain for the mountain climber, Rymer is monumentally there. Furness, for instance, reproduces a substantial passage from Rymer complaining about Desdemona's pleas for Cassio (I quote the passage in chapter 4) and then says, "It is to be hoped that the reader comprehends the motive which prompts the occasional insertion of these criticisms by Rymer. He has read his Shakespeare to little purpose who does not appreciate the relief, amid tragic scenes, afforded by a dash of buffoonery" (167). Comic relief in this sense is a form of motiveless benignity, but motivelessness is not meaninglessness, and Kirsch, commenting on the same passage, gets at the meaning—namely Iago: "To stage or read those scenes in which [Desdemona] pleads for Cassio as the exercises of a wilful woman or a domineering wife is to misconstrue her motives and to become as subject to Iago's inversions as Othello does" (17). If Rymer is just "a kind of critical Iago" (Newman, "And Wash," 152), then behind Rymer, the original impulse still driving a perverse critical tradition, is Iago himself.

But then how do we explain Iago's power to shape belief? Kirsch himself acknowledges that the play itself is responsible for Iago's initial power ("Shakespeare has deliberately implicated us in ... primordial prejudice"). He claims this is only to engage us actively in the process of reevaluation ("We ourselves thus experience, we do not merely witness, the process of perception Desdemona describes"); but if "that process is kept constantly in our consciousness by Othello's literal appearance, by the pervasive imagery of blackness and fairness and of true and false vision, and by Iago's increasingly ominous and explicitly diabolic threats" (21), why is the effect not to reinforce rather than to disconfirm the original impression?

It is precisely this process—first in, last out; not disconfirmation, but reconfirmation—that Michael Neill claims to be operating in our perception of *Othello's* opening movements:

> The play thinks abomination into being and then taunts the audience with the knowledge that it can never be *un*thought.... Since the audience is exposed to [Iago's] obscenities before it is allowed to encounter either Othello or Desdemona in person, they serve to plant the suggestion, which perseveres like an itch throughout the action.... The scenes that follow contrive to keep alive the ugly curiosity that Iago has aroused.[27]

Disconfirmation assumes a mind free and open to new evidence, but the model Neill describes here, "a technique that works close to the unstable ground of consciousness itself" (395), accounts for the generation of belief as a fundamentally irrational process.

This model too is not only enacted but thematized in the play, in Brabantio's initial response to Iago's appalling first image: "This accident is not unlike my dream, / Belief of it oppresses me already" (1.1.140–141). Brabantio is persuaded, even before he acts on Roderigo's advice to see if Desdemona is at home, by the subconscious fear of an apparently recurring nightmare. His conviction of female betrayal is not the product of conscious assent; he seems to have no choice but to yield to its oppressive anxiety. Once convinced, he looks for and of course finds confirmation in the idea of witchcraft to explain what has happened:

> Is there not charms
> By which the property of youth and maidhood
> May be abused? Have you not read, Roderigo,
> Of some such thing? (1.1.169–172)

At first just another straw at which Brabantio grasps, witchcraft is quickly transformed to a plausible hypothesis ("I'll have't disputed on, / 'Tis probable and palpable to thinking" [1.2.75–76]) and then elevated to the absolute certainty of a self-evident fact: "For nature so preposterously to err / Being not deficient, blind, or lame of sense, / Sans witchcraft could not" (1.3.63–65).

If we are meant to see through Brabantio's "superstition," then the Duke's skepticism—

> To vouch this is no proof
> Without more certain and more overt test
> Than these thin habits and poor likelihoods
> Of modern seeming do prefer against him. (107–110)

—and senatorial due process should act out the triumph of rationality.[28] But the resolution represented at the end of act 1 produces profoundly equivocal effects. The legal resolution somehow misses the point, a legal fiction.[29] It cannot altogether eliminate the intense fear and anxiety Iago has generated at the beginning, or totally erase the memory of Iago's suggestion that senatorial impartiality is a hypocritical facade ("the state . . . Cannot with safety cast him" [1.1.145, 147]).[30] The Duke's comforting maxims at the end of the scene do not satisfy Brabantio, whose sarcastic echoes seem designed to emphasize their banality. The elaborate suspense raised about Desdemona's "fit disposition" is left unresolved. The Duke simply avoids a decision, pleading time constraints.

Even more troubling are the suggestions that senatorial due process is significantly similar to the irrational epistemological model developed in Brabantio. Despite the sober reflection and the careful examination of contradictory hypotheses at the beginning of the scene, the Duke becomes convinced of Turkish intentions before confirming evidence comes in the form of the messenger. As with so many of the "preposterous" acts of judgment Altman and Parker describe in the play, the Duke seems to have leaped to a "foregone conclusion." He is apparently "driven by impulse" (to recall Kirsch's phrase for the perversity of *Othello* commentary), a preconception which (like Brabantio's dream) may itself be inaccessible to rational scrutiny. He believes the messenger, who is himself no closer to events or personally more authoritative than the sailor, presumably because the messenger's version conforms to what he already believes—that the Turks are a violently threatening force: "the main article I do approve / In *fearful* sense" (1.3.11–12). Senatorial judgment seems to be determined by a variant of the same frightful nightmare oppressing Brabantio.[31]

The element of time is crucial here, as always in dramatic experience. We of course know there's a lot more play to come, and the signals of an ultimately tragic denouement by themselves make suspect the stability of the generically comic resolution we have apparently negotiated here. The rapidity and volatility of the action in the first act of *Othello* are bound to leave remnants of disquietude. That Iago has residual authority even through the Senate's resolution is entirely reasonable. "Primordial prejudices" are not so "easy to abandon"; anyone who has experienced "the grip of a guilt" knows better than to expect immediate release. We need some time to get more distance from Iago's contaminating malice. But that's not what the play gives us. Instead of time and distance, the play restores Iago to a commanding presence at the end of act 1. Then it awards him almost sole proprietorship of the second act.

NOTES

1. See Webster's *White Devil*, 1.2.239, a play saturated with *Othello* echoes, for what the editor, Christina Luckyj, calls "the obvious pun" on ewe/you. See also Neill ("Changing Places," 122).

2. The standard account emphasizes the dislocation of social and economic life in sixteenth-century England, when an agrarian society, characterized by relatively stable and familiar relationships, began to give way to a more urban market economy inhabited by strangers bound tenuously to each other by money.

3. Much has been made of an increasingly appalled fascination with the favoritism of the Jacobean court, but this connection shouldn't be pushed. For one thing, *Othello* may be an Elizabethan play. Though it is usually dated 1603–4, Honigmann offers strong arguments for 1601 (344–350), and in any case a sense of arbitrariness in James's court took some time to develop. Besides, the Malcontent's role was substantially formed in Elizabethan drama. The designation is taken from the title of Marston's play of 1599 (though there are Malcontents taking shape before this), which seemed to inspire a renewed interest in revenge plays and therefore probably contributed to the production of *Hamlet*, which in turn led to the productions of *The Revenger's Tragedy* (probably by Middleton, around 1607) and Webster's *White Devil* and *Duchess of Malfi* (around 1612), with the grandest and most resonant of the Malcontents, Vindice, Flamineo, and Bosola.

4. According to George Best's more or less standard sixteenth-century account, "all these blacke Moores which are in Africa" trace their origin to the time of the great flood. Entering the ark, Noah "strictly commaunded his sonnes and their wives, that they . . . should use continencie, and abstaine from carnal) copulation with their wives," but his "wicked sonne Chain disobeyed," tempted (like Adam

earlier) by "our great and continuall) enemie the wicked Sprite," and convinced that he would sire "the first childe borne after the flood" who would therefore "by right and Lawe of nature . . . inherite and possesse all the dominions of the earth." As a punishment, God made this child (Chus) and all his posterity "so blacke and loth-some, that it might remaine a spectacle of disobedience to all the worlde." Best was writing about his travels in a book published in 1578 and reprinted in Hakluyt's enormously popular compendium of such writing in 1600. For details and more of Best, see Newman, "And Wash," from whom the quotation is taken (146–147).

5. Any attempt to recapture the play's experience for the original audiences is bound to be speculative and should allow for the counterintuitive. Lupton offers an interesting and plausible argument that Othello's Moorishness would be felt as more threatening than his black identity, the reverse of nineteenth-century and later senti-ment; her basic claim is that the Moslem *refusal* of the New Law, like the Jewish, "might actually challenge more deeply the integrity of the Christian paradigms set up in the play as the measure of humanity" than the image of the black Othello as barbarian, unexposed as yet to the revelation of Christ (74). Bak demonstrates that color signified differently in different discursive and rhetorical contexts and sees the drama as taking advantage of these differences for its own purposes.

The topic of race is of course very controversial in current criticism, and not everyone would agree with my emphasis on the distinctly "pre-racialist" quality of Renaissance belief (I take the word as well as the basic analysis from Appiah). For claims that Renaissance audiences had a more fully developed and generally dispersed sense of racial categories, see Hall, especially 254–268, and Shapiro, especially his critique of Hunter, 83–85. Perhaps they are right. In distinguishing Renaissance pre-racialism, nineteenth-century racialism, and current post-racialist belief (as it might be called), I do not mean to deny clear elements of continuity, still less to suggest that we have liberated ourselves from the prejudices of a benighted tradition. Although biologists now tell us that racial differences are too trivial to count as scientifically significant, race obviously remains a category with immense social significance. In a stunning recent book, Walter Benn Michaels argues that contemporary critics arguing for multiculturalism and ethnicity in specific opposi-tion to racial agendas in fact radically depend on and therefore effectively sustain the idea of race they wish to eradicate. According to Young, "if there is one constant characteristic of the history of the use of the word 'race,' it is that however many new meanings may be constructed for it, the old meanings refuse to die. They rather accumulate in clusters of ever-increasing power, resonance and persuasion" (83). Whether we emphasize continuity between us and the Renaissance (like Hall and Shapiro) or discontinuity (like Hunter and Appiah) depends on critical purpose. For an astute analysis of what is at stake for our own politics as well as for the peculiari-ties of *Othello* for its original audiences, see Chaudhuri.

6. For this material, see Vaughan, 13–34, and D'Amico, 7–40.

7. For the wealth of the Levant trade, which far exceeded trade in the Americas, see Davis. According to Brenner, the real forces driving English eco-nomic expansion were the "new-merchants," essentially freebooters who tended to undermine the authority of the aristocratic and officially sanctioned merchant com-panies, and who therefore had the effect, comparable to the Barbary pirates evoked in *Othello* and elsewhere in Shakespeare (as by Hal to Francis in *1 Henry IV*, 2.4), of threatening established order. This blurring of distinctions might lead to a version

of Portia's question in the Trial Scene of *The Merchant*: who is the Merchant here, and who the pirate?

8. See Lacey Baldwin Smith, who is chiefly concerned with child-rearing practices, the sorts of things that led Lawrence Stone to conclude that Tudor England was a "low-affect society" (*The Family, Sex, and Marriage*). As Maus argues, however, the peculiarly intense level of anxiety and suspicion reflected in Elizabethan and Jacobean textual, cultural, and political practice must have been "overdetermined" by a vast number of "mutually interacting social and ideological factors," and she too is inclined to emphasize the influential consequences of religious differences (*Inwardness and Theater*, 14 ff.). Patricia Parker similarly points to "the context of this paranoid atmosphere" generated out of religious differences in late Elizabethan and early Jacobean England ("*Othello* and *Hamlet*," 62). In "Torture and Truth," Elizabeth Hanson brilliantly analyzes the jurisprudential consequences of this uniquely threatened situation in late Tudor and early Jacobean England: the only period when torture was systematically and institutionally legitimated.

9. For a fascinating argument claiming that Shakespeare's geography is consistently and fundamentally symbolic, see Gillies.

10. For the Renaissance context, see Greenberg (6 ff.), Jones, David McPherson, and Vaughan (13–34). For later, see Tanner.

11. This idea is brilliantly developed by Neill with special reference primarily to the protagonist's story ("Changing Places") and by Genster with special reference to the audience's unstable position.

12. I quote the maxim from Jonson's *Volpone* (2.1.1) where, unfortunately for my purposes, it is spoken by Sir Politic Wouldbe. For the history and authority of the idea, see Kerrigan and Braden (18–19).

13. I am particularly indebted here to Newman's argument that the "play is structured around a cultural aporia, miscegenation" (145).

14. In declaring that his services will out-tongue Brabantio's complaints, Othello imagines his actions speaking for him, as if he existed in an objective form. A moment later he uses a similar formula to describe not his actions but his inner qualities: "My parts, my title, and my perfect soul / Shall manifest me truly." Like private self and public order, subjective and objective existence seem to merge into an integrated consciousness. The breathtaking wholeness with which Othello experiences his life gives a nontheological way of understanding Othello's "perfect soul." (See 5.c and 5.d in the revised *OED*. Cf. Hamlet's more ambiguous "perfect conscience" [5.2.67]. Cf. Calderwood: "By 'my perfect soul' Othello probably means completeness of self, perfect in the sense in which Macbeth uses the term" 3.4.20 [13]). Ulysses' address to Achilles as "thou great and complete man" (*Troilus and Cressida*, 3.3.181) is ironic, for Achilles' sense of self-worth depends on the unstable and arbitrary fashions of public reputation; but Othello is the thing itself.

15. For an interesting discussion of Dickens's opening, see Nuttall (*Openings*, 172 ff.).

16. Honigmann points out that "Say it, Othello" at the beginning of the speech is part of a short line. In his edition, he speculates about missing words, but in his book on the text, he speculates about short lines as contributing to emphatic effects (*The Texts of "Othello*," 103–26).

17. According to Hunter, these "complicating factors" include "Renaissance primitivism." See his discussion, 47 ff.

18. Romantic comedy, Shakespearean and otherwise, typically writes us into sympathy with the undutifully, desiring daughter against the oppressive father (think of Hermia and Egeus in *A Midsummer Night's Dream*), but *Othello* has evoked darker feelings. Although Brabantio resembles the blocking father of Shakespearean comedy, his grief ("And what's to come of my despised time / Is nought but bitterness" [1.1.159–160]) and loving concern ("O unhappy girl!" [161]) endow him with authority well beyond the insufferably self-absorbed Egeus or even Leanato in *Much Ado*. The news of his death at the end, "pure grief / Shore his old thread in twain" (5.2.203–204), should seem shocking but not surprising.

19. "(Roderigo stumbles, speaking hastily): he means 'your daughter *has been* transported . . . *than* with a knave'": Honigmann's clarifying note.

20. "Transported" regularly means passionately carried away in Shakespeare (see Spevack). In Webster's *Duchess of Malfi*, a play that frequently echoes *Othello*, Ferdinand's imagining of "some strong-thigh'd bargeman" (2.5.43) as one of his sister's succession of lovers may owe something to the gondolier here.

21. The standard Renaissance story—dominating if not wholly constituting the category of gender—represented women as weaker vessels, less able to master passionate feelings and more highly sexed than men, therefore requiring supervision ("guardage," as Brabantio says), the enclosure of their wandering appetites both for their own good and for the good of the men they might tempt into unmanly sexual interest (see Stallybrass and Ziegler). By the time of the Victorians, these views would be transposed—women are naturally demure and undersexed compared with men. To the extent that we are still enthralled by residual nineteenth-century thought, it may take some work to be able to acknowledge the emotional power of Iago's views in the play. Brabantio's anxiety may inspire coarse and sadistic laughter ("O heaven, how got she out? O treason of the blood!" [1.1.167]), like so many of Iago's productions, but for Shakespeare's audience, the old man's horror at Desdemona's escape from within evokes a fearful threat to the foundations of legitimate order no less serious than Othello's assault from outside.

Renaissance models of manliness are also likely to seem bizarre. The Lothario or Don Juan figure, heroic in sexual conquest, another Victorian (or perhaps eighteenth-century) residuum for us, would have probably been rendered as perverse in the Renaissance, when sexual conquest was typically understood as the reverse of manly—a conquest *by* the sexual appetite, always gendered female, over the rational self-command of true masculinity. Hence the two images of Hercules in *Much Ado About Nothing*, one in which Omphale has made him do women's work in women's clothes and "cleft his club," the other as "the shaven Hercules [whose] codpiece seems as massy as his club" (2.1.254 and 3.3.136–138), are not contradictory but emphatic: both of them, the massy as well as the cleft club, are images of emasculation.

22. Desdemona's behavior may have evoked echoes (with the gender changed) of Genesis 2:24, "Therefore shall a man leave his father and his mother, and shall cleave unto his wife; and they shall be both one flesh," and Paul in Ephesians 5:31, "For this cause shall a man leave his father and mother, and shall be joined unto his wife, and they two shall be one flesh."

23. I have used Q1 here, departing from Honigmann, who follows F's "Nor would I there reside."

24. In sum: many sixteenth-century Protestants vigorously contested the older view, associated with Saint Paul's "better to marry than burn," which they regarded as part of the monastic ideal of medieval Catholicism. Seeking to legitimate the

active life and to redeem the natural sphere, they reconceptualized marriage as a positively virtuous relationship in its own right. Without abandoning the idea of parental consent, they emphasized the value of marriage partners freely choosing each other. Still committed to the supremacy of husbandly authority, they nonetheless recentered marital relations in terms of companionship, a mutual affection, including sexual intimacy, sustained over a lifetime between two equally (though differently) contributing partners. This new concept achieves its climactically triumphant expression in *Paradise Lost*, a poem heavily invested in marriage as a sanctified relationship ("Hail, wedded Love," [4, 736]) conspicuously including a mutual sexual delight (see 4, 492–501).

The inaugurating modern research on these topics was performed by Mandeville and William Haller. For an excellent recent exposition of these ideas and their literary and dramatic implications, see Rose. Companionate marriage generated an enormous amount of critical excitement in historical criticism during the 1980s but is now either ignored or relegated to the trivial, as in Diana Henderson's remark that "for all the post-Reformation talk of companionate marriage, household management was modeled not upon collaborative equality but upon monarchy" (175). This may be true, but it seems odd for literary scholars to dismiss so much discourse ("all the . . . talk") as inconsequential. Over- and then under-investment in the discursive is coming to feel like the business cycles of academic life under late capitalism.

25. Coleridge anticipates John Holloway, who (as we saw in the previous chapter) presumes to possess the "simple facts" of "everyone's familiar knowledge about love, marriage, and affection between men and women." Both of them are anticipated by Othello himself, who adopts the generalizing tone of the canny insider at the very moment he abandons his love for Desdemona in order to credit Iago: "O curse of marriage / That we can call these delicate creatures ours / And not their appetites!" (3.3.272–274). All three make ridiculous spectacles of themselves, and this may suggest some practical advice along the lines of one of the three "very instructive" morals Rymer found in the play: "a lesson to Husbands, that before their Jealousie be Tragical, the proofs may be Mathematical" (132). The problem is that mathematical proofs in the sense of a totally disinterested (unprejudiced) perception of an external reality is impossible. "Generalizations are bad" may be a good thing to say, but it's a paradox which cannot provide a basis for behavior. Shakespearean tragedy is not very good at furnishing role models.

26. Kirsch is talking about "theological" or "psychological" criticism, but these terms pretty well cover the field in general. The Dexter-Olivier *Othello*, to which I shall want to return, is an interesting anomaly. It self-consciously goes with the flow of academic criticism out of Leavis but with surprisingly stunning results.

27. "Unproper Beds," 395–397, Neill's emphasis. I am deeply indebted to Neill's brilliant essay as to the Burke essay Neill acknowledges.

28. Honigmann suggests that the Duke's words may explicitly constitute "an appeal against racial prejudice." "Superstition" is Edwin Booth's word, commenting in his promptbook that "the dream is convincing proof" only "to the superstitious Italian" and that witchcraft, similarly, is generated out of "the superstition that pervades" such a mind (Furness, 24, 27). There is something self-contradictory about Booth's dependence on ethnic prejudice as a way of distinguishing himself from superstition. "Reflections like these," he adds, "help the actor to *feel* the character he assumes"; but why does he have to feel his way into an assumed role?—in a sense he's already there.

29. That Brabantio's case collapses with Desdemona's testimony seems oddly literal. Desdemona was not of course actually drugged, but Othello certainly charmed her in a metaphorical sense, and his sexual charisma could fairly be described as magical in its ability to transform her nature into a passionate arousal quite beyond the culturally constructed norms of dutiful daughterhood.

30. The play apparently wants to keep Iago's suggestion available. Consider the bathetic drop from the Duke's unqualified assurance early in the scene that Brabantio will get full satisfaction "though my proper son / Stood in your action" (69–70) to the response after Brabantio identifies Othello as the offending party: "We are very sorry for't" (74). A much more noncommittal response, this, and its attribution to "ALL" makes the reduction in commitment more emphatic. "ALL" is not uncommon as a speech prefix in Shakespeare, and there are divergent hypotheses about its implications for performance. See Honigmann, "Re-enter the Stage Direction," and Parker's edition of *Coriolanus*, 93–94.

31. For Altman, the Duke's judgment is "driven by the unspoken need to believe that the Turks behave like the Venetians" (136), but "fearful" allows us to be more specific about the feeling generating the behavior. According to Altman, "that the Duke's composition turns out to correspond, in large part, to the shape of external events does not lessen its fictive status; it merely suggests that probabilities are more reliable in public matters than in private" (153). Brabantio's domestic anxieties also turn out to be justified—Desdemona *has* eloped. Even paranoids have enemies; even people with enemies may be paranoid. As Neill remarks, "It is difficult to say whether" these "anxieties are ones that the play discovers or implants in an audience" ("Unproper Beds," 395).

ROBERT N. WATSON

Othello *as Reformation Tragedy*

"I too dislike it," admits Marianne Moore about "poetry"; but she adds that it may still offer "a place for the genuine," or at least something "useful." I want to say the same about factional and allegorical reading of Shakespearean drama. Such readings flatten while claiming to reveal profundity, and are soon dismissed, as they have dismissed the readings preceding them. From Keats's praise of Shakespeare's "negative capability" to recent criticism's devotion to nuance, paradox, and multiplicity, grand procrustean interpretations have been in disgrace. Yet, in these thoughts my claim almost despising, I still think it worthwhile to suggest that the many critics who have detected a Christian allegory in *Othello* are all right, and each wrong, because they have overlooked the polemical function of that allegory *within* Renaissance Christianity.[1]

Though far from perfect, the allegory is persistent and tendentious, and though its version of Catholic theology is a caricature, similar caricatures populate Elizabethan Protestant polemics.[2] If "Shakespeare and his successors recreate the Reformation image of Italy,"[3] perhaps such plays also recreate the Reformation image of Roman religion. *Othello* never attacks Catholicism directly, but "war with Spain, which had made anti-Catholic satire and polemics acceptable in the drama, ended in 1604"—the likely date of *Othello*'s composition—and "this tended to make the expression of militant

From *In the Company of Shakespeare: Essays on English Renaissance Literature in Honor of G. Blakemore Evans*, edited by Thomas Moisan and Douglas Bruster, pp. 65–96. © 2002 by Rosemont Publishing and Printing.

anti-Catholic, radical or skeptical viewpoints less easy and less direct than it had been."[4] Nonetheless, drama remained an important medium for Protestant propaganda, and, "[f]rom 1602 to 1605, the period following the Essex rebellion, a spate of plays about the Reformation appeared in the public theatres of London," including contributions by Dekker, Webster, Heywood, and Rowley.[5] If *Othello* is Shakespeare's contribution to this "spate," many of the play's anomalies begin to make sense.

"Much virtue in If," as Touchstone remarks (*As You Like It*, V.iv.103). My argument is speculative and provocative, and while readers will surely find some pieces of the evidence unconvincing, I hope that enough pieces remain standing to support the thesis collectively. Readers not convinced that the play actively advocates Protestantism may nonetheless recognize significant analogies between the dramatic conflict and the chief theological conflict agonizing Shakespeare's society: whether to accept heavenly love as an irreversible miracle of charity, or instead to measure it as the contingent reward of demonstrated merits. That would surely have been the deepest discursive context of Othello's tragic error for Jacobean audiences, and the play insistently evokes that context, often with specific echoes of contemporary anti-Catholic propaganda.

Recent scholarly practice favors declaring only that the text participates in some charged cloud of nebulous cumulative cultural meaning—which is surely true, accommodates complexity, and leaves questions open. But do we really serve our colleagues best by risking no answers that could be proven false, by obliging those colleagues to provide articulation and hence commitment to our playfully elusive wonderings at a multiple and paradoxical world, by mimicking the irresolution we sought in the literary texts? Isn't the collective enterprise often better served by assertions sufficiently clear as to be susceptible to refinements and refutations?

Othello's tragedy transposes solifidianism—salvation by faith alone—into the realm of marriage. What Martin Luther prescribes for the human soul resembles what audiences for centuries have silently urged on Othello: a belief that, though he may not deserve the redemptive love, the pity, even the body of this divine creature, God has given it to him, and now all he needs is absolute faith in that gift.[6] Though my evidence can certainly be read in the opposite direction, as Shakespeare using the Protestant sympathies of his audience to reinforce their approval of this incongruous love affair, I believe the play uses the appeal of romantic love to enhance the appeal of Protestantism, by repeatedly associating Desdemona with this pitying Christ, and Othello with her doubtful worshiper. Pride is as fundamental to the tragedy of *Othello* as jealousy, and the psychological melodrama comports a lesson in soteriology—the theology of salvation.

I am reluctant to make the logical deduction that Shakespeare was a Protestant in 1604—but not because I accept the strict current taboos against intentionalist reading. Though we can never know with absolute certainty what Shakespeare intended, neither can we be certain precisely what any given audience, past or present, would have perceived; and what is meant by the assertion that the text undertakes some project I doubt anyone really knows. Intentionalist assertions, like others, can fall anywhere on the continuum from near impossibility to near certainty; and the worth of any argument is a multiple of its probability and its importance. Still, I would demand grounds far more relative than the allegorical aspects of *Othello* before claiming to have caught Shakespeare's own religious conscience.[7] I have found considerable evidence of the play's theological valence, but that is what I was looking for. What follows is a brief for the view that, in composing this tragedy, Shakespeare was at least subliminally attuned to Protestant valuations of faith and Protestant fears about Jesuitical seductions.

Desdemona and Holy Matrimony

In suspecting that his wife has been unfaithful, Othello only demonstrates his own lack of faith. This domestic paradox carries over to the secondary, allegorical level of the play, where the marriage between Othello and Desdemona represents the passionate but troubled marriage between the sinner's soul and its Savior. This allegory is not far-fetched. Wedding services began with a reminder that "holy matrimonie" symbolizes "the misticall union that is betwixte Chryste and hys Churche"; and Luther writes, "Faith unites the soul with Christ as a bride is united with her bridegroom . . . human marriages are poor reflections of this one true marriage."[8] When Othello imagines Desdemona performing the Last Judgment on his soul—"When we shall meet at compt, / This look of thine will hurl my soul from heaven" (V.ii.271–72)—when he realizes that, in casting her aside, he, "[l]ike the base Judean, threw a pearl away, / Richer than all his tribe" (V.ii.343–44; cf. Matt. 13:46), and when he asserts that her death should be accompanied by "a huge eclipse / Of sun and moon, and that the'affrighted globe / Should yawn at alteration" (V.ii.100–102, recalling the report in Luke 23:45 that "the Sunne was darkened, and the vaile of the Temple rent thorow the middes" at the moment of Christ's death), our attention is surely drawn to this allegory, to the Christlike role she often plays.[9]

Cassio turns his case for redemption over to Desdemona, hoping "[t]hat, by your virtuous means, I may again / Exist, and be a member of his love":

If my offence be of such mortal kind
That nor my service past nor present sorrows,

> Nor purposed merit in futurity,
> Can ransom me into his love again,
> But to know so must be my benefit.
>   (III.iv. 104–13)

The diction is insistently theological. Characteristically over-reliant on his own merit and on the Catholic category of merely venial sins, this excommunicant begs ransom for the immortal part of himself.[10] Othello, at the height of his dignity and power, temporarily occupies the role of judging deity in this triangle, which allows Shakespeare to situate Desdemona as that deity's forgiving avatar. The play will triply and forcefully elide this earthly lord with the heavenly one at V.ii.85–86.

Desdemona intercedes with the angry lord on behalf of one fallen from grace: "Good my lord, / If I have any grace or power to move you, / His present reconciliation take" (III.iii.45–47); to borrow a sentence from a Renaissance convert from Catholicism, "This Mediatour is Christ himselfe [who] hath performed our reconciliation."[11] Desdemona, too, uses her surplus grace to redeem fallen souls by "not imputing their sinnes unto them, and hathe committed to us the worde of reconciliation" (2 Cor. 5:19, Geneva Bible).

To achieve this redemption she must invite the wayward soul to the lord's supper—"Shall't be tonight at supper? . . . Tomorrow dinner then?"—and in urging this communion her timing, oaths, and exculpations of the "trespass" all have Christian resonances: "let it not / Exceed three days. In faith, he's penitent" (III.iii.58–67).[12] Even when "the letter" stirs that judgmental lord's wrath, the spirited and merciful Desdemona announces that she "would do much / T'atone them, for the love I bear to Cassio" (IV.i.220–21; cf. Rom. 5:11).

Perhaps, on a theological as well as a psychological level, this eagerness to effect atonement helps to explain why Othello suspects she has been dispensing her love too freely, to the point of imagining hypothetically that "the general camp, / Pioners and all, had tasted her sweet body" (III.iii.346–47). The traces of ucharistic reference in this speculation add meaning to Othello's resulting determination to keep for himself her blood if not her body—as Catholic priests kept the wine, a practice vilified by English theologians.[13] Desdemona's insistence that Cassio never "used" her "unlawfully" (V.ii.69–70) echoes Protestant doctrine concerning "the Sacramentall union" which "in the lawfull use" is "conferd and given to every faithfull and worthy receiver."[14] Christ's church is "most trew," according to Donne's paradox, "[w]hen she is embrac'd and open to most men"[15]—a paradox more tolerable for a heavenly husband than for an earthly one.

This Reformation allegory offers a happier interpretation of Desdemona's very last words, which have seemed so unappealing when read, from the standpoint of sexual politics, as valorizing complete wifely self-abnegation: "Nobody; I myself. Farewell. / Commend me to my kind lord" (V.ii.125–26). Christ dies "commending" himself to his Lord (Luke 23:46); and Luther writes, "By the wedding ring of faith [Christ] shares in the sins, death, and pains of hell which are His bride's. As a matter of fact, He makes them his own and acts as if they were his own and as if He himself had sinned."[16] Desdemona's last words are thus kin to the equally astonishing last words of the murdered landlord in Herbert's "Redemption": "Who straight, 'Your suit is granted,' said, and died."

Of course the theological allegory is much further in the background of Shakespeare's work than of Herbert's, and I would not claim (for example) that Brabantio's paternal call for lights identifies him with God the Father's *fiat lux*. This allegorical level is secondary, recessive, and protean; it quickly becomes absurd if attached to every turn of phrase or plot. However, though some critics would (in the spirit of Doubting Thomas in John 20:25) forbid discussing Desdemona as a Christ-figure unless Othello were to nail her palms to the headboard, a fairer test is whether the areas where the analogies and allegories do function properly are signaled, phrased, and clustered in ways that could affect at least the subconscious minds of an audience for whom these theological questions were matters of eternal as well as temporal life and death.

Iago and Catholicism

Thus far I have contrived not to mention the name of Iago, but now I want to confront that name directly, by linking it with Saint James the Apostle, known at his burial site in Spain as Santiago Matamoros: Saint James the Moor-slayer.[17]

This site was a favorite destination for Catholic pilgrims in the Renaissance, and Martin Luther repeatedly condemns the tendency to "run to St. Iago" for help, instead of trusting in Christ's love.[18] The doctrinal significance of St. James amplifies the historical one, because his Epistle (2:14–26) contains the clearest scriptural obstacle to solifidianism. Martin Luther therefore refuses to "regard it as the writing of an apostle.... [I]t is flatly against St. Paul and all the rest of Scripture in ascribing justification to works."[19]

This chain of associations may explain a peculiar moment in Dekker's *The Whore of Babylon* (1607?), based on an historical murder plot the Jesuits "thought a sacrifice" (V.ii.65). Convinced by Jesuits that killing Titania (Queen Elizabeth) will be "an action full of merit," Palmio plans to ambush her in St. James' Park in London, which he calls "Saint Iago's park—a rare, rare, rare altar! / The fitt'st to sacrifice her blood upon. / It shall be there, in Saint Iago's park" (V.i.67–69).[20] The justice of it pleases him.

Iago may represent many forms of evil, but he is particularly opposed to the Pauline construction of goodness.[21] Shakespeare's text repeatedly calls Iago a devil, but a famous 1602 Protestant tract warns: "The divell under the habit of the Jesuits, doth goe about to circumvent all the world," and one critic has observed that Iago resembles the specifically jesuitical Machiavellians who appear in polemical tracts of this period.[22] Phillip Stubbes warned that "Jesuites" were "hollow harted friends [who] when they intend destruction then will they cover it with the cloke or garment of amity & friendship."[23] Iago covers his misdeeds with clever equivocations, proselytizes for his destructive assumptions about congruity and condignity, and makes his victims pay and empower him for these illusory blessings. By associating such Jesuits with Catholicism in general and by misrepresenting that doctrine as sharing the Pelagian tendencies of prominent Jesuits such as Ignatius Loyola and Luis de Molina,[24] Shakespeare can make his audience into more committed Protestants. The transaction may be mostly subliminal—we think we are caring about human kindness rather than about factional theology—but the best propaganda always is.

Shakespeare, characteristically, uses the opening scene to establish the theme. The ostensible topic is Roderigo's erotic envy, but (unlike in the Cinthio source[25]) the primary focus is on a different form of unrequital: the villain Iago's anger that his lord has not honored his good works with the ascendancy he thought he had purchased. "By the faith of man," Iago asserts, "I know my price, I am worth no worse a place" (I.i.10–11). Surely it is no mere coincidence that Shakespeare has Iago incongruously invoke faith here (and "God's will" twice in three lines at II.iii.139–43), nor is it a mere coincidence that when the great poet of Protestantism John Milton creates his ultimate villain, Satan so closely echoes Iago's protestations of injured merit. Iago complains about predestination: that, having "already chosen" someone else, his lord has refused to listen to Iago's exalted "mediators" (I.i.16–17). Catholics viewed the radical Protestant emphasis on the words of sermons and Scripture, without the physical performance of sacraments, as "bookish theoric" and "mere prattle without practice"—exactly what Iago complains has superseded him in this "election" (1.1.24–27; cf. Rom. 9:11).[26]

Cassio soon makes the association between salvation and this earthly promotion explicit:

> *Cassio*: Well, God's above all, and there be souls must be saved,
> and there be souls must not be saved . . . I hope to be saved.

> *Iago*: And so do I too, lieutenant.
>
> *Cassio*: Ay, but, by your leave, not before me; the lieutenant is to
> be saved before the ancient. Let's have no more of this; let's to
> our affairs. God forgive us our sins!
> (II.iii.88–96)

But why even so much of this: why couch Cassio's exhibition of petty pride
in these holy terms? A prominent debunker of theological allegories forbids
us to ponder soteriology here, dismissing this conversation as mere drunken
prattle, as if it were an historical scene that Shakespeare had no choice but
to transcribe, in all its irrelevancy.[27] From my perspective, the conversation
connects the play's mistrust of pride with its theological allusions.

In seducing Cassio and Roderigo, Iago becomes what Protestants
claimed Catholic priests were: mediators apart from Christ, who damn souls
under pretense of protecting them.[28] In insisting that "the power and cor-
rigible authority" of becoming good or evil "lies in our wills" (I.iii.318), Iago
directly contradicts the last of Whitgift's nine, Protestant-minded Lambeth
articles: "It is not in the will or the power of each and every man to be saved."
As ensign, Iago displays "the very badges and ensignes of the Whore of Babylon, Crueltie, Treacherie, Flatterie,"[29] and his initial self-description echoes
condemnations of richly garbed Catholic priests, "trimmed in forms and vis-
ages of duty," greedily lining their own coats and worshiping themselves while
deluding the world with "shows of service" (I.i.49–55). By an act of polemical ventriloquy, Shakespeare thus obliges Catholicism to verify the standard
Protestant accusations.[30]

A 1601 tract accuses Jesuits of tactics highly reminiscent of Iago's with
Roderigo:

> An other yong Gentleman not long since, entring into this exercise
> under a yong Jesuite here in *England* was found by his meditations
> to have lands yet unsold, worth a hundred marks a yeare, which
> hindred his journey to heaven. Whereupon he offring the same to
> the sayd yong Jesuite, the good Father allowing the offer, sayd, that
> if he should receive the land, her Majestie would take it from him:
> but (quoth he) sell it, and then I am capable of the money.

Could this be why Shakespeare shows Roderigo agreeing to "sell all my
land" in order to "[p]ut money in [his] purse"—which ultimately means
Iago's purse (I.iii.364, 330)? The same tract observes that "in exchange for
their wealth and large possessions" new dupes of the Jesuits are often convinced "to be practisers for them" in risky deviltry the handlers would rather

not undertake themselves.[31] Dekker condemns the "Papist Couchant" who knows how to "Creepe into credit . . . his Armes thus part / One to embrace, t'other to Stab your heart."[32] So when Iago makes his fool his purse, makes the same fool his sword against Cassio, then stabs him under the guise of a protective embrace, Shakespeare's audience might have recognized a particularly jesuitical threat from the figure who erases men's consciences by promoting their brittle self-love (I.iii. 364–65, 308). Indeed, according to a 1604 polemic, the idea that Christ's love can be won by human favors is one the papists "have invented for filthy lucre sake," in order to rob "ignorant people";[33] Iago lures Roderigo into a parallel delusion about Desdemona's favors. Behind Iago's concern about the prospective "restitution large / Of gold and jewels that I bobbed from him, / As gifts to Desdemona" (V.i.15–17) lurks a caricature of Catholic complaints about Tudor seizures of monastic property.[34]

Similarly, the end of the play endorses standard Elizabethan persecutions of Catholics, eliding those persecutions with the punishment of the villainous Iago and the man who joined him in the wrongful rites:

> Gratiano, keep the house,
> And seize upon the fortunes of the Moor,
> For they succeed on you. To you, lord governor,
> Remains the censure of this hellish villain:
> The time, the place, the torture, O, enforce it!
> (V.ii.361–65)

Who could object to secular authorities seizing the property and punishing the bodies of those who undermine the precious bond of faith?[35] Heresy has been transfigured into something more indisputably criminal. Even Iago's stubborn silence in the face of these threats evokes the figure of the jesuitical conspirator[36]—especially since, lacking any co-conspirators to protect, there is no verisimilar explanation for that silence, only an allusive one.

By having the Turkish fleet produce "a pageant / To keep us in false gaze" (I.iii.18–19), Shakespeare underscores the Turks' kinship not only with Iago, but also with Catholicism as both an iconophilic and a political practice. The wreck of that fleet would certainly have recalled the similarly stormy wreck of the Spanish Armada threatening to impose Catholicism on England. And, as Iago is implicitly an avatar of the Turkish invasion, so "Robert Parsons' appeal to English Catholics to support Spain as the Armada sailed was merely the most public and notorious association of internal subversion with foreign attack."[37] The Turks provide another slightly displaced outlet—and amplifier—for anti-Catholic sentiment, which Shakespeare channels into his story through Iago.[38] Indeed, Luther claims that though "the Turks perform different works from the papists . . . the content remains the same, and only the quality is different." Therefore, those who "can freely judge that the Turk with his Koran is damned" can "[w]ith similar confidence . . . pronounce sentence against the pope."[39]

At about the time Shakespeare was writing *Othello*, King James was issuing a proclamation banishing Catholics and Jesuits for "perswading our Subjects from the Religion established, and reconciling them to the Church of Rome."[40] The play was written during an anxious era of royal succession which amplified the usual fear that Catholicism might recapture the soul of England; and it was set in Venice, which (according to Sir Henry Wotton's ambassadorial report of 1603) was itself "a Signory . . . almost slipped into a neutrality of religion," and rapidly slipping into conflict with the papacy.[41] We may therefore suspect that behind the devilish Iago whose "business is to reclaim infidels to the demonic faith"[42] lies a recusant Iago who tries to reclaim creatures of faith for a doctrine of works. He convinces Roderigo that Desdemona's divine love can be won by bloody deeds and expensive gifts, Cassio that his worldly merits can earn otherworldly salvation,[43] and Othello that his face rather than her heart—his purity rather than her generosity—will determine Desdemona's love. Like his near-namesake Iachimo in *Cymbeline*, Iago replaces the faith that sustains love with a need for ocular proof, certainty of adherence with certainty of evidence.[44]

With jesuitical guile, Iago subverts the religion of pure faith by converting it to credulity and subjecting it to parody. Regina Schwartz discerns an echo of the transubstantiation controversy in Iago's dismissive response to the claim that Desdemona embodies a "blest condition": "Blest fig's end! The wine she drinks is made of grapes" (II.i.238).[45] But it is a parodic echo, subverting the Zwinglian position by implying that this would preclude the wine from instilling a blessed condition. When Zwingli insists that Matt. 26 "shows us plainly that . . . this drink is really wine, and comes from the vine,"[46] he is nonetheless arguing that the Communion remains fully efficacious. Iago thus attempts what Protestants (in 1604) complained that Jesuits attempted: to brand anyone denying the full presence and potency of Christ's blood in the wine "a flat Arian, beleeving Christ to be pure man, and not God."[47] Jewel's *Apology of the Church of England* approvingly quotes Ambrose's insistence that "[b]read and wine remain still the same they were before, and yet are changed into another thing" during Communion;[48] and I am tempted to cast as a jesuitical Iago any metacritic who doubts that Desdemona can sometimes embody Christ since she always remains Desdemona.[49] By insisting that grapes cannot carry blessing if they remain grapes, and that love is not love if it is "but sign," Iago disables an extremely important piece of Protestant theology.[50]

Iago provokes Othello to suspect that he was never really given the body of Desdemona, and thereby a place in the body politic of Venice. As Luther writes,

> To receive this sacrament in bread and wine, then, is nothing else than to receive a sure sign of this fellowship and union with Christ ... as if a citizen were given a sign, a document, or some other token, to assure him that he is indeed a citizen of the city, and a member of that particular community.[51]

Iago destroys Othello's faith in marriage and communion, offering in their place eternal love and the use of his body (III.iii.469–86)—a version of the unholy homosexual bond that was allegedly the Jesuit alternative to holy matrimony.[52]

Iago also offers, for the sake of discrediting it, a version of Anglican adiaphorism—the argument that Christianity may be practiced in various ways without harm, so long as the core intention is holy and the conduct does not violate any explicit scriptural rule:

> *Iago*: What,
> To kiss in private?
> *Othello*: An unauthorized kiss!
> *Iago*: Or to be naked with her friend in bed
> An hour or more, not meaning any harm?
>   (IV.i.1–4)

By taking this position of radical trust, by refusing to add traditional inferences to literal facts, and by calling such misconduct (in a theologically loaded phrase) "a venial slip" (IV.i.9), Iago forces on Othello a conversely suspicious and empirical view.[53] He makes the *credo quia impossibile* into something unsustainable: the slogan of the pathetic Chaucerian cuckold January, rather than of the joyous Christian fideist Thomas Browne. Furthermore, this tactic closely resembles Thomas More's parody of the Protestant preference for the potentially erotic term "love" in place of the Catholic "charity," with its emphasis on good works: except for those "silly" enough to trust Tyndale's translation, "men be nowadays waxen so full of mistrust, that some man would, in faith, ween his wife were nought if he should but find her in bed with a poor frere."[54]

Iago thus burdens Othello's marriage with something resembling Calvinist salvation anxiety—or perhaps burdens Calvinism with Othello's marital anxiety, the endless "damned minutes" endured by the spirit that "dotes, yet doubts" (III.iii.169–72). No wonder Othello begins to refer to his marriage as "the business of my soul" (III.iii.183), and to suspect that the love of this savior is earned and therefore changeable, rather than predestined and therefore stable in perpetuity.[55] "Perdition catch my soul / But I do love thee" Othello exclaims in the midst of this temptation, "And when I love thee not, / Chaos is come again" (III.iii.90–92).[56] And no wonder Iago enters instantly on this line, not only to personate the loveless chaos, but also (like Marlowe's Mephistopheles) to divert the protagonist from the path back toward grace.

Iago's feigned resistance to Othello's inquiries parodies the Elizabethan reluctance, as Bacon put it, to "make a window in men's souls." As Puritans insisted that no one should "be examined upon secret thoughts of his heart, or of his secret opinion," so Iago provocatively denies that he is "bound to that all slaves are free to"; Othello cannot know his inmost thoughts "if my heart were in your hand" (III.iii. 134–64). What this master-equivocator here makes intolerable for Othello is virtually identical—and virtually identified— with the don't-ask-don't-tell theological compromise.[57] It is also a taunting reminder that the state cannot really control heresy even by having an executioner hold up the heretic's heart in his hand. This may seem a strained reading, but the image hardly admits a comfortable one, and the most compelling analogue in Shakespeare's society would have been these gruesome attempts to pluck out the heart of the recusant mystery.

Othello and the Crisis of Faith

Shakespeare's *Othello* is notable for transposing high tragedy to a domestic mode. It is also notable, though less noted, for transposing theology to that domestic mode. The title of a more overtly theological play by Shakespeare's prodigious contemporary Tirso de Molina, *The Man Condemned for a Lack of Faith*, fits Shakespeare's play as well.[58] The polemical function of Nathaniel Woodes's *The Conflict of Conscience* (1581), in which the protagonist is fatally diverted from Protestant to Catholic soteriology, recurs less explicitly in *Othello*, but it is still audible—or would have been, to Shakespeare's audiences. To avoid his fatal error, Othello would have needed more faith in his wife's virtue, but also less faith in his own.

It is easy to overlook the latter point in a modern culture more interested in psychology than theology. One critic sees that Othello can resist Iago only by "an affirmation of faith which is beyond reason, by the act of choosing to believe in Desdemona. Shakespeare's point is that love is beyond reason";[59] but in Shakespeare's society that point would have borne distinct doctrinal resonances. Another critic shrewdly observes that Othello "loses faith in part because he never really had any"[60]—a remark applicable not only to conjugal trust, but also to the Christian faith that Calvinists believed (and the fifth of the nine Lambeth articles confirmed) could never be lost once truly achieved. Describing Othello as "something of a 'romantic idealist' where human nature is concerned,"[61] without noting that Elizabethan theologians emphatically were not, is dangerously ahistorical. In other words, the aspect of *Othello* I am describing has not been unseen in the play's critical history, only unrecognized as doctrinally factional.

Shakespeare repeatedly portrays Othello's pride as a claim of earned immunity from condemnation, not simply a boast of personal excellence.[62] Like several of Shakespeare's other disastrously presumptuous figures, and like several Jesuit theologians, Othello appears to imagine that worldly achievements can overturn original sin.[63] Hooker warned that no good Protestant should imagine he "can do God so much service, as shall be able to make a full and perfect satisfaction before the tribunal seat of God";[64] but Othello insists that "[m]y services which I have done the signiory / Shall out-tongue his complaints," overruling any "demerits," and that "[m]y parts, my title, and my perfect soul / Shall manifest me rightly" (I.ii.18–32). Only later does he perceive cuckoldry as a "destiny unshunnable, like death" that attaches to us "[w]hen we do quicken" (III.iii.277–79), and he still fails to perceive damnation in those terms.

When first confronted by the force of paternal law, Othello concedes that "little shall I grace my cause / In speaking for myself," and asks the Duke to "[s]end for the lady to the Sagittary, / And let her speak of me before her father" (I.iii.88–89, 115–16). This resembles the recognition that compelled Protestants (as in Herbert's "Judgment" and "The Quip") to ask Christ to speak on their behalf, rather than offer any self-defeating self-defense. The only valid plea is that the redemptive love—Desdemona's or Christ's—was entirely voluntary.[65] Unfortunately, Othello forgets that Desdemona loves him less for any self-sufficient virtues than "for the dangers I had passed, / And I loved her that she did pity them" (I.iii.166–67). Her pity is roused by his having been "taken by the insolent foe / And sold to slavery"—a commonplace metaphor (drawing on texts such as Rom. 3:24 and 6:16, and Matt. 13:39) for the forfeiture of human souls to Satan, which provoked Christ's redemptive sacrifice.[66]

Luther warns that, if a Christian were to "grow so foolish, however, as to presume to become righteous . . . by means of some good work, he would instantly lose faith and all its benefits";[67] and that is precisely what befalls Othello. His steepest descent occurs when Iago first leaves him alone in the temptation scene and Othello muses,

> Haply for I am black,
> And have not those soft parts of conversation
> That chamberers have, or for I am declined

> Into the vale of years—yet that's not much—
> She's gone; I am abused, and my relief
> Must be to loathe her. O curse of marriage. . . .
> (III.iii.265–70)

Othello was right to trust "My life upon her faith" (1.3.289), but it depended upon his own faith as well. Outside the solifidian position, there is nothing but despair, about himself and his entire race:

> Her name, that was as fresh
> As Dian's visage, is now begrimed and black
> As mine own face. If there be cords or knives,
> Poison or fire or suffocating streams,
> I'll not endure it.
> (III.iii.387–91)

Though emphatic, this last sentence fails to clarify whom he intends to kill; we may imagine him with the traditional noose and dagger of the prospective suicide, since what has seized him is loathing of himself (as inadequate lover) as much as loathing of Desdemona (as unfaithful lover). As Calvin argues repeatedly, despair leads to hatred of God through the hatred of self.

This syndrome—as much as any domestic naiveté or unlucky coincidence—destroys Othello's faith in Desdemona. Iago may drop hints, but what sends Othello careening downhill on his own momentum is a constriction of his understanding of charity: instead of experiencing Desdemona's love as self-evident and self-justifying, a transcendent manifestation of the goodness of the universe, Othello is coaxed back into experiencing it as (like the rest of his acceptance in Venice) the contingent reward of merit. At first he resists this temptation:

> 'Tis not to make me jealous
> To say my wife is fair, feeds well, loves company,
> Is free of speech, sings, plays and dances well:
> Where virtue is, these are more virtuous.
> Nor from mine own weak merits will I draw
> The smallest fear or doubt of her revolt,
> For she had eyes and chose me.
> (III.iii.185–91)

In seeing Othello's "visage in his mind" rather than his face (I.iii.248), Desdemona provides him with the same imputed worth requested in Canticles

1:5, as paraphrased by Luther: "Turn your attention not to my blackness, but to the kiss which God offers me, and then you will see that I am comely and lovable."[68] As soon as Othello starts measuring Desdemona's love by his worthiness to receive it, he is doomed; the more he worships her, the more he is bound to doubt her. Many Renaissance tracts, Calvinist and Catholic alike, warned of this dangerous spiritual labyrinth.

While entirely plausible as sexual jealousy, Othello's anguished alternation between praising Desdemona and hating her—almost comic at IV.i.169–88—also suggests the way his admiration generates his mistrust, as it must under a doctrine of merit. Like Elizabeth Cary's *Tragedy of Mariam*, *Othello* thus analyzes the unhappily familiar figure of the husband who alternately worships his wife with lavish gifts and sentimentality, and beats her in brutal possessiveness, a crime that leads him back to melodramatic regret and self-justification. Reformation psychology, like modern psychoanalysis, often attributes this syndrome to a man's repressed suspicion that he is unworthy of love.

So the jealous Othello is exasperating in a depressingly familiar manner, but also in the manner of Bunyan in "Grace Abounding," repeatedly lifted into assurance by some striking manifestation of divine love, only to be plunged back again into the tangle of self-loathing by satanic reminders of his unworthiness. After one joyful reunion with his Savior, Bunyan recalls, "I saw myself within the arms of grace and mercy . . . now I cried, Let me die. Now death was lovely and beautiful in my sight," producing a happier assurance of divine inheritance "than ever I shall be able to express while I live in this world."[69] This invites comparison with Othello's rhapsody at his reunion with Desdemona after the storm:

> O, my soul's joy,
> If after every tempest come such calms,
> May the winds blow till they have wakened death,
> . . . .
> If it were now to die,
> 'Twere now to be most happy; for I fear,
> My soul hath her content so absolute
> That not another comfort like to this
> Succeeds in unknown fate.
>   (II.i.176–85)

Desdemona's amendment to this passionate sentiment—"The heavens forbid / But that our loves and comforts should increase, / Even as our days do grow"—is a good marital precept that again matches Luther's prescription for faith: "these riches must grow from day to day even to the future life."[70]

Yet somehow that divine love goes bankrupt. I will not further tax the allegory by claiming that Othello's sarcastic pretense of hiring Desdemona as a whore parodies the sale of indulgences that drove Luther to begin the Reformation; but Othello is surely offering an unwitting commentary on his own assumption that her love was to be purchased in the first place, whether with cash or works or words. Perhaps he takes her for a "cunning whore of Venice" (IV.ii.89) because he is half aware that he has made her into the Whore of Babylon. In his deadly mixture of pride and suspicion, he resembles the "papists" who—according to an attack probably written in the same year as *Othello*—"preferre their owne workes, and merites fore-seene, and doe perversely accuse God of infidelity and falshood," because their pride forbids them to "beleeve that God were faythfull and constant."[71]

The Handkerchief and the Function of Sacraments

If only Othello had converted in Renaissance Zurich instead of Renaissance Venice, Zwingli could quickly have dispelled his ruinous overvaluation of the handkerchief. Zwingli condemns the Catholic belief that the sacramental object (Communion wine or a bloody cloth) creates rather than memorializes the sacred bond, and he discusses Communion by an explicit comparison to tokens of faithfulness between spouses: "in much the same way as a groom, wishing to assure his bride (if she had any doubts), gives her a ring . . . she, accepting that ring, believes that he is hers, and turns her heart away from all other lovers." Like this ring, and those in the markedly theological *Merchant of Venice*, the handkerchief supposedly contains and controls the marital fidelity of those between whom it is exchanged:

> while she kept it,
> 'Twould make her amiable and subdue my father
> Entirely to her love; but if she lost it
> Or made a gift of it, my father's eye
> Should hold her loathed.
> (III.iv.54–58)

Othello thus makes it function as the covenant of works functions in the Old Testament: "Keep my commandements, & thou shalt live, and mine instruction as the apple of thine eyes. Binde them upon thy fingers, and write them upon the table of thine heart" (Prov. 7:22–23).[72] Othello tells Desdemona, "Make it a darling like your precious eye. / To lose't or give't away were such perdition / As nothing else could match" (III.iv.62–64).

Desdemona has a more Protestant understanding of what does and what doesn't cause "perdition." Her efforts to deflect the discussion from lost linen back to Cassio's redemption—"It is not lost, but what and if it were. . . . This is a trick to put me from my suit" (III.iv.79–83)—are psychologically realistic, but they are also theologically appropriate, marking the distinction between the adiaphoric and the essential in Protestant salvation. Othello's mechanistic insistence on this artifact parodies a Catholic tendency to honor the physical eucharist or relic rather than the spirit it signifies:

> *Desdemona*: You'll never meet a more sufficient man.
> *Othello*: The handkerchief!
> *Desdemona*: I pray, talk me of Cassio.
> *Othello*: The handkerchief!
> *Desdemona*: A man that all his time
> Hath founded his good fortunes on your love,
> Shared dangers with you—
> *Othello*: The handkerchief!
> (III.iv.87–92)

There seems little question which belief system is more humane, and more spiritual as well.

In Middleton's *A Game at Chess*, the Jesuits use a "magical glass . . . bought of an Egyptian" (III.i.330), supposedly capable of revealing secret desires and marital destiny, to compromise the Protestant heroine. In *Othello*, Iago uses a "magic" handkerchief that Othello's mother purportedly acquired from "an Egyptian" (III.iv.65,52) to distract Othello from his transcendent recognition of Desdemona's transcendent virtue. This relic from Othello's former religion (as Protestants would complain about bloody shrouds and sumptuous vestments) obstructs the love of the savior, trapping it in a superstitious tradition. As Samuel Harsnett asked in a book we know Shakespeare read at about the time he wrote *Othello*, "Who doth not bewayle the sely doating Indian Nation, that falls down and performs divine adoration to a rag of red cloth?"[73] Iago acknowledges the theological aspect of the handkerchief, remarking that such "trifles" can become, for vulnerable spirits like Othello's, "confirmations strong / As proofs of holy writ" (III.iii.323–25). This was exactly what the Reformers condemned about the sensual rituals and material artifacts of the Roman church: that they tended to eclipse Scripture.[74] At the martyrdom of Edmund Campion, furthermore, "A young man who dropped his handkerchief into the blood on the ground was taken and committed";[75] blood-spotted handkerchiefs were evidently powerful relics among English Jesuits.

So while Shakespeare associates this handkerchief with the wedding sheets, probably through the ritual of showing the blood-spotted sheets as proof of a bride's virginity,[76] he also gestures mistrustfully toward "the best and chiefest ornament of Poperie [which] is the garment spotted of the flesh . . . that is, they retaine many carnall rites, ceremonies, and usages borrowed of the Jewes and Gentiles."[77] Shakespeare thus aligns the theological level with a psychological level on which Othello seems determined to punish Desdemona for staining his sheets as much as for misplacing his other bit of cloth: "Thy bed, lust-stained, shall with lust's blood be spotted" (V.i.36).

Othello's conviction that Desdemona gave her maidenhead to Cassio seems far less explicable than his parallel conviction about her handkerchief. But Catholic doctrine condemning even married concupiscence as sinful may help to explain the psychological syndrome that Edward Snow and Stephen Greenblatt have brilliantly articulated, whereby Othello perceives Desdemona as corrupt precisely because she is sexual.[78] A Pelagian suspicion that if people are fallen, it must be because they have committed some evil work, may underlie Othello's conclusion that, if his wife's desire seems transgressive, it must mean that she has committed adultery.[79]

The dangers of Othello's vestigial paganism persistently resemble the dangers English Puritans saw in vestigial Catholicism, which supposedly (like the Othello Brabantio envisions accusingly) "enchanted" worshipers with "chains of magic . . . gross in sense" through "arts inhibited and out of warrant" (I.ii.63–79). The idolatry of the handkerchief is a logical extension of the idolatrous tendency Protestants commonly identified in uxorious passions like Othello's for Desdemona. As he prepares to kill his potential savior, Othello seems to be "enacting unwittingly a kind of *tenebrae* service"[80]—distinctly Catholic—and comes tantalizingly close to recognizing the archetypal crime he is thereby about to commit. Bestowing on Desdemona a treacherous final kiss, he says her "balmy breath . . . doth almost persuade / Justice to break her sword" (V.ii.16–17)—precisely what Christ's love was supposed to do to the Old Testament's strict covenant of works. Recalling this moment during his suicide ("I kissed thee ere I killed thee" (V.ii.354)), Othello will cast himself as Judas—the role Protestants persistently assigned to Jesuits.[81]

For the moment, however, Othello assumes he is being a good Catholic. If Desdemona is no longer a virgin, if she is not carved in "monumental alabaster" (V.ii.5), then he was wrong to worship her. Instead he will kill her proudly, on behalf of "the cause," on behalf of his long-suppressed sacrificial religion, because "she must die, else she'll betray more men" (V.ii.1–6). This resembles the rationale Iago provides Roderigo—"'Tis but a man gone" (V.i.10)—and both echo supposed Jesuit rationales for assassinating Elizabeth.[82] During the Gunpowder Plot trials, Henry Garnet was accused of assuring fellow Jesuits "with his ghostly counsel that it was both lawful and meritorious" to assassinate Elizabeth, that it was not murder but a sacrifice.[83] Such arguments had already been caricatured on the English stage in *The Troublesome Raigne of King John*—a clear exercise in Reformation propaganda, adapted more moderately in Shakespeare's *King John*—in the words of a regicidal monk.[84] Protestants associated these arguments with Caiaphas's logic in sacrificing Jesus because "it is expedient for us, that one man dye for the people, and that the whole nacion perish not" (John 11:50).[85]

Even after the murder, Shakespeare continues to tease us with hints that Othello is "almosting" (to borrow James Joyce's useful neologism) the Protestant conversion that could have saved his wife's life and might still save his soul.[86] Letting go of his "sword of Spain," Othello exclaims, "O vain boast! / Who can control his fate?" (V.ii.251, 262–63). This provides a theological mode of dramatic irony; he needs only to apply this conclusion about his temporal fate to his eternal one.[87] Emilia tells him, "This deed of thine is no more worthy heaven, / Than thou wast worthy her" (V.ii.159–60), as if Othello had indeed expected to earn salvation.[88]

Othello's need to feel justified by his works, evident in his first confrontation with the Venetian authorities, becomes almost grotesquely marked in the speech before his suicide, which begins by reminding everyone that he has "done the state some service," and suggests that they need "nothing extenuate" in order to react to his crime sympathetically.[89] Both T. S. Eliot and F. R. Leavis are appalled by Othello's egotism in recounting his slaying of the "circumcised" Turk who "beat a Venetian" in Aleppo, and then re-enacting that slaying as a suicide.[90] Perhaps Eliot's high-church affiliations discouraged him from noticing how much his attacks on Othello's boastfulness resemble Renaissance Protestant attacks on Catholic penitential and salvational theology. Eliot complains that Othello here "has ceased to think about Desdemona, and is thinking about himself. Humility is the most difficult of all virtues to achieve; nothing dies harder than the desire to think well of oneself";[91] change "Desdemona" to "Christ" and Eliot's complaint closely matches a standard Protestant complaint about any covenant of merit. Hooker, for example, argues that "[t]he enemye that waiteth for all occasions to worke our ruyne, hath ever founde it harder to overthrowe an humble synner, then a prowde Sainte: There is no mans case so daungerous as his, whome sathan hath perswaded that his owne righteousnes shall presente him pure and blameles in the sighte of god."[92]

Leavis observes that "in the new marital situation, this egotism [of Othello] isn't going to be the less dangerous for its nobility"; the same point applies to the New Testament situation, as articulated by the Reformers such as Hooker. If Leavis is right that there is something unappealing about the way "Othello dies belonging to the world of action"[93]—and there is certainly something of the antique as well as the modern Roman about him here— perhaps it is because he dies in a tragically misguided universe of works. So while this speech may be morally repugnant, it is also theologically revealing, if read in conjunction with Paul's argument concerning the divine love

> which is riche in mercie, through his great love wherewith he loved us.... For by grace are ye saved through faith, and that not of your selves: it is the gift of God. Not of workes, lest any man shulde boaste him self.... Wherefore remember that ye being in times past Gentiles in the flesh, & called uncircumcision of them, which are called circumcision in the flesh, made with hands, That ye were, I say, at that time without Christ, & were aliantes from the commune welth of Israel, & were strangers from the covenants of promes, & had no hope, & were without God in the worlde. But now in Christ Jesus, ye which were once farre of, are made nere by the blood of Christ. For he is our peace, which hathe made of bothe one.... Now therefore ye are no more strangers & foreners: but citizens with the Saintes, and of the housholde of God.
> (Eph. 2:4–9)

Interpreters of *Othello* need to be aware of the potential domestic tragedy of that household, played out in the domestic tragedy that was Tudor–Stuart England.

Othello thus enacts what Luther considered "the greatest tragedy" a human soul could endure, a sort of Protestant morality play:

> See him plaguing himself night and day ... wearing a hair shirt, and going on pilgrimages to St. Iago clad in armor. And yet it is in vain; with all these works he will merit nothing but hell-fire. He will not find Christ, who alone reconciles the father to us, forgives sin, brings God's grace, and leads us from hell to heaven. It is the greatest tragedy that we will go in quest of all this after we have thrust Christ aside.[94]

Reformation theology thus provides a theme for the Othello music, and it remains audible at the highest moments of dramatic emotion. Othello's furious condemnation of himself to diabolical torture and his final suicide appear as hopelessly self-referential acts of pride: further efforts to put on the new man by the wrong kind of sacrifice.[95] He explicitly reconsecrates his life to the Christian cause at the end, but in this unredeemed manner. One critic insists, "The audience knows that in his renunciation of evil, his penance and expiation, Othello has merited salvation";[96] but surely a Reformed audience would see the claim to merit as the problem, not the solution. Any audience, furthermore, must recognize that Othello is quite wrong to imagine Desdemona accusingly consigning him to damnation (V.ii.270–73).

In *Othello* as in *King Lear*, the proud protagonist wrongly believes that love can and must be measured and recompensed; the Christlike woman, Desdemona or Cordelia, is martyred trying to convince him otherwise. Desdemona seemingly tries to raise her Venice from Catholic to Protestant religion, as Cordelia tries to raise her England from paganism to Christianity. Lear wonders what could cause the "hard hearts" of his bad daughters, without asking what enabled the greater miracle of his good daughter's tender one. Critics have scrutinized the motives of Iago's hatred, without noticing that Desdemona's love is no more easily explicable. The impossibility of explaining charity rationally is no less significant for a Christian exegesis than the enigma of ruthlessness, which has at least some basis in creaturely self-interest.

In their determination to turn the Catholic-associated tradition of cycle plays "into vehicles of propaganda" for the Protestant cause, Tudor playwrights succeeded only "in boring their audiences rather than entertaining them, and drove them into the arms of the professional players."[97] Shakespeare was there to welcome them, as his first tetralogy demonstrates, "not repudiating the genre of religious drama, but giving it fresh vitality in the light of the ecclesiastical and aesthetic controversies generated by the Reformation."[98]

That Catholics felt oppressed by such tendentious literature is evident from a title page of the period:

> *The Discoverie and Confutation of a Tragical Fiction, Devysed and Played by Edward Squyer yeoman soldier, hanged at Tyburne the 23. of Novemb. 1598 Wherein the argument and fable is, that he should be sent from Spain to poyson the Queen and the Earle of Essex, but the meaning and the moralization therof was, to make odious the Jesuites, and by them all Catholiques.*[99]

If Jesuits felt they were being cast as the villains in grand tragedies for the sake of discrediting Catholic religion, then perhaps it was occurring in literal theaters as well as in the theaters of statecraft. By making Desdemona a Christlike heroine, Iago a jesuitical devil, and Othello an imperfectly reformed infidel, Shakespeare renews the polemical function of the morality play for a new theological era, depicting a Protestant ideal of marriage sustainable only through the Protestant version of love, as a gift that nothing earthly can earn or repay. I'm not entirely sure what Shakespeare believed in 1604, or wanted us to believe. But a Jacobean audience convinced to value spontaneous love above Venetian traditions, to condemn Othello for letting the dubious evidence of his senses distract him from the certain devotion of his heart, and to hate Iago for deluding Christians into believing in reward and retaliation rather than love, would have found itself endorsing the Protestant Reformation.

NOTES

An abbreviated version of this argument has been published as "*Othello* as Protestant Propaganda," in *Religion and Culture in Renaissance England*, ed. Claire McEachern and Debora K. Shuger (Cambridge: Cambridge University Press, 1997), 234–57. Kind permission to reprint is gratefully acknowledged.

   1. See, for example, Roy Battenhouse, "Shakespearean Tragedy: A Christian Approach," in *Approaches to Shakespeare*, ed. Norman Rabkin (New York: McGraw-Hill, 1964), 209; Paul N. Siegel, *Shakespearean Tragedy and the Elizabethan Compromise* (New York: New York University Press, 1957), 131; and J. A. Bryant, Jr., *Hippolyta's View*, 140. My argument opposes that of Robert H. West ("The Christianness of *Othello*," *Shakespeare Quarterly* 15 [1964]: 333–43), which claims that no systematic theology is discernible in the play, though I agree with him that the theology remains secondary to the realistic level of plot. Roland Mushat Frye (*Shakespeare and Christian Doctrine* [Princeton: Princeton University Press, 1963]), argues that Shakespeare's "references to the commonplace topics of theology are never introduced into the drama for doctrinaire reasons, and the action of the plays is never subservient to the presentation of any systematic theology" (9); one need not dispute the second half of that statement to dispute the first. For similar reasons (though my work benefits from his), I dissent from the opinion of Naseeb Shaheen in "The Use of Scripture in *Othello*" (*University of Mississippi Studies in English* 6 [1988]), that "the references make it clear that Shakespeare had no theological message to convey" (58).

   2. Martin Luther himself evokes this caricature: "The papists . . . still boast in these sacrilegious words, 'Whoever does this or that merits the forgiveness of sins; whoever serves this or that holy order, to him we give a sure promise of eternal life'" (*Works*, vol. 26, ed. Jaroslav Pelikan and Helmut Lehmann [Philadelphia: Muhlenberg], 140). And even so moderate a figure as Hooker similarly conflates Catholicism with Pelagianism; see his *Works*, vol. 5, ed. W. Speed Hill (Cambridge: Harvard University Press, 1990), 130, 153, 158–59. For comparable distortions in Shakespeare's culture, see note 24 below. It also seems probable that this vulgarization of their soteriology was used by Catholics to promote their religion as well as by Protestants to attack it.

   3. John N. King, *English Reformation Literature* (Princeton: Princeton University Press, 1982), 378.

   4. Margot Heinemann, *Puritanism and Theatre: Thomas Middleton and Opposition Drama under the Early Stuarts* (Cambridge: Cambridge University Press, 1980), 48. Peggy Muñoz Simonds, in *Myth, Emblem, and Music in Shakespeare's "Cymbeline"* (Newark: University of Delaware Press, 1992), discerns Protestant affirmation in

that play's iconography of birds; while conceding that references are not "systematically worked out as an allegory," Simonds notes that "questions of religious doctrine
could not legally be discussed in Jacobean theaters, despite the interest of such for-
bidden questions to audiences of the period. The poet's main recourse in the face of
this prohibition was the art of poetic allusion" (227).

5. Julia Gasper, "The Reformation Plays on the Public Stage," in *Theatre
and Government under the Early Stuarts*, ed. J. R. Mulryne and Margaret Shewring
(Cambridge: Cambridge University Press, 1993), 190.

6. "He ought to think, 'although I am an unworthy and condemned man, my
God has given me in Christ all the riches of righteousness and salvation without any
merit on my part, out of pure, free mercy, so that from now on I need nothing except
faith which believes that this is true'" (Martin Luther, *The Freedom of a Christian
Man* [1520]; excerpted in Hans J. Hillerbrand, ed., *The Protestant Reformation* [New
York: Harper, 1968], 21–22).

7. Garry Wills, in *Witches and Jesuits* (New York: Oxford University Press,
1995), has argued that *Macbeth* is largely anti-Jesuit propaganda, responsive to the
Gunpowder Plot; my argument finds similar tendencies in Shakespeare a couple of
years earlier. For whatever conviction it might add, Heinemann, in *Puritanism and
Theatre*, reports that Shakespeare's patron Pembroke "is known to have been leader
of the anti-Spanish group on the Privy Council, and widely regarded as 'head of
the Puritans' (in the Venetian ambassador's phrase)" (168). Donna B. Hamilton,
in *Shakespeare and the Politics of Protestant England* (Lexington: University of Kentucky, 1992), notes on p. 22 that both Pembroke and Shakespeare's other patron,
Southampton, stood firmly on the Calvinist side in England; on p. 28 she describes
"Pembroke's position as recognised leader of the Protestant (Calvinist and anti-
Arminian) and anti-Spanish faction of the Privy Council"; and on p. 163 asserts
that "[a]nti-Catholic rhetoric, appropriated in *Cymbeline* from the oath of allegiance
controversy, was one of the central discourses of English religious and political life
for three centuries." Certainly it is clear enough that much early Elizabethan drama
was fundamentally Protestant apologetic, so it seems plausible that Shakespeare
might incorporate a subtler version of that apologetic into his drama.

On the other hand, Thomas Rymer, a much better seventeenth-century Puritan than I am, certainly found nothing to like in *Othello*; and Shakespeare's other
plays and Stratford affiliations suggest Catholic sympathies. John Henry de Groot
(*The Shakespeares and "The Old Faith"* [New York: King's Crown Press, 1946]) insists
that he "does not intend to prove that William Shakespeare was a Catholic," only
that he "held a greater respect for the Catholic faith than is sometimes supposed"
(158). De Groot argues that Southampton would have been a Catholic sympathizer
(223). He notes that Shakespeare "did not follow the lead of the Puritan movement"
with its emphasis on Pauline texts (164), and that the evidence of Shakespeare's
preference for the Protestant Geneva Bible "can be overestimated" (160). In any case,
in dealing with Shakespeare, evidence that produces contradictions is probably more
accurate than that which produces any univocal theology.

Finally, since the question seems inevitable, I should say that, while my argument may be misguided, it is not driven by personal attachment to the Protestant
cause. The Shakespeare I am proposing is not made in my own image.

8. "The Fourme of the Solemnizacyon of Matrymonye," *The First and Second
Prayer Books of King Edward the Sixth*, 1549, 1552, ed. Ernest Rhys (London: J.
M. Dent, n.d.), 410; Martin Luther, *The Liberty of a Christian* (1520), citing Eph.

5:31–32; quoted in Alister E. McGrath, *Reformation Thought*, 2nd ed. (Oxford: Basil Blackwell, 1993), 99. Later in this passage Luther discusses the way Christ insists on entering the identity and sharing the painful struggles of his mortal spouse (Hillerbrand, *Protestant Reformation*, 11); this recalls Desdemona's wish that "heaven had made her such a man," and her related insistence on accompanying him, both for pleasure and for pain, in his voyage against the infidels. Her insistence on accompanying Othello to the wars, on the grounds that she will not abandon the intimate "rites for why I love him," resembles other important Reformation descriptions of this soteriological marriage as well. John Calvin says that the salvational "promises offer [Christ], not so that we may end up with the mere sight and knowledge of him, but that we enjoy a true communication of him." See similarly Philip Melanchthon: "Having ingrafted us into his body, Christ makes us partakers, not only of all his benefits, but also of himself" (quoted in McGrath, *Reformation Thought*, 100).

9. Irving Ribner, in *Patterns in Shakespearean Tragedy* (London: Methuen, 1960), argues that "[i]n the perfection of her love Desdemona reflects the love of Christ for man" (95). The reading "Judean" depends on the Folio text of the play, which is primary for my argument, though (aside from III.iii.388–93) nothing important to my argument disappears in the main Quartos. Citations are based on *Othello*, in the *New Cambridge Shakespeare*, ed. Norman Sanders (Cambridge: Cambridge University Press, 1984).

10. Cassio's worship of Desdemona has overtones of Mariolatry (cf. II.i.84–87), and he earlier endorsed a Catholic *via media* whereby heaven saves those who steer themselves (II.i.44–51).

11. Edmund of Beauval, in W.B. ed., *The Confession and Publike Recantation of Thirteene Learned Personages* (London, 1602), trans. from the 1601 Dutch text, sig. H3r; Martin Luther, *Commentary on St. Paul's Epistle to the Galatians* (1535), excerpted in Hillerbrand, *Protestant Reformation*, 105; see also p. 92. George Downame (*A Treatise of Justification* [London, 1639]) calls Christ "our Intercessor and Advocate to plead for us . . . Mediator and Advocate" to the Father who is "Judge" (10).

12. She then sends word to Cassio that "I have moved my lord on his behalf and hope all will be well" (III.iv.15–16), insisting that she has done her best for him, "So help me every spirit sanctified," but that her lord's anger means that she must put herself at risk as well to reconcile them. Othello insists he cannot forgive as unconditionally as Desdemona asks—perhaps a political necessity, but perhaps also a hint that he cannot understand the principle of absolute forgiveness, not earned with penance, that is essential to the Reformation understanding of salvation.

Desdemona's subsequent submission clearly announces its theological character (IV.ii.150–60). Innocent in thought as well as deed, Desdemona seems to understand the morality of the Sermon on the Mount, and has nothing to fear from it; yet she does not condemn. Her reaction to even the worst kind of villainy is "heaven pardon him" (IV.ii.134; the more human Emilia corrects this to "hell gnaw his bones"). Her insistence that her righteous behavior should have exempted her from her lord's cruel judgment (IV.ii.106–08) clearly echoes Christ (John 8:46). Similarly, she tells Othello, "And have you mercy too! I never did / Offend you in my life" (V.ii.59–60), echoing Christ precisely where He makes the point Othello's doctrine of works overlooks: "Be ye therefore merciful, as your Father also is merciful. Judge not, and ye shall not be judged" (Luke 5:36–37). She has loved according to the "general warranty of heaven" (V.ii.60), and in her brief resurrection she adds,

"A guiltless death I die" (V.ii.123). She cries out "O Lord, Lord, Lord," which one critic has identified as an echo of Christ's dying "Lord, Lord, why hast thou forsaken me?" (see Robert G. Hunter, *Shakespeare and the Mystery of God's Judgments* [Athens: University of Georgia Press, 1976], 151; this point depends on the Quarto text). Hunter, however, believes that finally "[t]he tragedy is entirely without a supernatural dimension" (129) and that it ultimately endorses Pelagianism—quite the opposite of the argument I perceive. Roy Battenhouse, in his *Shakespearean Tragedy: Its Art and Christian Premises* (Bloomington: Indiana University Press, 1969), argues that "[w]e need not infer that Shakespeare was equating Desdemona with Christ" (97); but it seems to me that we are repeatedly encouraged to do so.

13. If this seems a grotesquely literal reading of the Eucharist, it may be worth noting that the great Swiss reformer condemned the traditional notion of full transubstantiation as suitable only if "one is living among the Anthropophagi"—precisely where Othello has been (I.iii.143–44); see Huldrych Zwingli, *True and False Religion*, excerpted in Hillerbrand, *Protestant Reformation*, 112.

14. See, for example, Downame, *Treatise of Justification*, 12.

15. John Donne, "Show Me Deare Christ, Thy Spouse," lines 13–14 (*Complete Poetry*, ed. John T. Shawcross [New York: Anchor, 1967]).

16. Excerpted in Hillerbrand, *Protestant Reformation*, 11. "For what is the remission of sin," asks Downame (*Treatise of Justification*, 24), "but the not imputing of it"; cf. 1 Pet. 2:22–24, which describes Christ as one "[w]ho did no sinne, neither was there guile found in his mouth. Who when he was reviled, reviled not againe: when he suffred, he threatened not, but committed it to him that judgeth righteously. Who his owne self bore our sinnes in his bodie. . . ." (cited by Peter Milward in *Biblical Influences* [Bloomington: Indiana University Press, 1987], 104); see similarly "Of Charity," in *Certain Sermons and Homilies* (1603; rpt. Oxford: Oxford University Press, 1844), 57; and Hooker, *Works*, vol. 5, 112–13. Desdemona's self-accusation leads Othello to conclude that "she's like a liar gone to burning hell"—an echo of Revelations 21:8, but only valid in the sense that she is mercifully absorbing his sin. She is a savior gone to burning hell, temporarily, to harrow it, to keep him out of it.

17. Walter Starkie (*The Road to Santiago: Pilgrims of St. James* [London: John Murray, 1957]) reports that "Saint James the Apostle . . . became *Santiago Matamoros* or 'Moorslayer'"; see also 25–27. Lena Cowen Orlin, *Private Matters and Public Culture in Post-Reformation England* (Ithaca: Cornell University Press, 1994), 205, Barbara Everett, *Young Hamlet* (New York: Oxford University Press, 1989), 190, and Samuel L. Macey, *Notes and Queries* 25 (1978), 143–45, note a possible connection between Iago and Santiago, but none pursues the further connection to James's Epistle and its soteriological import; they recognize the anomalous Spanish aspect of some names in the play, but do not connect it to theology. Yet Santiago Compostela rivaled Rome as a center of Catholicism in the Middle Ages, and Santiago himself was believed to provide supernatural aid against religious enemies, like the storm in *Othello* that destroys the Turks; see Americo Castro, *The Spaniards*, trans. Willard F. King and Selma Margaretten (Berkeley: University of California Press, 1971), 386 and 225.

18. Luther, *Works*, vol. 23, 261. Cf. vol. 23, 24, 43, 121; vol. 5, 247; vol. 22, 51, 287, 405, 421, 502; and vol. 22, 365, where it is compared with the practices of Turks.

19. The grudge becomes clearer when Luther suggests ejecting the book from the Wittenberg curriculum on the theory that "some Jew wrote it"; and when he admits that "[t]hat Epistle of James gives us much trouble, for the Papists embrace it

alone. . . . I almost feel like throwing Jimmy into the stove" (see Luther, *Works*, vol. 35, 396; vol. 54, 424; vol. 34, 317). John Calvin (*Commentaries*, trans. John Owen [Edinburgh, 1855], 309–17) takes the other tack, trying to twist the text somehow into solid solifidianism; see similarly Hooker, *Works*, vol. 5, 128–29.

20. Thomas Dekker, *The Whore of Babylon*, ed. Marianne Gateson Riely (New York: Garland, 1980). Frank R. Ardolino, in "'In Saint Iagoes Parke': Iago as *Catholic* Machiavel in Dekker's *The Whore of Babylon*" (*Names: Journal of the American Name Society* 30:1 [1982]: 1–4), argues that Dekker is here drawing on the notoriety of Shakespeare's villain to make his own the more repellent. If Dekker is indeed alluding to *Othello* in this intensely anti-Jesuit allegory, it would prove that at least one contemporary recognized an anti-Jesuit element in Shakespeare's depiction of Iago. But even if there is no connection between the plays, Dekker's use of the name still indicates an expectation that it would have ominously jesuitical associations for the original audiences of *Othello*.

21. Harold Bloom, in his "Introduction" to *Iago* (New York: Chelsea House, 1992), argues that "Iago's marvelous boast: 'I am not what I am' . . . echoes and undoes St. Paul's 'By the grace of God I am what I am'" (2). The White Knight in Middleton's *A Game at Chess* feigns Jesuit tendencies by claiming that "[t]he time is yet to come that e'er I spoke / What my heart meant" (V.iii.145–46). Tactically, Iago resembles this play's villainous Jesuit confessors who, "Finding to what point their blood most inclines, / Know best to apt them to our designs" (*The Works of Thomas Middleton*, vol. 7, ed. A. H. Bullen [Boston: Houghton Mifflin, 1886], I.i.114–15); the earlier parts of this speech also echo Iago suggestively.

22. Etienne Pasquier, *The Jesuites Catechisme* (trans. 1602), sig. A2r. In Thomas Bell, *The Golden Balance of Tryall* (London, 1603), "A Counter-Blast" warns that "the Jesuites came into *England*, by the instigation of the Divell. These Jesuites make it an usual practise, to publish scandalous libels . . ." (43). For further evidence of this association, see Daniel Stempel, "The Silence of Iago," *PMLA* 84 (1969): 252–63, which further demonstrates (p. 256) that Catholics were associated with the doctrine of salvation by works in Protestant polemics of the period.

23. Phillip Stubbes, *Anatomy of Abuses*, vol. 2, 6–7, ed. F. J. Furnivall (London, 1877–82); quoted by Stempel, in "Silence of Iago," 260. Unlike the other enemies of Venice, Iago can pass as a loyal citizen, which was a common Elizabethan complaint about Jesuits; and, like them, he solicits confidences only to turn "the wife's against her husband: the husband's against his wife, and the servants of them both . . . to tyranize over them" (Christopher Bagshaw, *A Sparing Discoverie of our English Jesuits* [1601], 16).

24. Several of Shakespeare's countrymen encourage this confusion in pamphlets written about the same time as *Othello*. John Hull, in *The Unmasking of the Politique Atheist* (London, 1602), sig. B3r, asks, "Would you know where to finde *Pelagianisme?* then have recourse to popery." Herman Renecher, in *The Golden Chayne of Salvation* (London, 1604), asserts that papists "follow and maintayne the damnable opinion, and manifest dotage of the *Pelagians*" (172). Thomas Bell (*The Downefall of Poperie* [London, 1604], 61) claims that the Council of Trent allowed people to believe they could "truly merit the increase of grace." Of course these are all crudely popularized versions of the doctrinal dispute. See also Dudley Fenner's, *An Antiquodlibet, or Advertisement to Beware of Secular Priests* (Middleburgh, 1602), which claims that Catholics try to hide their most evil beliefs and tendencies from the English public by attributing them exclusively to Jesuits.

25. Michael Neill, in "Changing Places in *Othello*" (*Shakespeare Survey* 37 [1984]: 120), describes this deviation from the source plot, where Iago's primary motive appears to be erotic rivalry.

26. Echoing Catholic arguments from antiquity, Iago also grumbles that the "old gradation" of cumulative works has given way to a system in which "[p]referment goes by letter and affection" (I.i.36–37).

27. Frye, Shakespeare and Christian Doctrine, 23–24.

28. John Jewel (*An Apology of the Church of England* [1564], ed. J. E. Booty [Ithaca: Cornell University Press, 1963], 38), condemns Catholics for relying on "mediators" other than Christ.

29. Andrew Willet, *A Catholicon* (Cambridge, 1602), sig. A1v.

30. Downame similarly accuses Catholics of having "turned Religion into a meere outward formality" (*Treatise of Justification*, 12). Iago's is an iconophilic "Divinity of hell" who induces and performs "the blackest sins" under the cover of "heavenly shows" (II.iii.317–19).

31. Bagshaw, *A Sparing Discoverie of our English Jesuits*, 26–27; see similarly William Watson, *A Decacordon of Ten Quodlibetical Questions* (1602), 37–38.

32. "The Double P.P." (1606), in *The Non-Dramatic Works of Thomas Dekker*, vol. 2 (Huth Library; rpt. Ann Arbor: University of Michigan Microfilms, 1962), 172; see also p. 176 on the Jesuit use of surrogates to perform their murders.

33. Renecher, *The Golden Chayne of Salvation*, 177.

34. Roderigo complains that "[t]he jewels you have had from me to deliver to Desdemona would half have corrupted a votarist" (IV.ii.184–85), which directly evokes the familiar accusation of Catholic priestly greed, and indirectly evokes the no less familiar accusation of sexual corruption under the guise of monastic renunciation and charity. Hull argues that Catholics draw in converts primarily in order to "picke their purses" (*Unmasking the Politique Atheist*, sig. D3n); cf. I.iii. 381 and the confession of Melchior Romain, in W.B., *Confession and Publike Recantation*, sig. E3r: "golde, silver, favours, and liberalities with the Pope can worke much," as when the Jesuits offered a huge sum "that *Ignatius* their patron and first founder may be canonized."

35. Christopher Morrell, in *An Answer Unto the Catholique Supplication* (London, 1603), insists no Catholics "received the sentence of death onely for professing the Romish religion, except treason were thereunto also annexed" (sig. A4r); in the same way, the audience of *Othello* may be encouraged to think of the repression of Catholics as justified by the crimes of Iago, rather than motivated by mere sectarian bigotry. Robert Cecil, in *A Declaration of the favourable dealing of her Majesties Commission* (London, 1583), also argues that no one was tortured merely for Catholic beliefs. Father John Gerard (*The Condition of Catholics Under James I*, ed. John Morris [London: Longmans, Green, 1871], 31–35) offers a more plaintive view of the seizure of lands from Catholics by the government of King James.

36. John Gerard (*Autobiography of an Elizabethan*, trans. Philip Caraman [London: Longman, 1951]), 72–73) boasts that, despite all the "threats and tortures," neither he nor any of his fellow Jesuits "spoke a syllable that could be used in evidence against any of us" by the Elizabethan government (cited in Stempel, "Silence of Iago," 262).

37. Robin Clifton, "Fear of Popery," in *The Origins of the English Civil War*, ed. Conrad Russell (London: Macmillan, 1973), 155. In accusing Henry Garnet of complicity in the Gunpowder Plot, Edward Coke insinuated Garnet's complicity

with the Armada, among other subversions; see Philip Caraman, *Henry Garnet 1555–1606 and the Gunpowder Plot* (New York: Farrar, Straus, 1964), 397–99.

38. When Iago makes a dubious assertion, he swears it "is true, or else I am a Turk" (II.i.113); when he provokes the "barbarous brawl" in Cyprus, Othello thinks the participants have "turned Turks" (II.iii.151); and it seems clear enough that Iago serves as an agent of internal subversion who resumes—indeed, literalizes—the infidel assault that the Turkish armada had failed to complete. In Pasquier's *The Jesuites Catechisme*, "The Secular Priests Preface" identifies Catholic plots against Elizabeth as "cruell, barbarous, and Turkish stratagems"; see also p. 232. Willet similarly insists that both the idolatrous and the regicidal tendencies of Catholics "farre exceed the barbarous Mahumetans the Turkes," particularly in fomenting "mutins" (Willet, *A Catholicon*, sig. B1r).

39. Luther, *Works*, vol. 26, 10, 134; cf. 270, 400–401. Hooker (*Works*, vol. 5, 131–32) similarly speculates "whether the churche of Rome for this one opinion of workes maie be thought . . . no more a christian churche then are the assembles of Turkes or Jewes."

40. King James I, *A Booke of Proclamations* (London, 1609).

41. Sir Henry Wotton, *Life and Letters*, ed. Logan Pearsall Smith (Oxford: Clarendon, 1907), vol. 1, 318, 75–86 (cited in Stempel, "Silence of Iago," 262).

42. James Calderwood, *The Properties of "Othello"* (Amherst: University of Massachusetts Press, 1989), 9.

43. When he imagines that Cassio will fall into his clutches because, in flirting with Desdemona, "it had been better you had not kissed your three fingers so oft, which now again you are most apt to play the sir in" (II.i.167–69), we may recall Luther's warning (Hillerbrand, *Protestant Reformations*, 7) that the doctrine of works resembles "kissing one's own hand" (cf. Job 31:27–28); again the problem of personal vanity has a theological extension.

44. Simonds describes Posthumus's fall much as I describe Othello's: "once in Rome, Posthumus falls from grace when he seeks proof of his bride's virtue (or lack of virtue) . . . he enters into the despicable wager with Iachimo, the tempter, instead of having faith in his beloved. . . . From a theological point of view, Posthumus is here defying the Protestant belief that one cannot know what is in the mind of God beyond what is already revealed in the scriptures" (*Myth, Emblem, and Music*, 218).

On the difference between "Certainty of Evidence" and the superior "Certainty of Adherence" see Hooker, *Works*, vol. 5, 69–71; though the distinction is drawn from Aquinas, Hooker uses it to endorse Protestantism. Even Othello's seemingly defiant demand for "ocular proof" concerning Desdemona (III.iii.361) is an unwitting echo of Iago's own argument that he deserved "election" because Othello's "eyes had seen the proof" of his merits in settings "Christian and heathen" (I.i.27–30). Luther, in *Bondage of the Will* (trans. J. I. Packer and O. R. Johnston [London: Clarke, 1957], 101), warns that "[f]aith's object is things not seen."

45. Regina Schwartz, talk delivered at the 1994 Shakespeare Association of America Convention, Albuquerque, New Mexico. Luther (in Hillerbrand, *Protestant Reformation*, 25) reports that the enemies of Protestantism "do not care a fig for the things which are of the essence of our faith"; and the other time Iago exclaims to Roderigo about figs, it is again to deny that we must submit ourselves to supernatural forces to achieve goodness: "Virtue? a fig! 'Tis in ourselves that we are thus or thus" (I.iii.313). This raises, in an extreme form, an issue closer to the core of the play's action, and (for Luther if not for Zwingli) closer to the core of the

Reformation: whether we have any control over our prospects for salvation; see A. G. Dickens, *The English Reformation* (1964; rpt. New York: Shocken, 1976), 60. The notion that the human soul can achieve condign merit was associated with Catholicism, as it edged toward Pelagianism; and Iago's speech has analogues in Pelagius, according to Battenhouse (*Shakespearean Tragedy*, 382).

46. Huldrych Zwingli, "On the Lord's Supper," in *Zwingli and Bullinger*, ed. and trans. G. W. Bormiley, Library of Christian Classics 24 (Philadelphia: Westminster Press, 1953), 227. The Lollards had long maintained a similar view in England. See also Dickens, *The English Reformation*, 172.

47. Thomas Bell, *The Downefall of Poperie* (London, 1604) 19; for Bell's attack on Catholic literal-mindedness about transubstantiation, see pp. 19–27. For similar attacks in other works of the period, see John Rider, *A Friendly Caveat to Irelands Catholicks* (Dublin, 1602), sigs. B3v–G4r, esp. sig. F3r on "the blood of the grapes"; see also W.B., *Confession and Publike Recantation*, sigs. A1v and D3v.

48. Jewel, *Apology of the Church of England*, 33.

49. As Luther wrote in *The Blessed Sacrament of the Holy and True Body of Christ*, "In the sacraments we see nothing wonderful—just ordinary water, bread and wine, and the words of a preacher. . . . But we must learn to discover what a glorious majesty lies hidden beneath these despised things. It is precisely the same with Christ in the incarnation. We see a frail, weak, and mortal human being—yet he is nothing other than the majesty of God himself" (quoted in McGrath, *Reformation Thought*, 164). I hope the same point may serve to defend the notion that Shakespeare and his audiences could have accepted Desdemona as a provisional representative of Christ within the theatrical ritual.

50. Iago thus explains to Roderigo why he still appears dutiful toward the general he professes to hate: "I must show out a flag and sign of love, / Which is indeed but sign" (I.i.155–56). Again, the Zwinglian position does depend on interpreting the Eucharist as the sign rather than the reality of Christ's gracious presence—but without surrendering the authenticity of the divine love implied in the sacrament. No less provocative is Iago's argument to Cassio that wine is merely "a good familiar, rightly used"; the taint of petty magic, normally used by Protestants to condemn Catholic demonology, is here projected back onto the transactional aspect of Protestant eucharistic theory.

51. Quoted in McGrath, *Reformation Thought*, 164.

52. Calderwood, (*The Properties of "Othello,"* 116) calls the ritual that overrides Othello's marriage vows "a black mass parody of a wedding in which [Iago] takes Desdemona's place"; but Neill ("Changing Places in *Othello*", 129–30) demonstrates that it is also a substitute marriage. The homoerotics of this new marriage, as indeed of Iago's story about Cassio's lascivious dream, evoke the sodomital taint of antimonastic polemics. Alan Bray (*Homosexuality in Renaissance England* [London: Gay Men's Press, 1982], 20) argues that "it was the Jesuits above all who came to embody in popular mythology the identification of Popery with homosexuality."

53. This appears to be Shakespeare's only use of the word "venial." Bell, in *The Downefall of Poperie*, pp. 81–85, attacks the Catholic position that some sins are merely venial. Stephen Greenblatt, in *Renaissance Self-Fashioning* (Chicago: University of Chicago Press, 1980), interprets the same phenomenon I am describing from a slightly different angle, calling Iago's response here a "brutally comic parody of the late medieval confessional manuals," one that "assumes an extreme version of the laxist position in such manuals in order to impel Othello toward the rigorist version" (246).

54. Thomas More, *The Dialogue Concerning Tyndale*, in *The English Works of Sir Thomas More*, vol. 2, ed. W. E. Campbell (London: Eyre and Spottiswood, 1927), 209, 208, quoted by R. Chris Hassel, Jr., "Love Versus Charity in *Love's Labor's Lost*" (*Shakespeare Studies* 10 [1977]: 20).

55. The hints that Othello is repeatedly forestalled from fully consummating his marriage to Desdemona parallel the exasperating struggles reported by Puritans seeking the perfect bond with Christ that (Reformation theologians argued) put faith beyond change and therefore salvation beyond doubt. See also Bell (*The Downefall of Poperie*, 37–39), arguing that "wedlocke before consummation or copulation is firme and perfect," and that "not the deflowering of virginitie maketh wedlocke, but the conjugall covenant"; Iago teaches Othello the contrary, Catholic view.

56. He is almost saved by this recognition that his redemption lies in loving rather than in deserving, and that, if he were not loved, chaos would never have gone. Cf. the end of Herbert's "A True Hymn": "As when th' heart says (sighing to be approved) / *O, could I love!* and stops: God writeth, *Loved.*"

57. Hamilton (*Shakespeare and Protestant England*, 123), citing Strype, *Annals* 4:121; Morice, *A Remembrance*, 28–87; and 12 Coke 26. On p. 8 she notes that Puritans defended themselves against official oaths by "[c]iting Magna Carta chapter 29" to prove "that secret and private thoughts were property and thus under the protection of the law."

58. A section early in *El condenado por desconfiado*, where the protagonist agonizes over his prospects for salvation and the devil enters to exploit that doubt, offers suggestive parallels to *Othello*, though the play functions entirely within a Catholic universe.

59. Winifred Nowottny, "Justice and Love in *Othello*," *University of Toronto Quarterly* 21 (1951–52): 334.

60. Calderwood, *The Properties of "Othello*," 31; this observation fits my argument especially well, considering the common Protestant belief that anyone who truly achieved (i.e., received) faith cannot lose it.

61. Harley Granville-Barker, quoted in Ivor Morris, *Shakespeare's God: The Role of Religion in Tragedies* (London: George Allen and Unwin, 1972), 334. By the same token when Morris observes that falling in love with Desdemona causes Othello to "find with her a self unrealized before" (327), we may choose to associate that new self with the way "the new man is joined to the promise and to grace" in the love of Christ (Luther, *Works*, vol. 26, 7). Morris, on 323, quotes Helen Gardner's description of Othello as "a man of faith"—which seems to overlook some significant ways in which he is instead, fatally, a man of works. Jane Adamson, in her "'Pluming up the Will,': Iago's Place in the Play" (Bloom, *Iago*, 188–89), concludes that in "identifying himself with what he claims is his autonomous will, [Iago] sees himself as free, omnipotent [thus demonstrating] why human life cannot, for all its need to, insulate and defend itself in mere will."

62. Of course, not every earthly good work should be interpreted as a violation of the covenant of grace. But Shakespeare's language repeatedly invites us to read the story in theological terms, and Luther himself insists that "[t]hese words 'works of the Law' are to be taken in the broadest possible sense." Furthermore, Shakespeare has both Cassio and Othello phrase their pleas in precisely the terms that Luther allows only in prayers to Christ: mere human righteousness must not presume "any power to make satisfaction for sin, to placate God, and to earn grace" (Luther, *Works*, vol. 26, 122, 4).

63. Iago convinces Montano that Othello "Prizes the virtue that appears in Cassio, / And looks not on his evils" (II.iii.117–18); perhaps Othello takes this partial view of his own soul as well. On the transmission of original sin and tragic efforts to evade it in Shakespearean drama, see Robert N. Watson, *Shakespeare and the Hazards of Ambition* (Cambridge: Harvard University Press, 1984), 136, 219–32, 242–53, 264–65, 273, 275–77, 219–20, n. 20.

64. Richard Hooker, Sermon VI, Part 21, in *Works*, vol. 2, ed. John Keble (Oxford: Clarendon Press, 1888), 398, cited in Frye, 29. Even Othello's self-reassurance that Desdemona cannot be corrupt because that would reflect badly on the angels she outwardly resembles—"If she be false, O then heaven mocks itself" (III.iii.280–81)—is arguably a bad sign, reflecting our vain (in both senses) tendency to imagine ourselves worthy of salvation or capable of extorting it. Protestant writers (including Donne in the Holy Sonnet "Thou Hast Made Me" and Milton in *Paradise Lost*) often placed such arguments in the mouths of sinners deluded by pride into doubting that God could permit the damnation of creatures made in His own image.

65. For an audience attuned to these issues, Othello's subsequent comparison puts Desdemona's love in place of the absolution achieved, under the old religion, by confession:

> And till she come, as truly as to heaven
> I do confess the vices of my blood,
> So justly to your grave ears I'll present
> How I did thrive in this fair lady's love,
> And she in mine.
> (I.iii.122–26)

Milward (*Biblical Influences*, 69), notes that these words echo "the Catholic prayer of Confession." On his p. 93 he notes that the "solid virtue" Lodovico admires in Othello (IV.i.257) echoes Loyola's principles for Jesuits: *"Ad veras solidasque virtutes consequandas insistant"* (*Summ. Const.* 22).

66. Downame (*Treatise of Justification*, 9), analyzing Christ's "motives" for choosing to save humankind, cites first "man's misery." Cf. Bell, *The Downefall of Poperie*, 63, in which Bell cites Origen's insistence that God would not "give stipends to his souldiers, as a due debt or wage; but to bestow on them a gift of free grace, which is eternall life in Christ Jesus our Lord."

67. Martin Luther, "The Freedom of Christian Man," excerpted in Hillerbrand, *Protestant Reformation*, 14.

68. Luther, *Works*, vol. 15, 200. Cf. Anders Nygren, *Agape and Eros* (trans. Philip S. Watson [New York: Harper and Row, 1969]), in which Nygren quotes Luther's *Disputatio Heidelergae habita* xxviii: "For sinners are lovely because they are loved; they are not loved because they are lovely" (725). The echo of Canticles is more explicit in Shakespeare's other story of Venice, when the Prince of Morocco introduces himself by urging Portia, "Mislike me not for my complexion, / The shadowed livery of the burnish'd sun, / To whom I am a neighbor and near bred" (II.i.1–3).

69. John Bunyan, *Grace Abounding to the Chief of Sinners*, Everyman edition, ed. G. B. Harrison (London: J. M. Dent, 1928), 80. Of course, by the next paragraph, Bunyan announces that "the tempter did beset me strongly," and his agonizing

doubts begin again. For a similar example contemporaneous with the composition of *Othello*, see William Harrison, *Deaths Advantage* (London, 1602).

70. Hillerbrand, *Protestant Reformation*, 16.

71. Renecher, *The Golden Chayne of Salvation*, 79.

72. Milward (*Biblical Influences*, 90) notes that Othello "blasphemously equates his magic handkerchief to the divine law"; I would add that the version of the divine law he equates it to is an outdated one. Lynda E. Boose ("Othello's Handkerchief," *English Literary Renaissance* 5 [1975]: 369), observes how often the embroidery is referred to as "work," though she does not touch on the theological significance of the word.

73. Samuel Harsnett, *A Declaration of Egregious Popish Impostures* (London, 1603), sig. A2v–A3r; yet Catholics, he says, do the same thing in worshiping relics; thus "God hath given them over . . . to believe unsavory lies, for refusing in their pride to embrace the pure naked synceritie of the Gospell of Christ." The fact that the handkerchief falls into the hands of a whore, and that copies of the sacred original are easily made, may recall Protestant satires on the corrupt Catholic Church and its multiplying relics.

74. See, for example, Downame's (Preface, *Treatise of Justification*) condemnation of the Jesuits: "whosoever taketh upon him authority above the scriptures . . . is undoubtedly Antichrist." Bell (*The Downefall of Poperie*, 86–121), condemns Catholicism for leading Christians to value other things above Holy Writ.

75. Richard Simpson, *Edmund Campion* (London: Burns and Oates, 1907), 455. Wills, p. 99, cites this incident to support his claim that "[h]andkerchiefs were associated with the public execution of Jesuits" by this form of relic-making.

76. Boose ("Othello's Handkerchief," 360–74) has ably articulated this pattern.

77. Willet, *A Catholicon*, sig. M8r, 156. Richard Hooker (*Works*, vol. 3, 527) demands that cardinals "cease to dye their garments, like Edom, in blood."

78. Edward Snow, "Sexual Anxiety and the Male Order of Things in *Othello*," *English Literary Renaissance* 10 (1980): 384–412; Greenblatt, *Renaissance Self-Fashioning*, 247–52. Bell (*The Downefall of Poperie*, 41–42) condemns Catholics, so devoted to "their inherent purities," for denying that "originall concupiscence in the regenerate" still constitutes sin; Othello's marriage arguably suffers from a comparable untenable denial. In any case, marriage and Mariolatry here seem an awkward combination. For Desdemona to preserve the purity of this love-token (whose silk was soaked in a conserve of "maidens' hearts") would be to leave those wedding sheets sadly unstained.

79. Iago transmits to Othello his interpretation of love as mystified lust—a predictable corollary of a supposed Catholic tendency to understand religion as merely its sensual rituals. Richard Sibbs's sermon on the anniversary of the Gunpowder Plot, *The Ruine of the Mysticall Jericho* (London, 1639), warns that Catholicism exploits "all the senses of the body, they have something to delight them, to draw people from the power of Religion, to carnall outward worship" (77). Critics offended by Desdemona's frank declaration of sexual desire toward her husband (I.iii.243–55) should remember that Protestantism was actively changing the moral valence of such desire; see, for example, Mary Beth Rose, *The Expense of Spirit* (Ithaca: Cornell University Press, 1988), on the Protestant "heroics of marriage," contrasted with Catholic heroics of virginity. Surely Othello had ancestors among the more craven or suggestible of the married Edwardian clergy who, upon the

ascension of Queen Mary, abruptly abhorred and abandoned their wives under the new Catholic dispensation that identified holiness with celibacy. When he begins to doubt Desdemona, Othello says something very much like "Get thee to a nunnery," prescribing for her "[a] sequester from liberty, fasting and prayer, / Much castigation, exercise devout . . ." (III.iv.36–37); Milward (*Biblical Influences*, 89) reports that the term "exercise" had "in the time of Shakespeare . . . come to take on the special meaning of [Jesuit] meditation, as in *The Spiritual Exercises* of Ignatius Loyola"; he also cites two other works—Loarte's *Exercise of a Christian Life* (1579) and Persons's *Book of Christian Exercise* (1582)—both by Jesuits. In any case, this tirade shows how effectively Iago has Catholicized Othello's idea of female virtue.

80. Battenhouse, "Shakespearean," 210; see similarly his *Shakespearean Tragedy*, 100. Anthonie Ginestet, in W.B., *The Confession and Publike Recantation*, sig. G3v, proclaims, "Let the Papistes . . . exalt their ecchoing musick, the picturing & sculpture of their images: let them wonder at the greatnes of the sundry orders of their sacrifices . . ."; Othello's speeches surrounding this "sacrifice" resound with these sorts of grandeur. And, to the extent that Desdemona represents the Savior, and Othello the sinner on the brink of repenting his religion of blood-sacrifice, Othello will indeed "kill thee, / And love thee after" (V.ii.18–19): what was traditionally the guilt of the Jews here taints Catholicism as well.

81. Pasquier (*The Jesuites Catechisme*, sig. A2r) remarks, "so many Jesuites, so many *Judases*"; Willet (*A Catholicon*, sig. B2v) calls the sect "Judasites, for they imitate Judas, and not Jesus." Dekker (*The Whore of Babylon*, 166) describes the Jesuit as "*Envies* heart, and *Treasons* head, / For, *England* bout the neck hee clips, / And kisses. But with *Judas* lips." The translator's Dedicatory Epistle to Petrus Boquinus, *A Defense of the Olde, and True profession*, trans. T. G. (London, 1581), accused the Jesuits of working "to the entent that Jesus Christ may be the sooner betrayed, while these holy Jesuites give him a Judas salutation, and kisse." *A Letter written out of England* (1599), 9, calls a Jesuit trying to kill Elizabeth a "second *Judas.*" Battenhouse (*Shakespearean Tragedy*, 95–102) notes parallels between Othello and Judas; see also Milward, *Biblical Influences*, 62. In selling the "entire and perfect chrysolite" of Desdemona (V.ii.143), Othello also (like the Jesuits) destroys what Downame's Preface, in condemning Jesuit theology, calls the "entire and perfect rule of faith" which the play embodies in her love.

82. Cf. *A Letter*, 4: "After the *Jesuite* had at sundry conferences, discoursed . . . upon how few persons lives" the misery of Catholics depended, the Squire agrees to serve as an assassin, though at first deceived into thinking he will be killing Essex rather than Elizabeth.

83. Caraman, *Henry Garnet 1555–1606*, 399. Edmund of Beauval, in W.B., *The Confession and Publike Recantation*, sig. H3v, asserts that "(in the Romish Church) the Masse priest is reputed a Sacrificer," thus belittling Christ, an "intolerable blasphemy, never used among the Turkes . . ."; also Lewys du Boys, sig. Mir: "but why do I call it a sacrifice, when it is nothing els but a manifest devision of Christ and his merites."

84.

> Now, if that thou wilt look to merit heaven,
> An be canoniz'd for a holy saint,
> To please the world with a deserving work,
> Be thou the man to set thy country free.

This passage from *The Troublesome Raigne* is quoted by De Groot (*The Shake-speares and "The Old Faith,"* 201), as evidence of Shakespeare's efforts to moderate popular anti-Catholic sentiments.

85. Boquinus, *A Defense of the Olde*, 78, compares the Jesuits to "Cayphas." Othello kills because he believes he has the power to restore purity. Luther might have compared the crime to the destruction of Christ by zealots of the old dispensation: Paul himself initially set out "to persecute Jesus of Nazareth, to abolish the doctrine of Christ, to murder the faithful . . . he was so completely blinded by a wicked zeal for God that he regarded these unspeakable crimes of his as the height of righteousness and an act of worship and obedience most pleasing to God" (Luther, *Galatians*, in Hillerbrand, *Protestant Reformation*, 98–99). Othello likes the suggestion that he murder Desdemona in the candlelit cathedral of their bedroom because "[t]he justice of it pleases" (IV.i.197); and, as his remark about the stained sheets indicates, this is definitely talionic justice of the sort associated with the Old Testament God. He will punish her for being "false as water" (V.ii.134), as Reuben is punished for being "light as water" (Gen. 49:4). Even Iago's professed determination to get even with Othello "wife for wife" echoes the talionic covenant that required ill deeds to be repaid "life for life" in Exodus 21:23. When Othello proclaims, "This sorrow's heavenly, it strikes where it doth love," as he prepares to sacrifice Desdemona, we may be reminded of the way passionate Protestant converts such as John Donne portrayed the tough love offered by their redemptive God. And the force that led them to focus on their own merits, instead of having absolute faith in divine love, they called the devil, as Othello calls Iago. John O'Meara ("'And I Will Kill Thee . . . ,'" *English Language Notes* [September 1990]: 35–42) argues that Othello here resembles Abraham in sacrificing a beloved; but if so, Othello should recognize that a humble faith offers the only hope of saving that beloved.

86. The temptation scene is full of such examples. In struggling to defend the faith of his marriage, Othello associates it with the transcendent importance of religious faith:

> If thou dost slander her and torture me,
> Never pray more; abandon all remorse;
> On horror's head horrors accumulate;
> Do deeds to make heaven weep, all earth amazed;
> For nothing canst thou to damnation add
> Greater than that.
>   *Iago*: O grace! O heaven forgive me!
> (III.iii.370–75)

The conduct Othello proposes is precisely the kind of morally despondent behavior that Catholic propagandists claimed Protestant doctrines of predestination would produce (cf. Downame [*Treatise of Justification*, 6], struggling to refute that claim), and Iago answers with oaths that underscore the irony. Later in the scene, Othello declares, "All my fond love thus do I blow to heaven," but he means only to disperse it; he commands, "Yield up, O love, thy crown and hearted throne," but he remains congruent with a religion that (from a Protestant perspective) cared too much about crowns and thrones, and too little about love; and he exclaims, "O, blood, blood, blood!" without thinking about the heavenly blood that was shed in love and defeats the evil tempter.

87. Othello also dismisses a piece of traditional Catholic demonology as merely "a fable" (V.ii.283), and—no longer supposing that Desdemona "did gratify his amorous works" (V.ii.212)—he manages simply to ask "pardon" of Cassio (V.ii.297); the wrong source, but the right request.

88. Cf. Matthew 10:38: "And he that taketh not his crosse, & followeth after me, is not worthy of me." Furthermore, when Emilia recalls a lady who "would have walked barefoot to Palestine" for a kiss from Lodovico (IV.iii.36), she not only extends her well-documented function as a moral middle ground into the doctrinal area I have been sketching, she also confirms the parallel between earthly and Christian love that underlies my argument; cf. also her claim that she would "venture purgatory" to make her husband a monarch, even if that meant making him a cuckold also (IV.iii.73).

89. Othello may certainly be accused of egoistically justifying himself rather than confronting his guilt and his wife's innocence—"an honorable murderer, if you will"—but in doing so he is behaving in the way that Romans have behaved, according to Luther, from St. Paul's time to his own: "the hypocrites are always righteous in their own sight, and thus always sinners outwardly" (quoted in McGrath, *Reformation Thought*, 106; this aspect of Othello's thinking should not, of course, erase the fact that he soon kills himself in remorse). Luther therefore warns that even those who successfully simulate righteousness "cannot trust in it or stand up before the judgment of God on the basis of it" (*Galatians*, in Hillerbrand, *Protestant Reformation*, 89).

90. Battenhouse's reading on p. 98 of *Shakespearean Tragedy*—"uncircumcized dog"—would work well for my argument, since Othello would then be making precisely the error Paul warns against, basing judgments of salvation on physical works of expiation, rather than on the inner, spiritual circumcision Paul emphasizes. But he offers no justification for the emendation, and I can find none.

91. T. S. Eliot, "Shakespeare and the Stoicism of Seneca" (1927); rpt. in John Wain, ed., *Othello: A Casebook* (London: Macmillan, 1971), 70.

92. Hooker, *Works*, vol. 5, 114.

93. F. R. Leavis, "The Diabolic Intellect and the Noble Hero" (1952); rpt. in Wain, *Othello: A Casebook*, 130, 142.

94. Luther, *Works*, vol. 23, 263.

95. Calvin sees a comparable "repentance of the law" in misguided scriptural figures such as Cain and Saul as well as Judas: "While Scripture recounts their repentance to us, it represents them as acknowledging the gravity of their sin, and afraid of God's wrath; but since they conceived of God only as Avenger and Judge, that very thought overwhelmed them. Therefore their repentance was nothing but a sort of entryway to hell, which they had already entered in this life . . ." (Calvin, *Institutes*, III, iii, 4, ed. John T. McNeill, trans. Ford Lewis Battles, Library of Christian Classics XX [Philadelphia: Westminster Press, 1960], 1:596). Compare Othello's foul accusations, tragic acts, and hopeless repentance, with Ginestet, in Raben, *The Confession and Publike Recantation*, sig. G4v, urging Catholics to go to Mount Sion and

> taste of her savorous fruite of life . . . forsaking the venemous Cisterns of the world: a desert not of sinne, but a desert of justice. To this effect, we from the bottome of our heartes, make our humble petitions to the most high; the inward companions of our soules,

making our eyes melt into fountaines, & our better partes yeelding forth unspeakable dolors, considering (in the Theatre of the world) that the greatest multitude, by the violent stormes of seduction, be enticed and ravished to be trayned & finally to be throwne headlong into perdition.

96. Ribner, *Patterns in Shakespearean Tragedy*, 113. S. L. Bethell ("The Diabolic Images in *Othello*," *Shakespeare Survey* 5 [1952]: 78) may oversimplify in declaring that Othello's "suicide, since he is a Christian, seals his fate"; but if the spectator is a particular kind of Christian, then it will seem to. See also Paul N. Siegel, *Shakespearean Tragedy and the Elizabethan Compromise* (New York, 1957) 131, on the way Othello's repentance is marked as merely "'Judas' repentance.'"

97. Glynne Wickham, *The Medieval Theatre* (London: Weidenfeld and Nicolson, 1974), p. 188; quoted by Hugh M. Richmond, "*Richard III* and the Reformation," *Journal of English and Germanic Philology* 83 (1984): 509.

98. Richmond, "*Richard III* and the Reformation," 510.

99. Martin Aray, *The Discoverie and Confutation of a Tragical Fiction* (Antwerp, 1599).

JOAN OZARK HOLMER

Desdemona, Woman Warrior:
"O, these men, these men!" (4.3.59)

> Unkindness may do much,
> And his unkindness may defeat my life
> But never taint my love.
> (4.2.161–63)

Othello is a tragedy that continually surprises us. Not only did Shakespeare make the blackest man on stage a white man (Iago), I would suggest that he made the bravest warrior onstage a woman (Desdemona). For only one other female character in his works does Shakespeare employ the descriptive term "warrior," predictably for the Amazon Hippolyta, the "warrior love" of Theseus (*A Midsummer Night's Dream* 2.1.71).[1] Because none of the acknowledged literary sources for *Othello* describe the heroine as a warrior, despite the popularity of the Ovidian trope of love as war, Shakespeare catches us off guard when Desdemona is identified as a warrior twice in the play, once by Othello who greets her on the seemingly peaceful battlefront of Cyprus as his "fair warrior" (2.1.180) and once by herself when she calls herself in the subsequent act an "unhandsome warrior" (3.4.152) for uncharitably arraigning Othello.[2] The Duke initially judged her husband "far more fair than black" (1.3.291), but by the end of the play Desdemona proves herself the play's "fair" warrior in both senses of outer beauty and inner virtue.

From *Medieval and Renaissance Drama in England* 17 (2005) 132–64. © 2005 by Joan Ozark Holmer.

185

In his *Artificial Persons: The Formation of Character in the Tragedies of Shakespeare* Leeds Barroll rightly observes, "Desdemona, rather significantly, is Othello's 'fair warrior,'" and "the relationship between Desdemona and Othello's military profession also proceeds through some complexities, for if he sees her as 'warrior,' he also sees her as a possible agency of Cupid's 'toys' in his speech to the senate."[3] As would most critics in responding to this play, Barroll finds that "the motif of Desdemona as 'fair warrior' receives only rudimentary development in the play" (183). It is precisely this important motif that I wish to re-examine in light of some new contexts (Edmund Spenser and Desiderimus Erasmus) and some reconsidered sources (Giraldi Cinthio, Geoffrey Fenton, and Matteo Bandello). Although Othello is a literal warrior in both the Christian and secular senses, Desdemona is literally a warrior in the Christian sense, with faith as her shield (Eph. 6.17), but figuratively a warrior in the secular sense since her tongue is her sword or her only weapon, used defensively against Othello and offensively on behalf of Othello. As moderns we need to recapture an older habit of reading literally and figuratively while we wrestle with Shakespeare's wordplay and the richer meanings then of "common" words we tend to take for granted, such as "honesty" and "honor," both of which have both outer (reputation) and inner (character) nuances.

I

Although Desdemona is no medieval Joan of Arc, Renaissance Britomart, or modern G. I. Jane, her true faith and enduring love in her relationship to Othello and his occupation as a warrior may be surprisingly illuminated by Edmund Spenser's portrayal of Una (truth) and the Redcrosse Knight (holiness) in the first book of *The Faerie Queene*. This contextual relationship of heroines and heroes has been overlooked despite Charles Prouty's earlier argument that Spenser's Archimago helps us to understand better Iago, even though one character inhabits an allegory and the other a drama.[4] Despite the major differences in genres and styles between Spenser's romance epic and Shakespeare's love tragedy, and Spenser's climactic versus Shakespeare's initial presentation of marriage, larger patterns of meaning link the warriors and their lady companions as they venture forth together to engage the enemy, ultimately in the typical one-on-one combat of spiritual warfare. Like Una, Desdemona is no "moth of peace" (1.3.257) to stay at home. Both ladies bravely accompany their beloveds to the field and lovingly "suffereth all things . . . hopeth all things . . . endureth all things" (1 Cor. 13.7) during trials that include temptations to jealousy and suicide. Throughout these trials the women triumph with love that never alters "when it alteration finds" (Sonnet

116) as they attempt to aid, even save, their less steadfast men who afflict them in return with unmerited suffering.[5]

Most significantly, these martial exploits occur within a marital context in which the lovers face challenges to the type of faithful love that constitutes true marriage. The love relationships, therefore, are not supposed to be divorced from the warrior's occupation, as we might typically expect. Hotspur, that warrior of warriors, voices just such an expectation when he prioritizes military over marital duty: "Away, you trifler! . . . / I care not for thee, Kate . . . / And when I am a' horseback, I will swear / I love thee infinitely" (1 Henry IV 2.3.90–102). If a warrior were asked what he most fears losing, Hotspur's answer might serve: not the loss of "brittle life" but the loss of "proud titles" (1 Henry IV 5.4.79), or his honors. Like Hotspur who divides the duties of war and love into different camps, Othello also reflects the typical awareness of how wives can function as "feathered" Cupid's "light-winged toys" (1.3.269–70) to distract a warrior from his proper business so that "housewives make a skillet of [his] helm" (1.3.273). Once in Cyprus, however, Emilia has to "pray heaven" that "no jealous toy" concerning Desdemona infects Othello (3.4.155–56). The play's shift of locale from Venice to Cyprus ominously suggests potential danger because of its mythological association with Venus. Cyprus is one of the two islands sacred to Venus, Cythera being the other; hence, Venus was frequently called either the Cyprian or Cytherea.[6] In The Tempest Shakespeare prevents some "wanton charm" being done by Venus and Cupid on another (unnamed) Mediterranean isle because they are sent "dove-drawn" back to Paphos on Cyprus where Cupid will break his arrows and instead "play with sparrows" (4.1.87–100).

Spenser, however, charts another course in which the love of a good woman is not to be feared for its effeminate potential but is to be integrated into the good man's life as a source of strength, and the betrayal of this love constitutes the knight's *greatest shame*:

> Young knight, what euer that dost armes professe,
> And through long labours huntest after fame,
> Beware of fraud, beware of ficklenesse,
> In choice, and change of thy deare loued Dame,
> Least thou of her beleeue too lightly blame,
> And rash misweening doe thy hart remoue:
> For vnto knight there is no greater shame,
> Then lightnesse and inconstancie in loue;
> That doth this *Redcrosse* knights ensample plainly proue.
> (1.4.1)[7]

This stanza appears after the Redcrosse Knight has broken faith with Una because the disguised, and newly met, tempter Archimago used witchcraft, somewhat akin to Iago's "wit-craft," to seduce the Redcrosse Knight to fall for false ocular proof (sprites masquerading as humans) that his beloved "doth her honour staine" (1.2.4.9) in bed with another man whom the Redcrosse Knight does not know. Shakespeare stacks the deck more against Othello by employing insider betrayal. We may overlook that Othello, unlike the Redcrosse Knight, has some legitimate grounds for suspicion. His friend and lieutenant Cassio did indeed betray his trust on the watch; therefore, Othello has a reasonable basis to distrust him in other situations, especially when his ensign Iago, universally reputed for honesty, leads the charge. When Cassio departs from Desdemona "so guilty-like" (3.3.39), he probably does look guilty, not with lust for Desdemona but with shame for having failed Othello. The Redcrosse Knight has known Una for only a short time at the beginning of their journey, but he has already witnessed her brave goodness in action when she helped him defeat the monster Error in "the wandring wood" (1.1.13.6). Othello has had nine months in Venice (1.3.85) to get to know Desdemona, and he too witnesses her courage in action when she wisely testifies on his behalf before her father and the Venetian senate (1.3.180–89) and then eloquently implores the Duke to allow her to stand by Othello's side in war-threatened Cyprus (1.3.244–60).

Othello, for all the criticism accorded his too rapid surrender to jealousy, looks better in comparison to the Redcrosse Knight, the future St. George. Indeed, despite the reputation Moors had for jealousy,[8] our "black Othello" (2.3.29) also looks far fairer than the white Venetian merchant, Corvino, in Jonson's *Volpone*, a comedy written about a year after Shakespeare's tragedy.[9] "With sword in hand" the Redcrosse Knight *immediately* burns with "gealous fire" at the false sight so that "the eye of reason was with rage yblent," and he would have *slain* both his beloved and her squire in his "furious ire" if Archimago had not restrained him (1.2.5.1–9). Archimago, of course, deters the jealous man for no moral purpose but to avoid the exposure of his deception because spirits cannot be slain. Iago similarly suggests to Othello ocular proof too painful to view and too impossible to catch—"Would you, the supervisor, grossly gape on? / Behold her topped?" (3.3.398–99)—knowing that not even a deft director like himself can stage such a scene.

The Redcrosse Knight consequently deserts Una, "flying from his thoughts and gealous feare" so that "will" became his "guide" and "griefe led him astray" (1.2.12.4), and like the Redcrosse Knight, Othello's rational eye becomes blinded by rage once his "clear spirit" is "puddled" (3.4.144) by Iago's temptation to foul jealousy: "O blood, blood, blood!" (3.3.454). Moreover, just as Iago perversely elevates "will" over right reason (1.3.320–22) in self-determination and denigrates "love" as "a lust of the blood and a permission of the will" (1.3.333–35), so also Othello begins unwittingly to incorporate Iago's philosophy as his own rude will, in conjunction with his tormented grief, contribute to leading him astray once he allows his mind to be tainted by "the green-eyed monster" (3.3.168). However, of his own accord Othello intermittently and repeatedly reverts to the right path to love and value Desdemona (e.g., see 4.1.176–85), and left alone, he might have kept to that path, were it not for Iago's persistent plotting. Whose "will" will be done—man's or God's? Both Una ("sore grieued" [1.2.8.8]) and Desdemona ("How have I been behaved that he might stick / The small'st opinion on my greatest misuse?" [4.2.110–17]) are baffled as to what they could have done wrong, knowing in truth their own loyal love. Una even experiences near despair and curses light when she mistakenly thinks the Redcrosse Knight is dead (1.7.20–23), but she spiritually rallies herself to continue the quest (1.7.24–28). Desdemona avoids near despair, but her most "perplexed in the extreme" (5.2.344) moment registers psychosomatically as a "half-asleep" daze in which she claims to have no lord (4.2.99–104). However, she too rouses herself in mid-speech by commanding her wedding sheets to be put on her bed (4.2.107), and then she continues to assert her innocence (4.2.109–66).

Despite the men's betrayals and their failures to resist temptations, neither Una nor Desdemona breaks faith with her beloved. Like their knights, both heroines experience great grief, but both refuse to capitulate to "will" or "wrath." Recognizing his errors in love, the Redcrosse Knight would have taken Despair's proffered "dagger" (1.9.51.2) and committed suicide, but Una saves him by snatching the dagger out of his hand and sharply reprimanding her knight to remember God's mercy: "Ne let vaine words bewitch thy manly hart / Ne diuelish thoughts dismay thy constant spright. / In heauenly mercies hast thou not a part?" (1.9.46.6–9). Othello, likewise tormented by his failure in love, has no lady love living to prevent the hand that threw her away from finding his hidden dagger of suicide.[10] Not only does Spenser seem to be suggestive for various aspects of a love relationship tested by spiritual warfare, but also he may influence some ways in which Shakespeare conceptualizes and images the passion of jealousy.[11]

Spenser's emphasis on spiritual warfare comprises the very emphasis Shakespeare carefully cultivates throughout his play, and it is precisely this emphasis that is lacking in his main literary source of Cinthio's novelle. This same spiritual orientation, with its concern for souls and eternal consequences, also is absent in modern analytical comparisons of O. J. Simpson to Othello and his murdered wife Nicole to Desdemona, such as that of Elaine Showalter.[12] Given the religious history of the Renaissance, we should not be surprised to find such a strongly spiritual emphasis, and perhaps not even too surprised to find in reformed England authors who appreciate the vocation of companionate marriage, rather than the more typical solitary male hero-ism, for militancy against evil. The martial unit becomes the marital one. But the love relationship of a man and a woman needs to prove true in order to triumph, losing some battles along the way but ultimately winning the war. Pity cushions the falls of the Redcrosse Knight and Othello because, like the original fall of Adam and Eve, they fall tempted primarily by another, not themselves. So Milton's God in *Paradise Lost* will grant grace to humanity but not to fallen angels because the latter fell "self-tempted, self-depraved" while man "falls deceived / By the other first" (3.130–31).[13]

Unlike the Redcrosse Knight who is a warrior in the making, Othello enters his play as a tested and proven hero on the martial (not the marital) front, and he is more than a brave warrior like Hotspur (although both men at death are praised as being "great of heart") because his "patience" (4.2.54) has overcome on numerous occasions "the slings and arrows of outrageous fortune" (*Hamlet* 3.1.57). His adventures have withstood adversity's assaults, and because of his "solid virtue" (4.1.266), because he is "so good" (5.2.288), he has been a "man / That is not passion's slave" (*Hamlet* 3.2.72) until he becomes "much changed" (4.1.268) when he faces the ultimate tempter and succumbs to his temptations to do evil, as does everyone else in the play, except Desdemona. Like the Redcrosse Knight, however, Othello values his soul. One of the deepest ironies, so often overlooked in the criticism on *Othello*, is how much this warrior values *spiritual* qualities, in particular "the worth of [his] eternal soul" (3.3.361). And indeed, one of the reasons Desde-mona loves Othello so much is because of the perceived nobility of his "per-fect soul" (1.2.31): "I saw Othello's visage in his mind, / And to his honours and his valiant parts / Did I my soul and fortunes consecrate" (1.3.253–55). This virtuous conception of himself is underscored by Othello's recurrent ref-erences to his soul, even valuing Desdemona as his "soul's joy" (2.1.182), and the language of "soul" and its variants is used more often by Othello than any other character in the play.[14] Othello should be praised because he values man's soul, but does he rightly "know" or "understand" his own soul? That knowledge of self and discovery of "truth" through "trothplight" is similar to what the Redcrosse Knight has to fight to learn.

Although they undergo no major falls, both Una and Desdemona also learn through adversity. Una learns not to trust too readily (1.7.38), benefits from Arthur's wisdom (1.7.40–42), and in the final canto rightly identifies the hypocrite Archimago, which she failed to do in canto 1, as the "fals-est man alive," despite his assumed role now as a "craftie messenger" or a "false footman, clokt with simplenesse" (1.12.34). In the final act Desdemona learns what she denied as possible earlier, namely that "[her] noble Moor" is

not so "true of mind" that he cannot fall to "such baseness / As jealous creatures" (3.4.26–28), even though she has in truth given him no cause. Both
Spenser's and Shakespeare's paired protagonists try to fight the good fight
in which trials test and refine their virtue. The women, forsaken yet faithful
and forgiving, persevere. When their heroes fall, their men incorporate the
vice to which they are tempted until they attempt to purge their sin through
remorseful recognition. While Spenser's *The Faerie Queene* stresses the human
inability to do good without divine grace, Shakespeare's *Othello* seems to
allow more possibility for human agency to seek divine grace and to do good
under adverse circumstances. That amazing agency he stunningly ascribes to
a *woman* warrior.

II

I will begin somewhat perversely at the play's end with Desdemona's
ending, but before commencing that consideration, the more obvious ways
in which Desdemona might be seen as a woman warrior, prior to her death
scene, should be indicated, especially in light of the critical trend to see Desdemona as too "passive" or, in Iago's words, "'too gentle'" (Honigmann 56–58).
First, in keeping with the natural desire of a lover to partake of the beloved's
identity, Desdemona sees herself in warrior terms for wanting to accompany her husband to the battlefield, and so she "may *trumpet* to the world"
(1.3.249, my italics) her love to live with him. Because Othello and the Duke
expected Desdemona to remain in Venice (1.3.236–41), the play treats her
request as unusual and unexpected. The Duke says the matter should be
settled "privately . . . / Either for her stay or going" (1.3.276–77), but Othello
determines it publicly once the command for departure "tonight" (1.3.279)
is given: he assigns Desdemona to Iago's escort in a separate ship (1.3.291).
This contrasts with Cinthio's novelle, the main literary source, in which the
wife Disdemona, needing no approval from the Venetian authorities, expects
to accompany her husband to Cyprus—she "could hardly wait for the hour
when . . . she would accompany him to that honourable post"—where the
Venetian Signoria has made him the "Commandant of the soldiers whom
they sent there," but where there is no threat of imminent war.[15] Cinthio's
Moor, on the other hand, is concerned about the peril of the journey for his
wife so that either he must cause her "this hardship" and himself "extreme
anxiety" on her behalf, or he must leave her behind, which would be "hateful"
to him because she represents his "very life" (Bullough 243). Shakespeare's
Desdemona wants to brave the dangers of both journey and war, and her
extraordinary speech about how and why she physically and spiritually loves
Othello persuades him to change his mind and champion the request she
directed to the duke's "prosperous ear" (1.3.245). To Othello's credit, he

thinks he is being "free and bounteous to her mind" (1.3.266), which contrasts with her disappointed father's refusal to emulate that attitude in rejecting her apparent need for "accommodation" (1.3.239, 241) and in projecting his distrust of Desdemona onto Othello (1.3.293–94). In response, Othello wagers his "life upon her faith" (1.3.295), speaking more prophetically than he knows.

Once on Cyprus Desdemona not only fights on behalf of Cassio, but more importantly she fights for the right reason. Cinthio's Disdemona gives up pleading for the reinstatement of her husband's officer as soon as the Moor becomes angry with her: " . . . but rather than have you angry with me I shall never say another word on the subject" (Bullough 245). Shakespeare's Desdemona, however, retreats in order to reengage repeatedly (3.4, 4.1) despite her husband's temper: "As I have spoken for you [Cassio] all my best / And stood within the *blank* of his displeasure / For my free speech" (3.4.128–30, my italics). Realizing that as a wife who should be obedient to her lord she appears too "free," Desdemona's own generous nature, "framed as fruitful / As the free elements" (2.3.336–37), to do good—abetted by the intercessions of Cassio, Emilia, and Iago—motivates her. She pleads not for her own good but for Othello's own good that he reinstate a man who "truly loves" him (3.3.48), as she rightly interprets Cassio's friendship. Indeed, against the backdrop of racial prejudice that Shakespeare develops in the play, Cassio's true love for his friend and general, like Desdemona's true love for her husband, shines all the brighter. In pleading for Cassio, Desdemona wisely distinguishes between seeking a "boon" for herself, which this is not, and doing "a peculiar profit / To [his] own person" just as she would naturally entreat him to "feed on nourishing dishes, or keep [him] warm" (3.3.76, 78–80). Despite her careful explanation, Othello simply repeats, "I will deny *thee* nothing" (3.3.76, 83, my italics), revealing that "his soul" may be, as Iago believes, "so enfettered to her love," perhaps even enough "to renounce his baptism" (2.3.338–40). Yet he does not seem to understand truly his wife and her good reasoning even before Iago begins his direct assault. In a play permeated with rich structural patterns, Desdemona's "vow" of "friendship" (3.3.21) that opens this crucial scene is offset by Othello's "sacred vow" of "capable and wide revenge" (3.3.462–64) that closes it.

Although some find her "too reticent" in the brothel scene,[16] Desdemona—like Emilia before her—asks the sensible questions regarding "to whom" and "with whom" (4.2.41), adamantly proclaiming Othello does her "wrong" (4.2.81–86), but the general's accusation remains too general because he withholds the specific name of Cassio so that she, unlike Othello when on trial before the senate, cannot summon Cassio as the key witness on her behalf. Only moments before Othello executes her does Desdemona learn from her husband "the cause" of his jealousy. Now she realizes that Othello somehow has become deceived about the missing handkerchief and the true nature of her relationship with Cassio. Complementing her verbal battle to live (5.2.35–83), Desdemona physically fights to live as Othello's textual clue—"Nay, if you strive—" (5.2.80)—indicates. Her will to live is so strong that even the physically superior strength of Othello has to be exerted a second time to silence her: "I that am cruel am yet merciful, / I would not have thee linger in thy pain. / So, so" (5.2.86–88). Nor does Desdemona passively submit after appearing dead; instead, she revives to use, presumably in some pain, the only weapon barely left her—her voice—so that her woman's words "out-tongue" (1.2.19) man's deeds.

Like the final silencing of her voice, critical commentary on her final lines has been relatively muted. How important is it to see and hear Desdemona's revival and not have it cut, as is the case in the 1995 film "Othello," directed by Oliver Parker (starring Irene Jacob, Laurence Fishburne, and Kenneth Branagh) and in the recent adaptation of *Othello* for modern teens, directed by Tim Blake Nelson and titled "O"? Although there may be several ways to read Desdemona's final utterances when she momentarily revives to speak,[17] I would like to offer a reading that, to the best of my knowledge, has not been presented and that illuminates how the play and early modern audiences might have perceived Desdemona as a fair warrior far more readily than we moderns may. Scholarly editions of the play are curiously silent about the blatant contradiction between the revived Desdemona's first two utterances and her last two lines. When Desdemona recovers enough breath from Othello's suffocation of her, her first concern is not to pray but to clear her name, that is, to reaffirm her innocence of adultery to her lord while she properly defines his attempted ritual sacrifice as actual murder: "O falsely, falsely murdered!" (5.2.115). But during the time Desdemona has seemed dead or been unconscious, the situation in her bedroom has changed unbeknownst to her, changed from a private scene with only her husband present to a public one with Emilia's entrance. As Desdemona regains consciousness, her cry that she has been falsely murdered is probably intended for Othello's ears.

But Emilia is the one who responds to Desdemona's cry and opens the bedcurtains that Othello had drawn (5.2.103), begging her "sweet mistress" to "speak again" (5.2.119–20). Now, directly to Emilia, Desdemona asserts, "A guiltless death I die" (5.2.121). Emilia specifically inquires, "O, who hath done / This deed?" (5.2.122). Naming "who" would affix blame for the deed of being "falsely murdered." After her double admissions of honesty, Desdemona's answer does, and should, stun us: "Nobody. I myself. Farewell. / Commend me to my kind lord—O, farewell!" (5.2.122–23). How might this reply, which appears to be a lie and so Othello interprets it—"she's like a

liar gone to burning hell" (5.2.127), cue us as to how an early modern audience might have seen her despite her gender, more readily than we do, as
not only Othello's but indeed the play's "fair warrior"? Honigmann interprets
Desdemona's final line as a "lie" in order to "protect" Othello (56), a lie that
almost "sanctifies" her (58); and I concur. So does Othello *after* he becomes
enlightened about the truth, changing his view of Desdemona from damned
to saved as he simultaneously changes his view of himself from saved to
damned: "When we shall meet at compt / This look of thine will hurl my soul
from heaven / . . . Whip me, ye devils, / From the possession of this heavenly
sight!" (5.2.270–76).

But how and why has Shakespeare scripted for his heroine such a
remarkable ending when deathbed speeches are traditionally noted for their
veracity? A brief review of possible sources helps to sharpen our awareness of
Shakespeare's originality in crafting Desdemona's ending.[18] In Cinthio, there
is no revival of the lady who is bludgeoned to death, although she does manage to pray for herself during her death throes: "The wretched Lady, hearing
this and feeling herself near to death (for the Ensign had given her another
blow), called on Divine Justice to witness to her fidelity, since earthly justice
failed, and as she called on God to help her, a third blow struck her, and she
lay still, slain by the impious Ensign" (Bullough 251). But two other possible
sources—Bandello's Italian tale and Fenton's English translation of it—present
an innocent wife who appears dead but briefly revives to speak after her jealous
husband, an Albanian captain, has stabbed her and then himself to death.[19] I
suspect the differences between these two versions may suggest that Shakespeare was familiar with both. In Fenton's English translation of Belleforest's
French translation of Bandello's original Italian story, the good wife "with
great ado to speake" salvages some time to pray for herself and to request that
her body be laid in the tomb of her first, good husband: " . . . the want of breath
abridged her secret shryft and confession to God, with lesse leasure to yield
her innocent soule (wyth humble praier) into the handes of her Redemer and
commende the forgevenes of her synnes to the benefit of his mercie."[20] Several
critics have argued that Shakespeare most likely used Fenton, especially at
the end of his drama.[21] If Shakespeare knew Fenton, he might recall the verb
"commend" for Desdemona's final line; although "commend" is a common
enough word in Shakespeare, in this play he uses it only in this one instance.
His Desdemona, however, had begged for time to pray, unlike Fenton's lady
who did not know she was about to be slain. Despite Othello's initial good
intention, he denies her time for even one prayer (5.2.82), although he knows
she had already prayed before going to sleep (5.2.25).

Desdemona's, "O Lord! Lord! Lord!" (5.2.83) as Othello smothers her,
a line that appears in the Quarto and not the Folio, sounds like a cry that is a

prayer, unlike Emilia's repetition of calling "my lord" in the subsequent line in order to be admitted by Othello to the bedroom.[22] This prayerful repetition of "Lord" might recall for the audience the Lord's Prayer, which concludes with an emphasis on the human need for forgiveness—"And forgiue vs our dettes, as we also forgiue our detters" (Matt. 6:12). This call for mercy Desdemona has explicitly invoked moments earlier: "The Lord have mercy on me . . . / And have you mercy too" (5.2.57–58). But when Shakespeare's Desdemona revives, she does not pray for herself, as does Fenton's lady, but rather she asserts her innocence twice (once privately to Othello, once publicly to Emilia) before she literally lies about *who* "falsely murdered" her. Nor does she then commend herself to God but rather to Othello, her "kind lord." Does Desdemona's own awareness of her essential innocence, despite her former white lie about the handkerchief not being "lost" (3.4.85–90) and her present lie about the identity of her murderer, indicate that she knows she does not need to pray again at the hour of her death? Does her faith justify her belief in her own salvation because she honestly knows that she has fulfilled the primary commandment to love charitably?

Unlike Nathaniel Hawthorne's Hester who concludes in *The Scarlet Letter*, "But a lie is never good, even though death threaten on the other side,"[23] the less puritanical Shakespeare often allows for deception as a means to greater good, especially to do good lovingly for the welfare of another.[24] This is not surprising given his medium of drama because the make-believe art of theater uses lies or fictions to convey truths, whereas the real world's use of lies usually promotes falsehoods. Indeed, the etymology of "hypocrisy" tends to capture this tension in its meaning of "actor."[25] Likewise, Emilia's "theft" of Desdemona's handkerchief to please her husband Iago (5.2.227–29), as well as her deliberate silence about this impropriety despite her intuitions of Othello's jealousy (3.4.29, 100) and her firsthand witnessing of Othello's anger and Desdemona's distress about the missing handkerchief (3.4.51–107), do not deter Emilia's hope for salvation as she transfers her allegiance from her "pernicious" (5.2.151) husband to her "heavenly true" (5.2.133) mistress and tells the truth, and nothing but the truth: "So come my soul to bliss as I speak true!" (5.2.248). Genre, however, generally governs consequences, and while well-intentioned deceptions in comedy produce prosperous outcomes, similarly motivated deceptions in tragedy litter the stage with multiple deaths.

Bandello's original Italian version presents more to the matter, and I am inclined to agree more with Shaheen who suggests Shakespeare read Bandello in Italian than Honigmann who remains unconvinced.[26] Suggesting that if Bandello is not a source then at least an "interesting analogue" (205), Bullough provides the pertinent translation, noting that in Bandello the wife gets to make a confession to a priest, insists her husband is not to blame for

her death, blames her death on her own misfortune, and asks to be buried in
her first husband's tomb: "The wife, returning somewhat to consciousness,
sent for one of the priests of Saint George, and made confession, pardoning
her husband with all her heart, not willing to let anyone speak ill of him, and
accusing *nobody* but her own misfortune" (261–62, my italics). I think the
overlooked word "nobody" ("*nessuno*") seems deliberately echoed by Shakespeare in Desdemona's few and significantly chosen words, as she painfully
draws her last breath.[27] Moreover, Bandello's wife disallows ill speaking of
her husband, which is recalled in Desdemona's "Let nobody blame him, his
scorn I approve" (4.3.51). This line, which develops Desdemona's attitude
of forbearance a few lines earlier (4.3.17–18), gains significance as an addition to the willow song, and Desdemona self-consciously catches her own
improvisation—"Nay, that's not next" (4.3.52).[28] Although Fenton's version
omits the priest, the pardoning, and the wife's blaming her own misfortune,
keeping only her personal prayer and burial request, in both Fenton's and
Bandello's versions an emphasis is placed on how "unfortunat" (Fenton 188)
is the unnamed lady in her "misfortune" (Bullough 262), which may recall for
Shakespeare the meaning of Desdemona's name as "unfortunate," provided
by Cinthio (Honigmann 386).

    However, Shakespeare creates two strikingly original additions for Des-
demona's last two lines: (1) the "lie"—Desdemona's assumption of blame for
her own death in what amounts to an admission of suicide and no general
scapegoating of fortune—"Nobody. I myself"; and (2) the nature of her farewell—"Commend me to my kind lord—O, farewell!" Given the tradition of
deathbed veracity, the magnitude of Shakespeare's innovative assignment of
tragic blame as a bold lie has not been critically considered. Desdemona's
"I myself" amounts to self-slander of self-slaughter, rendering her a suspect
suicide. By explicitly pinning the blame for her death on herself, Desdemona
is "undone" (5.2.75). She courageously sacrifices the loss of her good name—
"the immediate jewel" of her soul (3.3.159)—and gains the infamous reputation of a suicide, who like Ophelia in *Hamlet* could expect maimed burial rites
or even burial at a crossroads with a stake in her heart.[29] Although Desdemona lies about her death and never about her chastity, she dies knowing that
she has tried but failed to convince Othello that she is no strumpet so that
not only does her lord think her a whore, but now the world will brand her a
suicide. Insult is added to injury.[30]

    In this play so vitally concerned with "reputation" (a word repeated nine
times, excluding synonyms like "good name," "opinion," or "estimation"),
what man would so bravely and generously sacrifice the honor of his reputation? Othello, like Hamlet, expends some of his final breath in attempting to
clear the air about his wounded name and establish the truth as he sees it. As

Honigmann observes, Shakespeare probes many stereotypes in this play (56, 60–61), and here a woman sets an example of moral courage to which the men can only aspire. If men, especially warriors, were supposed to die for the honor of their reputations, how exceptional is Desdemona to lay down the honor of her reputation to try to save Othello? Shakespeare crafts a fitting exit for Desdemona. She deceived her father in order to marry Othello, and now she deceives the world in order to love Othello ideally, especially from an Erasmian perspective as I will explain later. She enters the play with an act of deception (her adventuresome elopement out of honorable love for Othello), and she exits the play with a verbal deception—the saving grace of her lie out of "humble love" (3.3.461) for Othello that risks her own self-abasement in the eyes of the world. Unlike Fenton's heroine who immediately earns "due fame ... after her deathe, beinge worthelye invested wythe the wreathes of honoure amonge all the ladies of that contreye" (191–92), Desdemona risks that very fame, risks having "her name, that was as fresh / As Dian's visage" now become "begrimed and black" (3.3.389–90).

Why lie? As mentioned earlier, Desdemona is probably trying to shield Othello. From what? Several possibilities. She probably hopes to defend Othello's physical life from the rigor of the law. Although some critics have suggested that Venice would tolerate, even approve in some cases, a jealous husband's taking of the law into his own hands and executing his wife suspected of adultery, this does not seem to be the expectation for Othello's case in this play.[31] In the first place, Desdemona is innocent so Othello would not be excused for taking an innocent life. Secondly, the Venetian authorities who have arrived in Cyprus, along with the Cyprian governor Montano, voice their disapproval. Ludovico is appalled that Othello slapped his wife in public (4.1.241–43, 272); Gratiano and Montano are stunned that Othello has murdered his wife (5.2.182–86, 204–07); and Gratiano cries shame upon Iago (who moments later brands his wife a "villainous whore") for drawing his sword upon his wife (5.2.222–27), even though Emilia rebels against Iago's commands to be silent and go home; and Montano pursues Iago as a "notorious villain" (5.2.237–41) for killing his wife and tempting Othello to kill his wife, not yet knowing Iago's role in the murder of Roderigo and the maiming of Cassio. Most importantly, Montano puts Gratiano in charge of guarding Othello, commanding that Othello be *killed* rather than allowed to escape (5.2.239–40), and once the full extent (although not the motive) of Iago's villainy is discovered, Ludovico continues to keep Othello a "close prisoner" for the Venetian state (5.2.333–35).

What might Othello's penalty be? More historical work needs to be done regarding the possible legal consequences, but given English law, an English audience would probably expect Othello to be judged guilty of the felony of murder, and he could receive the death penalty.[32] Under Venetian law, neither jealous rage nor injured honor would suffice to excuse Othello who would not have gone unpunished, and although the council would decide the precise penalty, the conviction of murder usually resulted in "either the serious mutilation of the criminal or his execution."[33] Because Desdemona now realizes that Othello has somehow been deceived about the true nature of her relationship to Cassio, she probably expects that if Othello's life is spared, he has more time to discover the truth and repent. Given Desdemona's faith in her husband's essentially noble nature, she would expect him to repent his "fall," which he does indeed once his error in judgment has been exposed to him. Therefore, her lie may also anticipate Othello's concern about damnation (5.2.65, 135–37) and attempt to preserve him for spiritual salvation.

The character most militant against slander ironically lies stifled on her deathbed after slandering herself with a lie that not only illuminates her magnanimity but also triggers ultimately the stifling of Iago's slanders through Othello's immediate truth-telling that in turn enables Emilia's unraveling of Iago's web of lies. With positively shocking irony, it is precisely Desdemona's lie that provokes Othello's self-confession of truth: "'Twas I that killed her" (5.2.128). Othello's voluntary correction of Desdemona's lie with his admission of guilt deserves much credit, but is often overlooked to find "Othello's death speech serves as his confession" (Honigmann 74). Shakespeare seems obsessed with having the truth come to light, in contrast to Cinthio whose Moor never confesses. Not only do Roderigo's letters supply new evidence in the play's closing minutes, but like Desdemona, Roderigo revives after appearing dead and vocally tells the truth that exonerates Cassio. But *how* the truth begins to emerge is crucial. Had Othello's own love of honesty never exposed Desdemona's lie, Emilia would have been constrained to report Desdemona's lie as truth—"She said so; I must needs report the truth" (5.2.126). When Othello takes this first step of self-conviction, the pieces of the puzzle can begin to fall into place as Emilia rises to take down the culprits. Emilia's "iterance" of "my husband" (5.2.137, 142, 145) ironically parallels Iago's "iterance" of "honest" and "think" (3.3.104, 108) as Shakespeare uses this same speech strategy for *peripetia*, reversing now Iago's deception with Emilia's clarification. Her moral and physical heroism is inspired by that of her mistress, whose song she dies singing as she requests to be laid on the same bed by her side. Her request perhaps allies the two women in a positive parody of marriage that visually reverses and replaces the negative parody of marriage in the alliance of Othello and Iago who kneel together, Othello vowing revenge and Iago vowing obedience: "I am your own forever" (3.3.482).

It is easy to fault Desdemona for not being less naive like the more worldly wise Emilia. However, all of Emilia's sophisticated assets—her incisive intuitions about jealousy (3.4.29, 100), her awareness of her husband's waywardness (3.3.296) and accusation of adultery with Othello (4.2.149), her observations of Othello's changed behavior over the missing handkerchief (3.4.100), her knowledge that he now regards Desdemona as unchaste (4.2.12–19), and her instinct for smelling out villainy (4.2.132–35; 5.2.188–89)—do not suffice to enable Emilia to connect the dots and detect Iago as *the* villain: "I know thou didst not, thou'rt not such a villain" (5.2.170). Despite suspicions, no one sees through "honest" Iago until too late, and appropriately it is Iago's first victim, Roderigo, who first sees through the Ensign's false signs. Unlike the more "divine" (2.1.73) Desdemona, the more earthly Emilia approves the payback of revenge (4.3.91–01) and does not forgive (5.2.156–57) the "cruel Moor" (5.2.247), even though she witnesses, as Desdemona could only imagine, his agony of remorse upon realizing the truth. Desdemona can even pray for the villain abusing her husband's conception of her, "If any [villain] such there be, heaven pardon him" (4.2.137), whereas Emilia speaks for most of us mortals, "A halter pardon him, and hell gnaw his bones!" (4.2.138). Bemoaning "why should honour outlive honesty" (5.2.243), Othello decides to "let it go all" (5.2.244), but he ends up trying to salvage some of his honor (reputation) through his honesty (character) and how he interprets the truth about what he has done and why. Desdemona's paradoxical "dishonesty," on the other hand, is truly honorable in attempting to be honest ("kind") to Othello.

Let us now consider Desdemona's final line. When Desdemona seeks to save Othello with her dying breath, she purposefully ends with a goodwill wish that speaks volumes: "Commend me to my kind lord." Why "commend"? Why "kind"? As noted earlier, Shakespeare may be simply echoing Fenton's verb choice in his selection of "commend." But the fact that Desdemona's line is a death utterance might also recall for Shakespeare's audience the most biblically famous of all death utterances, namely Christ's "Father, into thy hands I *commend* my spirit" (Luke 23:46, my italics).[34] The gloss in the Geneva Bible refers the reader to Psalm 30.8 (misprinted as 6): "Then cryed I unto thee, o Lord, and prayed to my Lord." This psalm could remind one of Desdemona's prayerful cry—"Lord, Lord, Lord"—when Othello stifles her. The reiterated emphasis on Othello's intended "sacrifice" would linguistically signal a parallel between the sacrifice of innocent victims who die as scapegoats assuming others' guilt for salvific purposes.[35]

Why "my kind lord"? Other monosyllabic adjectives would have worked poetically, e.g., "good" or "dear." This is significantly the only time in the play when Desdemona explicitly addresses Othello as her "kind lord, " even though elsewhere the play's rhetoric of "kindness" (2.3.315) and "unkindness" (3.4.153, 4.1.225, 4.2.161–62) does get associated with Desdemona.

The adverb "unkindly" in the play's very first line keynotes the opening mood as Roderigo complains against Iago: "Tush, never tell me, I take it much unkindly / That thou, Iago, who hast had my purse / As if the strings were thine, shouldst know of this" (1.1.1–3). Who knows what and when in this tragedy of epistemology and theology—of knowing and believing—a tragedy long valued for its powerful psychology? Othello's "dear heart strings" (3.3.265), like Roderigo's purse strings, will be untied maliciously by Iago. Yet Iago cannot unmoor "true hearts" (4.2.119) like Desdemona's because, among its many virtuous attributes, love truly defined is kind (1 Cor. 13:4–7). The language of kindness is crucial in the play (and as we will discover in Erasmus); "kindness" as a word was richer then than now, having the meanings of "naturalness" as well as "benevolence." In fact, Othello has been unkind in both senses. Othello could have condemned her supposed adultery but forgiven the adulterer. Othello has at least one nonlethal option, and he knows it. He initially thinks of divorce: "If I do prove her haggard, / . . . I'd whistle her off and let her down the wind / To prey at fortune" (3.3.264–67). Likewise, when she discovers he intends to kill her, Desdemona begs, "O, banish me, my lord, but kill me not!" (5.2.77). Earlier even Iago anticipated this possibility: "[Brabantio] will divorce you" (1.2.14). However, Othello spirals downward to murder with Iago's pestilent persistence as Iago follows his own advice to "plague him with flies" (1.3.70). Unlike Desdemona, why does Othello fail to consider the option of forgiveness for either her or himself? No longer suborning the witness as the "unhandsome warrior" she had envisioned herself as in act 3, Desdemona now admits Othello's life-threatening "unkindness" (4.2.161–62) as she recognizes that his "soul" may not be as "perfect" (1.2.31) as either of them had thought.

Although both spouses need to grow in wisdom, they do recognize the existence of evil. Desdemona distinguishes between those who err in "ignorance" as opposed to those who err in "cunning" (3.3.48–51), and Othello knows "the tricks of custom" adopted by "a false disloyal knave" (3.3.121–27). But they, like everyone else in the play, cannot be expected to detect Iago's hypocrisy, "the only evil that walks Invisible, except to God,"[36] until the hypocrite slips up and tips his hand. They also deserve credit for how genuinely they value the human soul. Despite Othello's change for the worse, or as Emilia puts it, "Here's a change indeed!" (4.2.108), Desdemona maintains her undying love so that she appears to love him more knowingly now than she did earlier. When Othello makes his intent of killing known to her, Desdemona correctly instructs him about the unkindness of such mistaken behavior that punishes "loves" as "sins" (5.2.40): "That death's unnatural that kills for loving" (5.2.42). However, in publicly identifying him to Emilia as her "kind" lord, she shows she has forgiven his unnaturalness and hurtfulness, and she does so not naively, but *knowingly*. Bandello's heroine closes with an explicit articulation of forgiveness. Shakespeare grants his heroine less breath and less time, preferring to indicate directions by indirections, characteristically leaving more open to his audience's fertile imagination. Like Prospero, whose rejection of magic demonstrates self-mastery in recognizing the superiority of the power of virtue over the virtue of power, Desdemona, whose rejection of revenge demonstrates knowledgeable forgiveness, understands that "the rarer action is / In virtue than vengeance" (*The Tempest* 5.1.27–28). Desdemona sets the example of Christian kindness for Othello regarding how to avoid hate, whether of self or other, in love that is both giving and forgiving. In so doing, she upholds Erasmus's conception of the woman warrior.

III

An especially fruitful, yet neglected, context for understanding Shakespeare's construction of Desdemona as a woman warrior, who is both "fair" and "unhandsome" in the play's two references to her as a "warrior," is Erasmus's *Enchiridion Militis Christiani*, that is, *The Handbook of the Christian Soldier* (first published in February 1503 by Martens). Erasmus told Thomas More that this book became "'universally welcome'"; he described it to John Colet as "'a method of morals'" (for matters of religion "'that have to do with true goodness'") and to Maarten van Dorp as "'the pattern of a Christian life.'"[37] Although the metaphor of the "Christian soldier" is as old as the New Testament, receiving its first expression from Paul,[38] Erasmus pointedly gives it fuller meaning in his own treatment of the spiritual warfare against the allurements of vice that should be the life of the Christian. Earlier, medieval drama presented such warfare in the *psychomachias* of the morality plays that staged the conflict necessary to drama either between humans and supernatural powers or within human nature as strife between body and soul. Erasmus, however, self-consciously affirms that his *Enchiridion* presents the reader with "the method and rules of a new kind of warfare" (126).

In his version of our spiritual combat, Erasmus specifically redeems Eve, allegorically our "carnal passions" (48), through the marriage trope and the figure of the obedient wife as a heroic female warrior:

> Paul wishes the woman to be subject to her husband.... The carnal passions are our Eve [Sir 42:14], whose glance the clever serpent attracts daily.... But what do you read about the new woman, the one who is obedient to her husband? "I shall create enmity between you" (obviously the serpent) "and the woman, and between your seed and her seed. She will crush your head, and you will strike insidiously at her heel." [Gen. 3.15] ... The serpent has

been thrown down on his belly ... All he can do is lie in wait to strike blows at her heel from ambush. But by the power of faith the woman has been turned into a female warrior and with great heroism crushes his poisonous head. Grace has been increased; the tyranny of the flesh has been diminished. (48)[39]

If Shakespeare had Erasmus's description of the Fall in mind, he would find here both the old nature of woman as corrupted temptress and the new nature of woman as heroic warrior. Shakespeare captures this contrast by combining two characters in Cinthio to create the single character of Bianca (Bullough 249) so that she embodies onstage the idea of woman as "whore" (carnal passions). While Bianca is no spouse, despite her desire for Cassio as a husband (4.1.128–30), she can be seen as a type of "enfleshed" Eve. None-theless, Bianca joins Desdemona and Emilia in demonstrating female brav-ery when she immediately withstands, far better than the male Roderigo has done, Iago's best attempt to intimidate her: "[Cassio] supped at my house, but I therefore shake not" (5.1.119). Moreover, Shakespeare would also find two notable elements that suit his play but that do not appear in Genesis 3.15, the biblical text to which Erasmus refers.[40] Erasmus's serpent needs "ambush" in order to strike "insidiously," and likewise Iago, called a "viper" (5.2.282) though but a man, uses the mask of honesty as his ambush for insidious attacks. The "poisonous head" of the serpent complements Iago's deliberate use of verbal "poison" (3.3.325) to strike at the Achilles' heel of the newlyweds so that the play ends with a scene that "poisons sight" (5.2.364).[41] Desde-mona is the only one of Iago's intended victims that he cannot corrupt but can only make to *appear* corrupt. She may lose the earthly battle for physical life, but more importantly she wins the eternal war for spiritual salvation. Emilia who rebelliously but justifiably transfers her allegiance from Iago to Desdemona in act 5 becomes the disobedient wife whose heroic champion-ing of the obedient wife ironically contributes to Iago's downfall.[42] But what I wish to emphasize here is not so much detailed as *general* applicability of Erasmus's version of the Fall and his significant and surprising depiction of the *woman* of faith as the heroic *warrior* over evil.

The *Enchiridion* might also shed light on Desdemona's surprising self-description as "unhandsome warrior" (3.4.152). Shakespeare uses the adjec-tive "unhandsome" only 3 other times in his canon, twice in the usual sense of "unattractive" (*Much Ado about Nothing*, 1.1.175; 1H4, 1.3.44) and once in the sense of "unfitting" (*As You Like It*, Epilogue 2P). In his careful note on "unhandsome" (250), Honigmann presents the possible meanings of "unhandsome," primarily as "unskilful" (noting that this is the first and only such instance cited in the *OED*), and secondarily as "unseemly, discourteous" and "unsoldierly" (noting that the first citation for "handsome" as "soldierly" is 1665). Because the etymological meaning of Desdemona's name is "unfortunate," as noted earlier, I would suggest that perhaps Shakespeare is also playing on the meaning of "unhandsome" as "unfortunate, unhappy" (*OED* 5), although the first instance cited is 1633. But I think it is the soldierly sense that a literal translation of Erasmus's Latin title conveys best. As Fantazzi observes, the first English translation, published by Wynkyn de Worde in 1533, was followed by a thoroughly revised edition in 1534, which translated the Latin original more literally and rendered the title: "'The hansome [ie ready to hand] weapon of a christen knyght'" (6). One meaning of "unhandsome" is "unhandy, inconvenient, ill-adapted" (*OED* 2) which complements the meaning of "inexpert, unskilful" thought to be the primary sense of Desdemona's term. As Fantazzi explains, the Greek word *enchiridion* has both the meanings of "'dagger'" and "'handbook'" that Erasmus earlier used in a letter to Jacob de Voecht to play on Menander's saying that "'virtue is mortal man's mightiest weapon'" and that a few years later he used again to entitle this treatise "to exploit its double-edged connotation, although in the context of the military metaphor the more concrete sense must have been uppermost in his mind" (2).

Erasmus cleverly took pains to create a handy handbook or weapon to be used for virtue and against vice by all Christian warriors. Desdemona, therefore, recalls Othello's description of her as his "fair warrior" when she finds herself unfair or unhandsome, not in the sense of physical but rather spiritual beauty, because she lets down her guard against imperfect charity and unskillfully wounds herself when she sought to wound Othello: "Beshrew me much, Emilia, / I was, unhandsome warrior as I am, / Arraigning his unkindness with my soul, / But now I find I had suborned the witness / And he's indicted falsely" (3.4.151–55). Throughout his treatise Erasmus emphasizes the heart of Christian *pietas* as the new law of love, as "kindness" (11, 97), as pure or perfect "charity" (94, 97), as "forgiveness" (123–25) so that when we err, we should try to err on the side of love (13–15, 19, 123–24).

Given Erasmus's rich wordplay on handiness, skill, dagger, and handbook for his *Enchiridion*, it should not catch us so much by surprise, as it might otherwise, to find Iago sneers at Othello for his lack of bookish knowledge as an appropriate self-defense regarding the vice of jealousy: "As [Cassio] shall smile, Othello shall go mad. / And his unbookish jealousy must construe / Poor Cassio's smiles, gestures and light behaviour / Quite in the wrong" (4.1.101–04).[43] Had Othello been fully armed with Erasmus's handbook as his dagger, as it can be argued his wife as the Erasmian fair warrior truly is, he might not have found his own dagger so ready to hand. Othello has already been doubly disarmed, once by Montano (5.2.238) and once by himself (5.2.268–69), but both times the weapons are significantly swords: (1) swords as stage props help to signify Othello's identity as a Christian Moor, unlike the scimitars that Honigmann notes are assigned to Moors in other plays (323); and (2) these two swords have personal meaning for Othello: the one Montano takes appears to be the sword he wears daily (its confiscation makes Othello see himself as no longer valiant), and the other seems to be a trophy sword that represents his glorious past victories, one that he initially flaunts but then permanently retires. Regarding the removal of his first sword Othello bemoans how "every puny whipster gets my sword" (5.2.242), and Ross glosses "puny" as "skilless," thinking "*puny* has the force of 'puisny' in *As You Like It* III.iv.39—'having but the skill of a novice'" (Ross 238). No one suspects Othello has another weapon (5.2.358), but the ever resourceful soldier produces a hidden dagger when he (self-divided in fighting simultaneously for and against himself) decides to kill himself as paradoxically both the Turk and the Christian Moor.[44]

Erasmus's *Enchiridion* also presents both a literal and figurative use of the Turkish threat that is not found at all in Shakespeare's main literary source, Cinthio, although one literal allusion to a past fifteenth-century Turkish siege appears in Fenton (165). Likewise, Shakespeare's use of contemporary historical sources regarding the Turkish-Venetian wars in the sixteenth century and his awareness of James I's poem on the Battle of Lepanto (Bullough 212–14) reflect a literal or factual representation of the Turks, but these sources tend not to emphasize a symbolic reading of the Turks.[45] In his preface Erasmus lays the groundwork for how he will use the Turk in his text, beginning with the historically literal to emphasize later the spiritually figurative significance, an organizational structure that Shakespeare reflects in his play because he begins with a strongly literal use of the Turks but shifts increasingly toward a figurative emphasis on "the Turk" as a symbol of evil that threatens not just Christendom but every Christian as the danger within us all, according to Erasmus: "this is ... a war with oneself, and the enemy battle line springs unbidden from our own entrails ..." (40–41; cf. 83).[46] Both Cinthio's and Fenton's (Bandello's) stories of a jealous soldier's murder of his innocent wife occur in times of peace. Shakespeare adds the emphasis on literal war between the Turks and the Venetians over the island of Cyprus. If "what's past is prologue" (*The Tempest* 2.1.253), Erasmus, in language that hauntingly recalls somewhat the 2003 international crisis over the war in Iraq, agonizes over the current (1518) Christian preparation for war against the Turks, worrying about the image and message Christians represent if they don't live up to their *true* ideals, should they physically triumph in literal battle but spiritually fail to convert their enemies to those ideals by living a good example of "a pure and simple life" (10).[47] Erasmus even contemplates staging first a paper war of "pamphlets" to win the minds and hearts of the Turks.[48]

Shakespeare, however, has his Turks take the offensive and, like Iago, use "a pageant / To keep us in false gaze" (1.3.19–20), but he avoids actual bloodshed by creating a tempest that destroys the external threat of the Turks while he allows the internal threat of the Turk—both in the person of Iago and the potential for darkness within each person—to breed on Cyprus. Hence, the curiously brief scene (3.2) of Othello's inspection of his outer fortifications ironically precedes Iago's attack on Othello's inner fortifications that he has not inspected sufficiently. So also in *Hamlet* Shakespeare shifted the threat from outside (Fortinbras) to inside (Claudius) the realm. Once Iago's engineered chaos begins on Cyprus, Othello remonstrates: "Are we turned Turks? and to ourselves do that / Which heaven hath forbid the Ottomites? / For Christian shame, put by this barbarous brawl" (2.3.166–68). Othello's metaphor of Christians shamefully "turning Turk" reflects the same idea of erroneous conversion that Erasmus articulates when he explains that "we shall degenerate into Turks long before we convert the Turks to our way of thinking" if Christian militants do not promote the flowering of "religion and charity and peace and innocence" (11).

The jewel of Erasmus's metaphorical uses of the Turk, who is the enemy of the Christian soldier, is a passage that relates most poignantly to both Desdemona's and Othello's final speeches, and the following context for that passage is very important. In his articulation of the "beliefs worthy of a Christian," Erasmus begins by emphasizing that we live not for ourselves, but for God, and charity is the rule: "Christian charity knows no exclusivity. Let him love the pious in Christ and the impious for the sake of Christ, who so loved us first when we were still his enemies that he expended himself wholly for our ransom [Rom. 5.10]. Let the Christian, therefore, embrace the former because they are good, and the latter as well so that he may render them good" (93–94). In his concrete example that Christian charity embraces all humans, regardless of race or nation, Erasmus explains: "It is not fitting for a Christian to entertain thoughts like this: 'What have I to do with this fellow? I don't know whether he is black or white [Catullus 3.2]. He is unknown to me, a total stranger. . . . he offended me once . . . ' None of this! Recall only for what merit of yours Christ bestowed all his gifts. It was his wish that the *kindness* he conferred upon you would be reciprocated not to himself, but to your neighbor" (94, my italics). These beliefs, then, frame the following passage on the Turk that pertains to *Othello* because Desdemona embodies them—she who has loved faithfully a black man, a stranger to her native city, a misled murderer, she whose romantic love manifests pure charity in returning kindness for "unkindness" (4.2.161–62) that defeats her life but never taints her love:

> [The Christian] should not hate any man at all in so far as he is a man, any more than a devoted doctor hates a sick man. Let him be the enemy only of vice. The graver the illness, the greater the care pure charity will administer. He is an adulterer, a sacrilegious person, a Turk; one should abhor the adultery, not the man; show one's aversion for the sacrilege, not the man, kill the Turk, not the man. He should make every effort that the impious man that the other has made of himself should perish, but that the man that God made should be saved. (94)

Over two decades ago I tried to study the importance of this passage for Othello's final speech in arguing for the Folio's "the base Judean" reading over the Quarto's "the base Indian," but I overlooked its significance then for Desdemona.[49] I would like to revisit briefly this difficult textual crux as well as suggest another possible reading in light of Desdemona as woman warrior. As I demonstrated in the earlier article, there is no philological evidence to show that "base" could mean "ignorant," either in Shakespeare's era or ours.[50] However, the interpretation of "base" as "ignorant" continues to prevail in criticism devoted to this textual crux. For example, Richard Levin glosses "base" as meaning "ignorant" if it modifies Indian, which is the reading he prefers.[51] M. R. Ridley emphasizes the aptness of the "Indian" reading on grounds of the Indian's "ignorance" because "'they know not the value of their own commodity.'"[52] Reading "the base Indian" in light of the contemporary stories about Indians who threw away jewels because they did not know the gems had any value whatsoever tends to predispose scholarly editors to interpret "base" as meaning "ignorant" even when that is not the specific gloss supplied by them. For example, Norman Sanders glosses "base" as meaning "'low in natural rank or in the scale of creation'" or as meaning "'deep-coloured, dark,'" but he concludes by finding that among other flaws "Othello is lamenting his ignorance."[53] Honigmann glosses "base" as "lowly" if it modifies "Indian" but "depraved, despicable" if it modifies "Judean" (330), but he too concludes that "the ignorance of Indians, unaware of the value of their gold and precious stones" defines Othello's action as similarly resulting from "ignorance" (342). Summarizing the arguments for and against "Judean" and the arguments for "Indian," Honigmann adopts the "Indian" reading and supports Levin's argument as the "best analysis" of this crux because it ends with a telling point: "It is appropriate for Othello to compare himself with the Indian, whose action results from ignorance, and 'very inappropriate for him to compare himself to Judas, whose action was regarded as a conscious choice of evil'" (342–43). While Othello may be "ignorant" in the sense of "stupid" or "foolish"—"O gull, O dolt, / As ignorant as dirt" (5.2.161)—he is not totally ignorant of the value of what he threw away, which is the sense of absolute "unknowing" that the "Indian" reading necessitates, but rather he believes Desdemona has betrayed or cheapened her original value so that he "will kill [her] / And love [her] after" (5.2.18–19).[54] Shakespeare's texts (Quarto and Folio), however, present the word "base," not "ignorant."

In addition to the inaccuracy of interpreting "base" as "ignorant," there is another problem that confronts us here. Whose Judas do we have in mind? We may think of Judas's choice as a deliberate or conscious choice of evil, but this overlooks the biblical presentation of Judas, especially in the gospels of Luke and John, as having been tempted, as having been corrupted from out-side influence, like Othello: "the devil had now *put in the heart* of Judas Iscar-iot . . . to betray him [Jesus]" (John 13:2, my italics). But unlike Othello, Judas encounters the devil himself and not a "demi-devil" (5.2.298) human: "Then entred Satan into Judas" (Luke 22:3); "And after the soppe, Satan entred into him" (John 13:27). Once deceived by the tempter and fallen to temptation, both Othello and Judas can be seen as having "changed" ("change" being a major theme in Shakespeare's play) because evil does "gnaw [their] inwards" (2.1.295) as they ingest the temptation fed them and respond to its poison. Thus Othello incorporates Iago's view that women are hypocrites (2.1.109–13) so that now he can "see" Desdemona as only seeming pure when she is really foul. Desdemona verbally refutes Iago as a "slanderer," but Iago parries, "Nay, it is true, or else I am a Turk" (2.1.113–14), which figuratively he is. Desdemona's life and death, however, offer the best rebuttal to Iago's slander-ing of good women.

But to return to "base." "Base" modifying "Indian" can mean "deep-coloured" or "lowly," and it might be argued, as it has not been, that both meanings could also possibly modify "Judean" if "Judean" refers to "Judas" because from an English or Venetian perspective Judeans would be consid-ered darker in skin color and Judas has humble origins. If "Judean" refers to Herod, who jealously killed his good wife Mariamne, then "base" as "lowly" could not be applied since Herod was a king. But do the senses of "lowly" or "deep-coloured" really suit the context of Shakespeare's simile that is meant to describe Othello as he now sees himself? Othello does not see himself as "lowly," but of "royal siege" (1.2.22). Moreover, Ludovico recognizes Othello as a wealthy figure or he would not be concerned enough to order Gratiano to "seize upon the fortunes of the Moor / For they succeed to [him]" (5.2.364–65). Sanders's "deep-coloured" seems to have more merit because darker skin color is characteristic of Othello, Indians, and Judeans.[55] If this is the literal meaning Shakespeare intended for "base," then I would suggest perhaps there is wordplay to suggest the "darkness" of the deed done by the dark-skinned man, as Shakespeare does, for example, in Emilia's "racist" condemnations of Othello as Desdemona's "most filthy bargain" (5.2.153) or "as ignorant as dirt" (5.2.160). However, this reading seems to invert priorities because the primary emphasis in Othello's simile is not on what is "external" to the man and over which he has little choice (skin color or natural/social birthright), but rather what is more "internal" and over which he has more choice: what he has done and why. What is at stake here is the nature of the deed done and how that deed reflects the doer's perceived identity of self and how he wants others to see him for the record.

Rhetoric might shed some light on these tough issues. Shakespeare's rhetorical strategy of *anaphora* (repetition) should be carefully considered regarding how it works and stylistically contextualizes meaning.[56] Othello insists, "Speak of me as I am," and if so, "then must you speak" (5.2.340) of one whom he describes in four successive, and I would suggest, *related* phrases that comprise one grammatical sentence in verse, each beginning with the phrase "of one" and each conjoined by colons in the Folio's punctuation as part of one sentence that arrives at a final period when the comparisons end in line 349. Shakespeare's figure of speech presents four different expressions that are connected by an introductory repetitive phrase and one governing idea, namely the description of one who *erred* and who now *realizes* that error. Therefore, Othello can describe himself *now* as one "that loved not wisely, but too well"; as one "not easily jealous" but once provoked capable of extreme distraction; as one whose hand "threw a pearl away / Richer than all his tribe" (the gem specifically recognized as a pearl and not just any pearl, but one of inestimable value); and finally, as one who does not easily weep, any more than he was one to be easily jealous, but who now weeps profusely in grief-stricken awareness of what he has done. Given the paralleled rhetorical structuring of Othello's self-conscious descriptions, the idea of "ignorance" as "destitute of knowledge" (*OED* 1) does not seem to suit this context any more than "ignorant" can be used to define "base," according to the *Oxford English Dictionary*. Unlike a Judas, a Herod, or an Othello, an "ignorant" Indian cannot judge and bewail his own action if he accords no significance or value to what he has done. Nor do we tend to feel tragic pity for a person who is indifferent to what he has done, who does not suffer *anagnorisis* as a result of his *hamartia* because ignorance is bliss: "He that is robbed, not wanting what is stolen, / Let him not know't, and he's not robbed at all" (345–46). The "Judean" reading, whether taken to refer to Judas or Herod, disturbs sensibilities because such a reading seems to preclude the response of "pity," or as Levin indicates, the Judean (Judas) reading treats Othello's killing of Desdemona "allegorically" as "meriting eternal damnation" whereas the Indian reading allows us to view Othello's murder "in literal terms as a tragic error committed by a particular man worked upon by a particular set of circumstances who merits some pity" (36). Need it be so starkly "either/or"?

Enter Desdemona, woman warrior. As I have tried to indicate throughout this essay, I do think Othello elicits pity, and in fact, I think Shakespeare deliberately cultivates our pity for Othello. Shakespeare assaults our senses with Othello's agony; our ears hear his moans and his anguished eloquence, and our eyes watch Othello's "subdued eyes" (5.2.346) rain tears, a sight rare to see for a military general of Othello's stature, whether onstage or in public life. Not to pity Othello would be not to pity ourselves, that is, not to pity anyone who falls to temptation. As mere mortals we are all sinners and err to varying degrees and for various reasons. Ross makes this idea even more explicit by not allowing us to demonize even Judas as dismissively "the other": " ... every mortal sinner could be regarded analogically 'as' a Judas and Judean ('they crucify unto themselves the son of God afresh' Hebrews 6:6)" (246). Desdemona responds with charitable wisdom to Emilia's understandable argument in favor of "revenge" (4.3.92): "God me such usage send / Not to pick bad from bad, but by bad mend!" (4.3.103–4). That response foreshadows her ultimate act of what Erasmus defines as "perfect charity" for a Christian warrior when one imitates Christ by overcoming evil with good (cf. Rom. 12:21): "Perfection is reached when, having indignation only against vice, you replace insult with an act of charity. . . . Not to be angry at all is to be most like God and therefore most beautiful" (126). Desdemona, therefore, proves herself to be the play's "fair warrior" in the "new kind of warfare" (126) Erasmus describes so that one might arm oneself against "the vices of detraction, obscenity, jealousy," vices being "the sole enemies of the Christian soldier" (126).[57]

Therefore, I suggest that Shakespeare may cultivate our pity for Othello *especially* through Desdemona's final response as an Erasmian woman warrior. Othello sees himself now as damned. But he earlier saw Desdemona as unchaste and was proven wrong. Othello mistakenly envisions Desdemona's "look" as that which "will hurl his soul from heaven" (5.2.272), but her "look" has already been contradicted by her voice because her dying words spoke for him in forgiveness, not against him. Desdemona wisely cautions that "we must think men are not gods" (3.4.149). Nor are women. No matter how greatly good Desdemona is, Shakespeare remarkably succeeds in making her human with recognizable fears, desires, and deceptions, or as Marvin Rosenberg states: "It seems to me as dangerous to rob Desdemona of her human frailty as it is to steal her essential goodness from her. . . . But we care intensely for this young, passionate woman who ran away secretly from her father's house to the arms of her lover, who has a healthy desire to be with her husband on her wedding night, who cries when she is struck, and who fears death terribly."[58] However, if she in her mortality can forgive Othello, does Shakespeare also invite us to ponder what God can do whose greater love far surpasses the pale reflections that even the best of humankind can mirror? The inebriated Cassio claims, "Well, God's above all, and there be souls must be saved, and there be souls must not be saved" (2.3.98–100). Fortunately for us fallible folk, that ultimate judgment rests not with us but with an infallible God whose perfection of both justice and mercy challenge human comprehension. Although Ludovico voices dismay for the ending of Othello's peroration, "O bloody period!" and Gratiano objects, "All that's spoke is marred" (5.2.355), Shakespeare's play leaves us with thought-provoking possibilities and avoids the kind of definitive judgment found at the end of Marlowe's *Dr. Faustus* with the despairing protagonist dismembered and dragged down to hell.

Given the insistence on jealousy as a "base" passion (3.4.27–28) and given Erasmus's association of this weakness especially with women,[59] Shakespeare's use of jealousy in connection with Desdemona should also surprise us. In a play more than any other in Shakespeare's canon that explores negative jealousy, Desdemona refreshingly exemplifies positive jealousy in the biblical sense of "godly gealous," that is, jealousy in the sense of being "zealous . . . for the well-being of something possessed or esteemed" (*OED* 3). Whether Desdemona tries to be kind to her father by not provoking impatient thoughts (1.3.242–43), speaks up publicly on behalf of Emilia (2.1.102, 162–63), befriends Cassio (3.3.21), or prays for villains (4.2.137), she evinces a positive jealousy that Iago ironically apes in presenting the quality of his "love" for Othello—"oft of my jealousy / Shape faults that are not" (3.3.150–55). Given the tragic trajectory of evil coming out of good, Desdemona's good jealousy on behalf of Othello ironically provides the "ocular proof" (3.3.363) he demands. After being exposed to Iago's germ of jealousy, Othello struggles to "not believe't" (3.3.283), and Desdemona, noting Othello's uncharacteristically faint speech, inquires about his health. He complains of a headache, and Desdemona immediately seeks to heal him by binding his head with the handkerchief that he then brushes aside as insufficient or "too little" (3.3.291) so that Desdemona drops it. Both are so preoccupied—he with negatively jealous thoughts, she with positively jealous concern—that neither observes what happens to the "fallen" handkerchief that Emilia picks up to please Iago's "fantasy" (3.3.303).

In the next scene Othello asks for her handkerchief because he feigns a specific illness that indicates to Shakespeare's audience, as it does not to us, the psychological change Othello is undergoing in his fall to false jealousy. James Winny explains that Othello's complaint, "I have a salt and sullen rheum offends me" (3.4.52), warns that "Othello's habitually phlegmatic nature" that is "temperamentally cold despite his torrid background" and makes him "a man most unlikely to commit crimes of passion" is about to undergo a dangerously passionate change to choler because in humoral theory, as explained in Timothy Bright's treatise on melancholy that Shakespeare used for *Hamlet*, "a salt phlegm" changes a phlegmatic temperament: *"then approacheth it to the nature of choler, and in like sort thereof riseth anger and frowardness."*[60] Winny also observes that in addition to seeing the storm (2.1) "as a symbol of disorder" in general, Bright clarifies how this storm imagery, common to "sixteenth-century treatises of the passions," has "pointed relevance" for Othello's later tempestuous rage given the Elizabethan belief in the "sympathetic link" between human nature and Nature: *"those domestic storms that arise more troublesome and boisterous to our nature than all the blustering winds in the ocean sea"* (15). Desdemona could tame Nature's storm: "Tempests themselves, high seas, and howling winds / . . . As having sense of beauty, do omit / Their mortal natures, letting go safely by / The divine Desdemona" (2.1.63–73). But her husband's jealous tempest did not let her body go safely by, although he could not drown her godly jealous love.

Shakespeare's praise for the nobility of an honorable woman, like the Christian soldier Desdemona, would not be lost on Shakespeare's audience, especially the female patrons who comprised a significant portion.[61] Honigmann observes that Desdemona may "seem passive" once her "self-confidence is checked" by Othello's rejection of her "handkerchief" in the third scene of act 3, and I agree with him that "it would be kinder to describe her as bewildered, out of her depth, not as defeated" (43). However, I would disagree that she "suppresses [her impulsiveness] and thus denies her own nature, almost becoming another person in the last two acts" (48), because that view of her "impulsiveness" does not do justice to Desdemona's charitable courage in sacrificing her reputation or "honor" as a self-proclaimed suicide in order to save Othello. Honigmann, however, astutely appreciates the "moral strength" of Desdemona's "'sweet soul'" (56–57), and my exploration of her heroism as a woman warrior hopefully supplements his awareness of the Christian view of heroism articulated by Milton when he finds "'the better fortitude / Of patience'" to be "'not less but more heroic than the wrath / Of stern Achilles'" (56). From the perspective of some in Shakespeare's audiences, Desdemona, as Emilia's human "angel" (5.2.128) but no modern "kickass" Charlie's angel, may well deserve a medal of honor for courage under fire on the moral battlefield.

NOTES

1. All citations from Shakespeare's works, except *Othello*, are to *The Riverside Shakespeare*, ed. G. Blakemore Evans, 2nd ed. (Boston and New York: Houghton Mifflin, 1997).

2. All citations from *Othello* are to *Othello*, ed. E. A. J. Honigmann, 3rd Arden (Walton-on-Thames, Surrey: Thomas Nelson & Sons Ltd., 1997).

3. See J. Leeds Barroll, *Artificial Persons: The Formation of Character in the Tragedies of Shakespeare* (Columbia: University of South Carolina Press, 1974), 183.

4. See Charles Tyler Prouty, "Some Observations on Shakespeare's Sources," *Shakespeare Jahrbuch* 96 (1960), 64–77.

5. Unless specified otherwise, all biblical citations are to *The Geneva Bible (a facsimile of the 1560 edition)*, intro. Lloyd E. Berry (Madison: University of Wisconsin Press, 1969).

6. See Edith Hamilton, *Mythology* (Boston: Little, Brown and Co., 1949), 45. In Ovid's story Pygmalion was a sculptor on Cyprus, and once Venus transformed his statue into a woman, Pygmalion and Galatea had a son named Paphos who "gave his name to Venus' favorite city" (145–50).

7. All citations from Spenser are to *The Faerie Queene*, ed. Thomas P. Roche, Jr. (Harmondsworth: Penguin, 1978).

8. See, e.g., Geoffrey Bullough, ed., *The Narrative and Dramatic Sources of Shakespeare* (London: Routledge and Kegan Paul; New York: Columbia University Press, 1973), 7:209–10.

9. The white King of Sicilia, Leontes, in Shakespeare's *The Winter's Tale* also falls to false jealousy much more rapidly than Othello does, and unlike Othello, Leontes also falls tempted by himself and not by another like Iago.

10. For the symbolic significance of Othello's suicide weapon, see Lawrence J. Ross, ed., *The Tragedy of Othello the Moor of Venice* (Indianapolis and New York: Bobbs-Merrill, 1974), 248 n. 352. In his book 1 Spenser presents Wrath with a dagger (1.4.33.8).

11. In a forthcoming essay I will examine this matter of influence.

12. In her newspaper feature article, Showalter quotes Lance Morrow as referring to O. J. Simpson as a "'Santa Monica Othello,'" and she suggests that "for many women, the case was another drama of female powerlessness, with Nicole the innocent Desdemona." See Elaine Showalter, "Othello of Santa Monica," *The Guardian*, 4 October 1995, T4. Cf. also, Anthony Hecht's interesting comparison of "uncanny" parallels between Simpson's letter (read by his friend Robert Kardashian) and Othello's final speech in Hecht's letter to the editor, *The Washington Post*, 4 July 1994, A18. Cf. also, Faith Nostbakken, *Understanding Othello: A Student Casebook to Issues, Sources, and Historical Documents* (Westport, CT and London: Greenwood Press, 2000), "Contemporary Applications," 171–85.

13. See John Milton, *Paradise Lost*, ed. Scott Elledge, 2nd ed. (New York and London: Norton, 1993), 3.130–31.

14. Of the play's forty instances of "soul" used either in the singular, the plural, or the possessive, Othello's speech accounts for fifteen references, Iago's for ten, Desdemona's and Emilia's for 5 each, and other characters are limited to a single usage (Roderigo, the Duke, and Brabantio) or two (Cassio). "Soul" interestingly appears in Emilia's discourse (3.4.159) only after Othello has begun to mistreat Desdemona due to jealousy.

15. See Giovanni Battista Giraldi Cinthio, *Gli Hecatommithi* (1566 edn.), The Third Decade, Story 7, in *Narrative and Dramatic Sources of Shakespeare*, ed. Geoffrey Bullough (London: Routledge and Kegan Paul, and New York: Columbia University Press, 1973), 7:242. All citations from Cinthio's novelle will be to this translation by Bullough (pp. 239–52).

16. See, e.g., Kenneth Gross, *Shakespeare's Noise* (Chicago: University of Chicago Press, 2001), 123.

17. For example, Desdemona's "lie" that she is to blame for her death might be interpreted as figuratively "true" from the perspective of the marriage mystery that two individuals become one flesh so that she could identify herself with Othello, but such an interpretation conflicts with Desdemona's preceding assertions of her own innocence.

18. Honigmann notes that in English domestic tragedy predating *Othello*, there occur two revival scenes in the anonymous *A Warning for Fair Women* (1599), a play that was performed by Shakespeare's own company, but he also observes that in one of those scenes the identification of the murderer by a servant *contrasts* with Desdemona's attempt "to shield her murderer instead of accusing him" (74).

19. See Bullough, 202–05.

20. Geffraie Fenton, trans., *Certain Tragical Discourses of Bandello* (1567; repr. New York: AMS Press, 1967): 1:189, my italics. All citations from Fenton will be to this edition.

21. See, e.g., Paul N. Siegel, "A New Source for *Othello*," *PMLA* 75 (1960): 480; Lawrence J. Ross, ed., *The Tragedy of Othello the Moor of Venice* (Indianapolis and New York: Bobbs-Merrill, 1974), 274–75; Naseeb Shaheen, "Like the Base Judean," *Shakespeare Quarterly* 31 (1980): 93–95, and *Biblical References in Shakespeare's Plays* (Newark: University of Delaware Press; London: Associated University Presses, 1999), 600–01.

22. Ross refers Desdemona's "prayerful iteration of the divine name" to Isaiah 42:8: "'I am the Lord, this is my Name'" (225). Honigmann cites Granville-Barker's defense of Q's line: "'Imagine it: Desdemona's agonised cry to God, and as the sharp sound of it is slowly stifled, Emilia's voice at the door rising through it, using the same words in another sense. A macabre duet'" (312).

23. See Hawthorne, *The Scarlet Letter*, ed. Seymour Gross, Sculley Bradley, Richmond Croom Beatty, and E. Hudson Long, 3rd ed. (New York and London: Norton, 1988), 132.

24. Hal, e.g., magnanimously "gilds" Falstaff's lie about the credit for killing Hotspur in order to befriend Falstaff or to do him "grace," thereby sacrificing the embellishment of his own reputation for killing the most reputed warrior in the realm: "For my part, if a lie may do thee grace, / I'll gild it with the happiest terms I have" (*1H4* 5.4.157–58).

25. See the etymology from the Latin and Greek of "hypocrisy" in the *OED*: "the acting of a part on the stage, feigning, pretence."

26. See Honigmann, 387. See Naseeb Shaheen, "Shakespeare's Knowledge of Italian," *Shakespeare Survey* 47 (1994): 161–69.

27. For Bandello's Italian, see Matteo Bandello, *Le Novelle*, ed. Gioachino Brognolio, 5 vols. (1910–12) (Bari: Gius Laterza & Figh, 1910), vol. 2, 230: "*Ella alquanto in sé ritornata, fece chiamar uno dei sacerdoti di San Giorgio e confessosi, di core perdonando al marito, non potendo sofferire che nessuno di lui dicesse male, non incolpando altro che la sua disgrazia.*" Bandello's story is numbered fifty-one.

28. For the full text of the willow song, see Honigmann, 392–93.

29. For practices regarding suicide burials, see Rowland Wymer, *Suicide and Despair in the Jacobean Drama* (Brighton, Sussex: Harvester Press Limited, 1986), 15.

30. Fenton's heroine cautions her husband against the loss of reputation—"a crowne of infamie" (184)—as a result of suicide due to unbridled passion; if he uses

"unnaturall force" against himself and sacrifices his body, he will certainly "leave to the remeinder of [his] house, a crowne of infamie in the judgement of the worlde to come, and put [his] soule in hazarde of grace afore the troane of justice above" (184).

31. See, e.g., Rodney Poisson, "Death for Adultery: A Note on *Othello*, III. iii.394–96," *Shakespeare Quarterly* 28 (1977): 89–92: "For a man of honor like Othello, who is presented as living in the Venetian world of the sixteenth century, the thought of executing his wife . . . would have been considered proper, even inevitable" (90); Sarup Singh, *The Double Standard in Shakespeare and Related Essays: Changing Status of Women in Sixteenth and Seventeenth Century England* (Delhi: Konark Publishers, 1988), 43: "Perhaps most husbands in that period—whether Venetian or not—did act as Othello did, if their sense of honour was as highly developed as his and they possessed his courage."

32. For evidence from English law that Othello would probably be judged guilty of the felony of murder, see Michael Dalton, *The Countrey Iustice* (1618; rpt. Amsterdam: Theatrum Orbis Terrarum; Norwood, NJ: Walter J. Johnson, 1975), 211. In his section on "Murder" in his chapter, "Of Felonies by the Common Law," Dalton (a gentleman of Lincoln's Inn) cites the case of a husband who was in a quarrel with his wife and who suddenly struck her, and she died. Even though the act was "done vpon the sudden, and vpon prouocation" with "no precedent malice" appearing, "it was adiudged Murder at the Assises at Stafford before Walmesley. 43 *Eliz.*" (211). The title page of Dalton's book indicates its focus and purpose: "*The Covntrey Ivstice, Conteyning the Practice of the Ivstices of the Peace out of their Sessions.* Gathered for the better helpe of such Ivstices of Peace as haue not beene much conversant in the studie of the Lawes of this Realme." My suggestion here contradicts the view presented by Sarup Singh that "for an Elizabethan audience . . . what Othello did was justified" (42). Cf. also J. H. Baker, *An Introduction to English Legal History*, 3rd ed. (London: Butterworths, 1990), "Homicide" (600–603); I am grateful to my colleague Lindsay Kaplan for this reference.

33. See Guido Ruggiero, *Violence in Early Renaissance Venice* (New Brunswick, NJ: Rutgers University Press, 1980), 171. Because of the political significance of Othello's case, the Avogadori and the Forty would probably handle it (171). For Venetian legal punishments of adultery during the Renaissance period, see Guido Ruggiero, *The Boundaries of Eros: Sex Crime and Sexuality in Renaissance Venice* (New York and Oxford: Oxford University Press, 1985), 66–69. Ruggiero notes that "lost honor was not in itself an excuse for murder in adultery cases" (67), and punishment was required for "passionate murders and rationally committed ones" (68) so that "neither offended honor nor jealous rage" (68) excused a crime. Ruggiero cites a case from 1441 in which a nobleman, Domenico Grimaldi, killed another young noble, Francesco Bembo, after Grimaldi caught Bembo with his wife in "a compromising moment" (68). Grimaldi fled the city, escaping Venetian justice, but he was "banned perpetually," and if he was caught, "he was to be taken to the scene of the crime, where his hand was to be cut off and hung around his neck," and then "he was to be taken between the columns of justice and decapitated" (68). Ruggiero finds that "only a slight inequality in penalties for women is a surprising indicator of female status in patriarchal Venice" (68) where "a certain independence for women in sexual matters, especially at the higher social levels" (69) obtained. Penalties for adultery for both men and women were "typically restrained and ameliorative" (68) and "seemed to be concerned not with eradicating a moral vice but with reconstituting the family unit and protecting property" (69).

34. The verb form "commend" is used surprisingly less than ten times in the Bible, and the only time "commend" appears in a death utterance is this instance in Luke's account of the crucifixion.

35. For William Tyndale's coinage of the word "scapegoat" and its biblical applicability to Christ as the innocent sacrifice for others' sins, see the present writer's *The Merchant of Venice: Choice, Hazard and Consequence* (Basingstoke and London: Macmillan; New York: St. Martin's Press, 1995), 239. For a study of religious imagery, the theme of sacrificed innocents, and parallels in scenic form between the mystery plays and the last scene of *Othello*, see Cherrell Guilfoyle, "Mactacio Desdemonae: Medieval Scenic Form in the Last Scene of *Othello*," *Comparative Drama* 19 (1985–86): 305–20. Although I agree with her emphasis on Desdemona as "innocent," I disagree with the emphasis on her "passivity" (306–07).

36. Milton, *Paradise Lost*, 3.684.

37. All citations, hereafter documented parenthetically, are to Erasmus, *The Handbook of the Christian Soldier (Enchiridion militis christiani)*, trans. Charles Fantazzi, in *Collected Works of Erasmus*, ed. John W. O'Malley (Toronto: University of Toronto Press, 1988), 66: 1–127; quotations are from Fantazzi, p. 3. Fantazzi suggests the composition of the *Enchiridion* dates from "between the early months of 1499 and the publication of the *Lucubratiunculae* in February 1503 (2); he has based his translation on the 1519 Schürer edition (7). By 1561 Erasmus's text had gone through eleven editions in England. John W. O'Malley cites Margo Todd's *Christian Humanism and the Puritan Social Order* for demonstrating the influence of Erasmus's text on Puritan social thought in England (xxxi). In his edition, John P. Dolan maintains that this text had "a lasting influence in the Church of England" (58). See Erasmus, *Handbook of the Militant Christian* (Notre Dame, IN: Fides Publishers, 1962).

38. See 1 Tim 1:18; 2 Tim 2:3–5, 4:7–8. See O'Malley's introduction, *Collected Works of Erasmus*, vol. 66, xliii and n. 78.

39. In a letter of 1523 to Johann von Botzheim, Erasmus interestingly explains that his *Enchiridion* originated from the request of a good wife, "a lady of a deeply religious turn of mind," who "was fearfully concerned for her husband's salvation" because he was "plunged in fornication and adultery," and she hoped that Erasmus "might get a little religion into the man . . . on condition that he must not know that this was his wife's initiative, for he was cruel even to her, to the extent of beating her, as soldiers will." See *The Correspondence of Erasmus: Letters 1252 to 1355 (1522 to 1523)*, trans. R. A. B. Mynors, in *Collected Works of Erasmus* (Toronto: University of Toronto Press, 1989), vol. 9, 321–322. For early English translations (1533 and 1534) of the passage cited from *Enchiridion* in the text, see Erasmus, *Enchiridion Militis Christiani: An English Version*, ed. Anne M. O'Donnell, S.N.D. (Oxford: Oxford University Press, 1981), 74. This translation does not use the word "warrior" in this passage; instead, " . . . the woman thrugh grace of fayth, *changed as it were in to a man*, boldly tredeth down his venymous heed" (74, my italics).

40. For Genesis 3.15, Erasmus appears to be rather unique in gendering the victor as female and not specifically identifying that female as Mary but rather more generally as a faith-filled "woman" who is "a female warrior." The Geneva Bible (1560) genders the victor as male: "He shal breake thine head, & thou shalt bruise his heele." Biblical scholar and editor, Father James Walsh, S.J., informs me that the Hebrew is clearly masculine, but Jerome writes "*ipsa conteret*," following the Old Latin, and the feminine "she" has always been taken in a Marian sense.

41. Shakespeare may be adapting his earlier motif of literal poison in the ear in *Hamlet* for Iago's figurative poison in the ears of others. For example, just as Iago seeks to "poison [Brabantio's] delight" (1.1.68) with obscene accusations, so also he plots, "I'll pour this pestilence into [Othello's] ear" (2.3.356), rejoicing three scenes later that "the Moor already changes with my poison" (3.3.325). Although sin figured as disease is commonplace imagery, to the best of my knowledge, however, it has not been noted that Shakespeare's use of the disease nuance of "pestilence" may owe something to Fenton's translation of Bandello's story of the Albanese captain who murders his wife because Fenton consistently uses disease imagery for the passion of jealousy, as Shakespeare's main source, Cinthio, does not. See Fenton, e.g., "sickness" and "disease" (185–86), "traunce" and "fyttes of straunge and diverse disposition" (186), and "violence of sicknes" (187).

42. See Erasmus who objects to obeying "ungodly" commands by citing Acts 5:29: "'We ought to obey God rather than men'" (Fantazzi 23).

43. As Honigmann notes, "unbookish" is Shakespeare's coinage (261).

44. The hidden weapon is brilliantly concealed in Janet Suzman's film of *Othello* (1987) based on her direction of the play for the Market Theatre in Johannesburg. Jon Kani, who plays Othello, wears an African style metallic necklace that unclasps to reveal a hidden dagger so that the necklace literally "converts" to a dagger. The only drawback is that Kani's death gesture is a "slicing" of the jugular vein rather than the "smoting" that the play's language indicates.

45. For the figurative sense of "the Turk" as representing "all that was barbaric and demonic, in contrast to the Christian's civil and moral rightness" (13), see Virginia Mason Vaughan, *Othello: A Contextual History* (Cambridge: Cambridge University Press, 1994), 13, 23, 31.

46. Cf. Milton, *Paradise Last*, 9.348–49: " . . . within himself / The danger ties, yet lies within his power."

47. Erasmus cautions: "At this moment war is preparing against the Turks, and whatever the intentions of those who started it, we must pray that it may turn out well, not for a chosen few but for all in common. . . . We shall have found the most effective way to defeat the Turks, once they have seen shining forth in us Christ's teaching and example, once they realize that we are not greedy for their empire, we have no thirst for their gold and no desire for their possessions . . . Nor does it make sense to prove ourselves truly Christians by killing as many as we can, but by their salvation . . ." (10). The date of 1518 for war preparations against the Turks is derived from Erasmus's letter to his friend Thomas More, dated 5 March 1518. See *The Correspondence of Erasmus: Letters 594 to 841 (1517 to 1518)*, trans. R. A. B. Mynors and D. F. S. Thomson, annot. Peter G. Bietenholz, in *Collected Works of Erasmus* (Toronto: University of Toronto Press, 1979), vol. 5, 325–29. With this letter Erasmus also sent to Thomas More, Pope Leo X's "Proposals for a Crusade against the Turks" (issued 12 November 1517) as well as Luther's Ninety-five Theses ("the Conclusions on Papal pardons"), and a book by the Englishman Richard Pace (5: 327).

48. Although understandably writing with the religious bias of his era, Erasmus furnishes a pacifist opinion that it would be a good plan "long before we make attempt by force of arms, to seek to win [the Turks] by letters and pamphlets," of course, not political but spiritual documents that avoid scholarly, theological jargon for clear, pithy expression: "They are human beings, as we are; there is neither steel nor adamant in their hearts. It is possible they may be civilized, possible they may

be won over by kindness which tames even the wild beasts. And the most effective thing of all is Christian truth" (11).

49. See the present writer's "Othello's Threnos: 'Arabian Trees' and 'Indian' Versus 'Judean,'" *Shakespeare Studies* 13 (1980): 145–67.

50. I argued if "base" modifies "Judean," it means "low in the moral scale" (*OED*, *a*., 9), that is "ignoble" or "vile," which is the sense most frequent in Shakespeare (152–55). Cf. "base" as a synonym for "ignoble" in sixteenth- and seventeenth-century dictionaries. For example, John Florio, *A Worlde of Wordes* (London, 1598): "*Ignoble, ignoble, infamous, unrespected, base, dishonored*"; John Bullokar, *An English Expositor* (London, 1616): "*Ignoble*. Base, that is not noble"; and John Minsheu, *Ductor in Linguas* (London, 1617): "*Base, vile, abject*" with synonyms being "*unnoble, vile*."

51. Richard Levin, "*Othello's* American Indian and the Nu Principle," *The Shakespeare Newsletter* 50:2, no. 245 (Summer 2000): 36.

52. M. R. Ridley, ed., *Othello*, 2nd Arden (London: Methuen, 1958), 196.

53. Norman Sanders, ed., *Othello*, New Cambridge Shakespeare (Cambridge: Cambridge University Press, 1984), 192.

54. See Holmer, 153.

55. The evidence cited in the *OED*, however, leaves much to be desired. Both sixteenth-century examples of "base" as "deep-coloured" refer medically to the color of urine, not to skin color. The *OED* questions whether this sense defines Shakespeare's use of "base" in *Titus Andronicus*, "IV ii.72: Is black so base a hue?" See *OED* 5. Given Aaron's response to the Nurse's view of his black baby as "loathsome as a toad / Among the fair-fac'd breeders of our clime" (4.2.67–68), I think that the "depth" of color is not so much the issue (black is the darkest color) but rather the sense of "base" as "befitting an inferior person or thing; degraded or degrading, unworthy" (*OED* 10) better suits the context. Although the *OED* questions the meaning of "base" in this line from *Titus Andronicus*, none of the seven recent editions of the play I checked (including the 1995 Arden) gloss "base."

56. For *anaphora*, see George Puttenham, *The Arte of English Poesie*, ed. Gladys Dodge Willcock and Alice Walker (Cambridge: Cambridge University Press, 1936). Regarding "*anaphora*" or "the Figure of Report" as one of the seven different figures of repetition, Puttenham writes that *anaphora* is "repetition in the first degree . . . when we make one word begin and . . . lead the daunce to many verses in sute" (198). The three English examples of *anaphora* furnished by Puttenham illustrate the idea that many verses perform "*one daunce*" (198, my italics). Moreover, this figure is singled out for eloquence and therefore contributes to the power of Othello's final self-report: "your figure that worketh by iteration or repetition of one word or clause doth much alter and affect the eare and also the mynde of the hearer, and therefore is counted a very braue figure both with the Poets and rhetoricians . . ." (198).

57. In emphasizing that the pious Christian soldier must "be gentle at heart" (15), Erasmus also illuminates the degree of Desdemona's generous mercy for even the "unworthy" (97–98), who might be "worthy of compassion, not punishment" (125), when he cites Augustine's evidence that "in the old days, even when criminals were justly condemned, bishops used their authority to appeal for them, and sometimes rescued a criminal from the hands of his judges . . ." (14).

58. Marvin Rosenberg, *The Masks of Othello* (1961; repr. Newark: University of Delaware Press; London: Associated University Presses, 1994), 209.

59. In the *Enchiridion* Erasmus discusses Paul's use of the terms "flesh" and "spirit," and he indicts the Christian who practices ceremonial observances (e.g., vigils, fasts) but who still indulges in "the works of the flesh," e.g., "jealousy worse than you find in a woman" (77). Regarding the baseness of false jealousy in love, Othello unwittingly prophesies what happens when he assures the senate that if he neglects his military duty for Desdemona, then "all indign and *base adversities* / Make head against [his] estimation" (1.3.274–75, my italics).

60. See James Winny, ed., *The Frame of Order* (London: George Allen & Unwin Ltd., 1957), 15. For the view that Bright's *A Treatise of Melancholy* (1586) is a "subsidiary source" for *Hamlet*, see Harold Jenkins, *Hamlet*, Arden Shakespeare (London and New York: Methuen, 1982), 108.

61. See Andrew Guff, *Playgoing in Shakespeare's London*, 2nd ed. (Cambridge: Cambridge University Press, 1996), 58: "women from every section of society went to plays, from Queen Henrietta Maria to the most harlotry of vagrants." See S. P. Cerasano and Marion Wynne-Davies, eds., *Renaissance Drama by Women: Texts and Documents* (London and New York: Routledge, 1996). Although the debate over the influence of the English theatre was "a controversy that was to coexist with the playhouses throughout this period up to 1642 when overwhelming puritanical sentiment forced their closure" (Cerasano and Wynne-Davies 157) and women were the subjects of much of this controversy, women did not vacate the playhouses until they closed for men too.

Chronology

1564	William Shakespeare christened at Stratford-on-Avon April 26.
1582	Marries Anne Hathaway in November.
1583	Daughter Susanna born, baptized on May 26.
1585	Twins Hamnet and Judith born, baptized on February 2.
1587	Shakespeare goes to London, without family.
1589–90	*Henry VI, Part 1* written.
1590–91	*Henry VI, Part 2* and *Henry VI, Part 3* written.
1592–93	*Richard III* and *The Two Gentlemen of Verona* written.
1593	Publication of *Venus and Adonis*, dedicated to the Earl of Southampton; the *Sonnets* probably begun.
1593	*The Comedy of Errors* written.
1593–94	Publication of *The Rape of Lucrece*, also dedicated to the Earl of Southampton. *Titus Andronicus* and *The Taming of the Shrew* written.
1594–95	*Love's Labour's Lost*, *King John*, and *Richard II* written.
1595–96	*Romeo and Juliet* and *A Midsummer Night's Dream* written.
1596	Son Hamnet dies.

1596–97	*The Merchant of Venice* and *Henry IV, Part 1* written; purchases New Place in Stratford.
1597–98	*The Merry Wives of Windsor* and *Henry IV, Part 2* written.
1598–99	*Much Ado About Nothing* written.
1599	*Henry V, Julius Caesar,* and *As You Like It* written.
1600–01	*Hamlet* written.
1601	*The Phoenix and the Turtle* written; father dies.
1601–02	*Twelfth Night* and *Troilus and Cressida* written.
1602–03	*All's Well That Ends Well* written.
1603	Shakespeare's company becomes the King's Men.
1604	*Measure for Measure* and *Othello* written.
1605	*King Lear* written.
1606	*Macbeth* and *Antony and Cleopatra* written.
1607	Marriage of daughter Susanna on June 5.
1607–08	*Coriolanus, Timon of Athens,* and *Pericles* written.
1608	Mother dies.
1609	Publication, probably unauthorized, of the quarto edition of the *Sonnets.*
1609–10	*Cymbeline* written.
1610–11	*The Winter's Tale* written.
1611	*The Tempest* written. Shakespeare returns to Stratford, where he will live until his death.
1612	*A Funeral Elegy* written.
1612–13	*Henry VIII* written; The Globe Theatre destroyed by fire.
1613	*The Two Noble Kinsmen* written (with John Fletcher).
1616	Daughter Judith marries on February 10; Shakespeare dies April 23.
1623	Publication of the First Folio edition of Shakespeare's plays.

Contributors

HAROLD BLOOM is Sterling Professor of the Humanities at Yale University. He is the author of 30 books, including *Shelley's Mythmaking, The Visionary Company, Blake's Apocalypse, Yeats, A Map of Misreading, Kabbalah and Criticism, Agon: Toward a Theory of Revisionism, The American Religion, The Western Canon,* and *Omens of Millennium: The Gnosis of Angels, Dreams, and Resurrection. The Anxiety of Influence* sets forth Professor Bloom's provocative theory of the literary relationships between the great writers and their predecessors. His most recent books include *Shakespeare: The Invention of the Human,* a 1998 National Book Award finalist, *How to Read and Why, Genius: A Mosaic of One Hundred Exemplary Creative Minds, Hamlet: Poem Unlimited, Where Shall Wisdom Be Found?,* and *Jesus and Yahweh: The Names Divine.* In 1999, Professor Bloom received the prestigious American Academy of Arts and Letters Gold Medal for Criticism. He has also received the International Prize of Catalonia, the Alfonso Reyes Prize of Mexico, and the Hans Christian Andersen Bicentennial Prize of Denmark.

R. A. FOAKES is a professor emeritus at the University of California, Los Angeles. He has been the editor of many Shakespeare plays. His publications also include *Shakespeare and Violence, Coleridge's Criticism of Shakespeare,* and many other titles.

JAMES L. CALDERWOOD is professor emeritus at the University of California, Irvine. He has authored *Shakespearean Metadrama, Shakespeare and the Denial of Death,* and several other titles on Shakespeare.

EDWARD BERRY is a professor at the University of Victoria. He has published numerous articles and chapters on Shakespeare and early modern English literature. Among his books are *Shakespeare and the Hunt: A Cultural and Social Study* and *Patterns of Decay: Shakespeare's Early Histories.*

THOMAS MOISAN was a professor at St. Louis University, where he also served as chair of the department for many years and later as graduate program director. He coedited *In the Company of Shakespeare*, published essays on many Shakespeare plays, and was editor of *Allegorica*, a journal of medieval and renaissance scholarship.

MAYNARD MACK was professor emeritus at Yale, where he also had been chair of the English department. He was coeditor of several volumes of *The Norton Anthology of World Literature* and other works and also edited several Shakespeare plays.

T. H. HOWARD-HILL is distinguished professor emeritus at the University of South Carolina. He has published concordances to many Shakespeare plays, including *Othello*, and also *Shakespearian Bibliography and Textual Criticism: A Bibliography* and other work.

EDWARD PECHTER is a retired professor of Concordia University, Montreal. Most of his publishing has been on Shakespeare. He is the author of *What Was Shakespeare? Renaissance Plays and Changing Critical Practice* and editor of *"Othello": A Critical Edition*, published by W. W. Norton.

ROBERT N. WATSON is a professor at the University of California, Los Angeles, where he has served as chair of the English department and chair of the faculty of the UCLA College of Letters and Science. His publications include *Back to Nature: The Green and the Real in the Late Renaissance*, *Shakespeare and the Hazards of Ambition*, and others.

JOAN OZARK HOLMER is a professor at Georgetown University. She published *The Merchant of Venice: Choice, Hazard and Consequence* and articles on Shakespeare, focusing particularly on *Romeo and Juliet*, *Othello*, *The Merchant of Venice*, and *Hamlet*.

Bibliography

Bartels, Emily C. *Speaking of the Moor: From Alcazar to Othello*. Philadelphia: University of Pennsylvania Press, 2008.

Berger, Harry, Jr. "Acts of Silence, Acts of Speech: How to Do Things with Othello and Desdemona." *Renaissance Drama* (2004): 3–35.

Bevington, David. *This Wide and Universal Theater: Shakespeare in Performance Then and Now*. Chicago: University of Chicago Press, 2007.

Bradbrook, Muriel. *Bradbrook on Shakespeare*. Brighton, Sussex: Harvester Press; Totowa, N.J.: Barnes & Noble Books, 1984.

Brown, John Russell, ed. Othello. New York; London: Applause, 2000.

Buccola, Regina, and Lisa Hopkins, ed. *Marian Moments in Early Modern British Drama*. Aldershot, England; Burlington, Vt.: Ashgate, 2007.

Collington, Philip D. "Othello the Traveller." *Early Theatre* 8, no. 2 (2005): 73–100.

Corporaal, Marguérite. "Women, Speech and Subjectivity in Shakespeare's *Othello*: A Comparative Analysis." *Shakespeare Yearbook* 14 (2004): 93–107.

Elliott, Martin. *Shakespeare's Invention of* Othello*: A Study in Early Modern English*. Basingstoke, Hampshire: Macmillan Press, 1988.

Erickson, Peter. *Citing Shakespeare: The Reinterpretation of Race in Contemporary Literature and Art*. New York; Basingstoke: Palgrave Macmillan, 2007.

Gajowski, Evelyn, ed. "Re-visions of Shakespeare: Essays in Honor of Robert Ornstein." Newark: Delaware University Press; London: Associated University Presses, 2004.

Garber, Marjorie. *Shakespeare and Modern Culture*. New York: Pantheon, 2008.

223

Guilfoyle, Cherrell. *Shakespeare's Play within Play: Medieval Imagery and Scenic Form in* Hamlet, Othello, *and* King Lear. Kalamazoo: Western Michigan University, Medieval Institute Publications, 1990.

Hadfield, Andrew, and Paul Hammond, ed. *Shakespeare and Renaissance Europe.* London: Arden Shakespeare, 2004.

Hall, Joan Lord. Othello: *A Guide to the Play.* Westport, Conn.: Greenwood Press, 1999.

Hays, Michael L. *Shakespearean Tragedy as Chivalric Romance: Rethinking* Macbeth, Hamlet, Othello, *and* King Lear. Cambridge, UK; Rochester, N.Y.: D.S. Brewer, 2003.

Honigmann, E. A. J. *Myriad-Minded Shakespeare: Essays on the Tragedies, Problem Comedies and Shakespeare the Man.* Basingstoke, England; New York: Macmillan; St. Martin's, 1998.

Kaul, Mythili, ed. Othello: *New Essays by Black Writers.* Washington, D.C.: Howard University Press, 1997.

Korda, Natasha. *Shakespeare's Domestic Economies: Gender and Property in Early Modern England.* Philadelphia: University of Pennsylvania Press, 2002.

Lim, Walter S. H. *The Arts of Empire: The Poetics of Colonialism from Raleigh to Milton.* Newark, Del.: University of Delaware Press; London: Associated University Presses, 1998.

Little, Arthur L., Jr. *Shakespeare Jungle Fever: National-Imperial Re-visions of Race, Rape, and Sacrifice.* Stanford, Calif.: Stanford University Press, 2000.

Logan, Sandra. "Domestic Disturbance and the Disordered State in Shakespeare's *Othello.*" *Textual Practice* 18, no. 3 (2004): 351–75.

Marienstras, Richard. *New Perspectives on the Shakespearean World,* trans. Janet Lloyd. Cambridge: Cambridge University Press, 1985.

McPherson, David C. *Shakespeare, Jonson, and the Myth of Venice.* Newark: University of Delaware Press; London; Cranbury, N.J.: Associated University Presses, 1990.

Montrose, Louis. *The Purpose of Playing: Shakespeare and the Cultural Politics of the Elizabethan Theatre.* Chicago: University of Chicago Press, 1996.

Nelsen, Paul, and June Schlueter, ed. *Acts of Criticism: Performance Matters in Shakespeare and His Contemporaries: Essays in Honor of James P. Lusardi.* Madison, N.J.: Fairleigh Dickinson University Press, 2006.

Newman, Karen. *Essaying Shakespeare.* Minneapolis: University of Minnesota Press, 2009.

Nordlund, Marcus. *Shakespeare and the Nature of Love: Literature, Culture, Evolution.* Evanston, Ill.: Northwestern University Press, 2007.

Nostbakken, Faith. *Understanding Othello: A Student Casebook to Issues, Sources, and Historical Documents.* Westport, Conn.: Greenwood Press, 2000.

Orkin, Martin. "Othello and the 'plain face' of Racism." *Shakespeare Quarterly* 28 (1987): 166–88.

Orlin, Lena Cowen. "The Domestication of Othello." *Shakespeare Jahrbuch* 144 (2008): 132–47.

O'Toole, Fintan. *Shakespeare Is Hard, But So Is Life: A Radical Guide to Shakespearean Tragedy.* London; New York: Granta, 2002.

Paster, Gail Kern. *Humoring the Body: Emotion and the Shakespearean Stage.* Chicago: University of Chicago Press, 2004.

Potter, Nicholas. Othello: *Character Studies.* London; New York: Continuum, 2008.

Raatzsch, Richard. *The Apologetics of Evil: The Case of Iago.* Princeton, N.J.: Princeton University Press, 2009.

Ronk, Martha. "Desdemona's Self-Presentation." *English Literary Renaissance* 35, no. 1 (2005): 52–72.

Rudanko, Juhani. *Pragmatic Approaches to Shakespeare: Essays on* Othello, Coriolanus, *and* Timon of Athens. Lanham, Md.: University Press of America, 1993.

Sadowski, Piotr. *Dynamism of Character in Shakespeare's Mature Tragedies.* Newark Del.: University of Delaware Press; London: Associated University Presses, 2003.

Sohmer, Steve. "The 'Double Time' Crux in *Othello* Solved." *English Literary Renaissance* 32, no. 2 (2002): 214–38.

Snyder, Susan, ed. Othello: *Critical Essays.* New York: Garland, 1988.

Snyder, Susan. *Shakespeare: A Wayward Journey.* Newark; London, England: University of Delaware Press, Associated University Presses, 2002.

Wells, Stanley, and Lena Cowen Orlin, ed. *Shakespeare: An Oxford Guide.* New York: Oxford University Press, 2003.

Wilson, Richard. *Secret Shakespeare: Studies in Theatre, Religion, and Resistance.* Manchester, England: Manchester University Press, 2004.

Zimmerman, Susan, ed. *Shakespeare's Tragedies.* New York: St. Martin's, 1998.

Acknowledgments

R. A. Foakes, "The Descent of Iago: Satire, Ben Jonson, and Shakespeare's *Othello*." From *Shakespeare and His Contemporaries: Essays in Comparison*, edited by E.A.J. Honigmann. © 1986 by Manchester University Press.

James L. Calderwood, "The Properties of the Play." From *The Properties of Othello*. Copyright © 1989 by the University of Massachusetts Press and published by the University of Massachusetts Press.

Edward Berry, "Othello's Alienation." Reprinted with permission of *SEL, Studies in English Literature*, 1500–1900 30, no. 2 (Spring 1990): 315–33. © 1990 by Rice University.

Thomas Moisan, "Reception and Interrogation in *Othello*: 'What needs this Iterance?' or, 'Can anything be made of this?'" From *Othello: New Perspectives*, edited by Virginia Mason Vaughan and Kent Cartwright. © 1991 by Associated University Presses.

Maynard Mack, "'Speak of Me as I Am': *Othello*." From *Everybody's Shakespeare: Reflections Chiefly on the Tragedies*, by permission of University of Nebraska Press. © 1993 by Maynard Mack.

T. H. Howard-Hill, "U and Non-U: Class and Discourse Level in *Othello*." From *Shakespeare's Universe: Renaissance Ideas and Conventions: Essays in Honour of W. R. Elton*, edited by John M. Mucciolo with the assistance of Steven J. Doloff and Edward A. Rauchut, published by Scolar Press. © 1996 by T. H. Howard-Hill.

Edward Pechter, "Disconfirmation." From *Othello and Interpretive Traditions*. ©
1999 by the University of Iowa Press.

Robert N. Watson, "*Othello* as Reformation Tragedy." From *In the Company of
Shakespeare: Essays on English Renaissance Literature in Honor of G. Blakemore
Evans,* edited by Thomas Moisan and Douglas Bruster. © 2002 by Rosemont
Publishing and Printing.

Joan Ozark Holmer, "Desdemona, Woman Warrior: 'O, these men, these men!'
(4.3.59)." From *Medieval and Renaissance Drama in England*, 17 (2005): 132–64.
© 2005 by Joan Ozark Holmer.

Every effort has been made to contact the owners of copyrighted material
and secure copyright permission. Articles appearing in this volume generally
appear much as they did in their original publication with few or no editorial
changes. In some cases, foreign language text has been removed from the
original essay. Those interested in locating the original source will find the
information cited above.

Index

Characters in literary works are indexed by first name (if any), followed by the name of the work in parentheses